10.90

ETHNOGRAPHY THROUGH THICK AND THIN

Key Text

REFERENCE

ETHNOGRAPHY THROUGH THICK AND THIN

George E. Marcus

PRINCETON UNIVERSITY PRESS   PRINCETON, NEW JERSEY

Copyright © 1998 by Princeton University Press
Published by Princeton University Press, 41 William Street,
Princeton, New Jersey 08540
In the United Kingdom: Princeton University Press, Chichester, West Sussex

Library of Congress Cataloging-in-Publication Data

Marcus, George E.
Ethnography through thick and thin / George E. Marcus.
p. cm.
Includes bibliographical references and index.
ISBN 0-691-00252-5 (cloth : alk. paper). — ISBN 0-691-00253-3
(pbk. : alk. paper)
1. Ethnology—Research. 2. Ethnology—Field work.
3. Ethnologists—Attitudes. I. Title.
GN345.M373 1998
305.8′007—dc21 98-21287 CIP

This book has been composed in Baskerville

Princeton University Press books are printed on acid-free paper
and meet the guidelines for permanence and durability of the
Committee on Production Guidelines for Book Longevity of the
Council on Library Resources

http://pup.princeton.edu

Printed in the United States of America

10 9 8 7 6 5 4 3 2 1

(Pbk.)
10 9 8 7 6 5 4 3 2 1

To Students and Faculty—Present and Former—
of the Rice Anthropology Department (1980–)

Contents

viii

Acknowledgments ────────────────────────────────

THE AUTHOR gratefully acknowledges previous publication for the following essays:

"Imagining the Whole: Ethnography's Contemporary Efforts to Situate Itself," *Critique of Anthropology* 9, no. 3 (1989): 7–30. Copyright © Sage Publications Ltd.

"Requirements for Ethnographies of Late-Twentieth-Century Modernity Worldwide," originally published as "Past, Present and Emergent Identities: Requirements for Ethnographies of Late Twentieth Century Modernity Worldwide," in *Modernity and Identity*, ed. Scott Lash and Jonathan Friedman (Blackwell 1991), pp. 309–30. Copyright © 1991 Blackwell Publishers, UK.

"Ethnography in/of the World System: The Emergence of Multi-Sited Ethnography," *Annual Review of Anthropology* 24 (1995): 95–117. Copyright © by Annual Reviews Inc. All rights reserved.

"The Uses of Complicity in the Changing Mise-en-Scène of Anthropological Fieldwork," *Representations* 59 (Summer 1997): 85–108. Copyright © The Regents of the University of California.

"Power on the Extreme Periphery: The Perspectives of Tongan Elites in the Modern World System," *Pacific Viewpoint* 22, no. 1 (1990): 48–64. Victoria University of Wellington, New Zealand.

"The Problem of the Unseen World of Wealth for the Rich: Toward an Ethnography of Complex Connections," *Ethos* 17, no. 1 (March 1989): 114–23. Copyright © 1989 American Anthropological Association.

"On Eccentricity," in *Rhetorics of Self-Making*, ed. Debbora Battaglia (University of California Press, 1995), 43–58. Copyright © The Regents of the University of California.

"On Ideologies of Reflexivity in Contemporary Efforts to Remake the Human Sciences," *Poetics Today*, 15:3 (Fall 1994), 383–404. Copyright © The Porter Institute for Poetics and Semiotics/Duke University Press.

"Critical Cultural Studies as One Power/Knowledge Like, Among, and in Engagement with Others," in *From Sociology to Cultural Studies: New Perspectives*, ed. Elizabeth Long (Blackwell 1997), pp. 399–425. Copyright © 1997 Blackwell Publishers, UK.

ETHNOGRAPHY THROUGH THICK AND THIN

About the Illustration

Stanford Carpenter, cartoon artist and graduate student in the Rice Department of Anthropology, has been interested in probing sources in popular culture of the current appeal of Afrocentric thought in the United States. His critical study of the production of particular comics with African-American characters has also led him for varying periods of fieldwork to sites in Africa and museums, some shared with the cartoon producers he is studying, some not, but all are part of the multi-sited canvas of his ethnography.

Introduction _____

Anthropology on the Move[1]

THIS VOLUME provides an opportunity to pull together and juxtapose selected papers of mine that have been published over the past decade in dispersed venues. As I discuss in the final essay of this volume, like many others and for interestingly complicated reasons that reflect both the changing objects of study and conditions of knowledge production in academia, my work has evolved primarily in the form of essays produced for occasions and invitations. While I have been aware of strong continuities in my thinking since the 1986 publication of *Anthropology as Cultural Critique* and *Writing Culture,* the crystallization through assemblage that this volume makes available has proved useful in demonstrating to me (and I hope to others) just how systematic this work has been. What the collection itself adds, I believe, is a chance to explore the connection between the two parallel tracks that my work has systematically taken.[2]

The papers of Part 1 trace my fascination, first registered in my piece in *Writing Culture* (not reprinted here), with the impetus, means, and implications of the emergence of, if not multi-sited fieldwork, then at least a multi-sited research imaginary in the pursuit of ethnography. Much of the experimentation and the working into the mainstream of ethnographic practice of different conventions and sources of authority went in a quite different direction following the critiques of anthropological representation in the 1980s from the one examined in these essays. While a sense of critical reflexivity, the complexity of voice, and subject position have transformed the terms in which ethnographic research is now undertaken and written about, the regulative ideals and framing presumptions of what it is to do fieldwork very much remain in place in anthropology's professional culture.

Thinking in terms of multi-sited research provokes an entirely different set of problems that not only go to the heart of adapting ethnography as practices of fieldwork and writing to new conditions of work, but challenge orientations that underlie this entire research process that has been so emblematic for anthropology. This thinking arises from the very practical need that anthropologists confront all the time these days to resignify habits of thought about fieldwork and adapt their emblematic method to objects of study that are not simply "peoples" in topical arenas that do not readily define themselves in terms of sites available for sustained participant observation. For me, it has been the multi-sited character of the challenges—the need in any project to keep in view and mind two or more ethnographically conceived sites juxtaposed—that has made the difference, that has raised new provocation beyond the trenchant critiques of anthropological practice of the 1980s, which nonetheless occurred within a sustained mise-en-scène of traditional research imaginary.

The essays of Part 3 reflect my unfinished ethnographic memoir of observation and participation in anthropology's changing professional culture over the past decade,[3] as it has related to (as well as kept its distance from) the strong inter- (some would say, anti-) disciplinary trend, first known diffusely as postmodernism and then more concertedly as cultural studies. Many norms have changed in the training of anthropology students. There is certainly more flexibility in the development of dissertations, and renewed curiosity about new topics and research possibilities. But, for better *and* worse, the regulative ideals and imaginary of ethnographic research remain deeply engrained and largely unchanged. Consequently there is much discussion, confusion, and negotiation going on in graduate departments of anthropology about how to resignify, indeed, reimagine, anthropology's emblematic research process. There is a lot of informal talk at present about this process, but very little formal articulation and analysis of it.

By working both sides of the boundary between anthropology concerned about itself as a distinct discipline with a tradition, and anthropology engaged within the arena of cultural studies[4] constantly seeking to stimulate itself by a rapid retailing of ideas, I have thought a lot about the ongoing shifts in the professional culture of anthropology. The multi-sited challenge can be seen to intrude at various points in the essays included here reflecting my concern with professional culture.[5] But the essays of Part 3 were largely developed according to their own agenda of assessing changes in academic styles, practices, and institutions on the borderlands between anthropology and relevant interdisciplinary movements since the critiques of the 1980s.

Therefore, what I would like to encourage here, as an opportunity occasioned by the making of this collection, is more thinking about the interpenetrations and connections between the changes in research practices implied and entailed by a multi-sited imaginary and the directions that the changing modes of production, demographics, and ethos of participation seem to be taking in what it has been to be a social or cultural anthropologist within established disciplinary traditions. My own contribution to this effort will be to think through in my own context of graduate teaching a very specific predicament of anthropologists-in-the-making in designing their first projects of research, raised as a focusing observation in the final essay that gives this volume its title, and the possible effects of a multi-sited research imaginary upon this most central of processes in the reproduction of professional culture. However, before turning to this, I want to provide a framing narrative for each of the essays selected for inclusion.

The essays of Part 1 probe multi-sited strategies of doing and writing ethnography primarily as a response to the understanding of cultures as increasingly in circulation, making all locales and sites of sustained fieldwork partial perspectives on what anthropology, at least in its traditional rhetorics and subjects as "peoples," promised to study, if not holistically, then more completely (which, in my view, does not entail the dreaded "totalism," so much the ideological enemy of cultural studies). This enduring commitment to a sense of holism within the finely observed particular case is the embedded functionalist ghost in ethnography that will not go away. The question is whether anthropological ethnography can, or should, be satisfied with "partial knowledge" thus ceding its contexts of holism, significance, and argument to given frameworks and narratives of theory in history and political economy that limit the scope of what ethnography can discover on its own, in terms of its own practices and the sensibilities that these encourage. This is an issue perhaps more relevant to an ethnography more oriented to elucidating contemporary processes emergent or unfolding than to locating present subjects within a past that holds the key to contemporary problems. At any rate these are the preoccupations that generated "Imagining the Whole: Ethnography's Contemporary Efforts to Situate Itself."

I composed "Requirements for Ethnographies of Late-Twentieth-Century Modernity Worldwide" to fit into a project on modernity and identity conceived by scholars associated with the journal *Theory, Culture, & Society* (such as Mike Featherstone, Scott Lash, and Jonathan Friedman, among others)—a group whose concerns with the tradition of social theory I have found most congenial and complementary to an ethnography, moved primarily by an interest in culture and a multi-sited research imaginary. This was a comprehensive effort to bring together in one essay many of the diverse conceptual implications of the interdisciplinary critiques of the 1980s for the future of fieldwork and ethnographic writing. One key idea here was that the critique of ethnographic writing was not just about writing as such, but had backward linkages and deep implications for the way fieldwork might be thought about and designed. The techniques are a composite, not all or any combination of which would characterize a particular work. As such, it

was an effort at sketching the unfulfilled potentials that might yet oc-
cupy the space for exploration in ethnography opened by the critiques
of the 1980s. The need for a multi-sited imaginary is very clear, without
being crystallized as such, in the techniques that discuss "redesigning
the observed." And the techniques that discuss "redesigning the observer" indicate the need to think through the corresponding changes
in the way that basic fieldwork relationships are conceived and what an
act of effectively communicated critique within the confines of ethnographic convention might entail.

The final two papers of Part 1 begin to provide the crystallizations
signaled in the first two papers. "Ethnography in/of the World System
. . . ," written for the same venue as "Ethnographies as Texts" (Marcus
and Cushman 1982) more than a decade earlier, is self-consciously
methodological in framing and is constrained to some degree by the
genre of a review article, but it effectively foregrounds the importance
of a multi-sited imaginary that had been percolating through my other
papers since *Writing Culture*. However, the importance of multi-sited
strategies as a research *imaginary* (provocations to alter or experiment
with the orientations that govern existing practices) rather than a set of
methods that are very specifically prescriptive for the conduct of fieldwork and writing might have been lost in the genre of a review article.
For example, the evocation of "circumstantial activism," sketched at the
end of this essay, raising the key issue surrounding ethics, moral ambiguity, and the reidentification of the ethnographer at the heart of pursuing multi-sited strategies of research, is methodological in intent,
rather than an appeal to rethink the ingrained regulative ideals of
fieldwork practice under differently posed conditions.

The paper on "The Uses of Complicity . . . ," written in response to
an invitation to contribute to an issue of *Representations* on the work of
Clifford Geertz, is an attempt to fill in more of what is at stake in the
sketch of "circumstantial activism." It is also meant to say more about
the changes in the nature of fieldwork relationships attendant upon
pursuing research in different sites that are not merely variants upon a
unified ethnographic subject (e.g., tracing a "people" or the cultural
artifacts that represent them in different locations, such as rural-urban), but lay across contested and conflicted social ground (e.g., working through ethnographic juxtaposition in expert and governmental
systems *and* in everyday lifeworlds *both* within the same research frame
of reference). "Complicity" rather than "rapport" signals the rethinking
that needs to be done about the primary conception of subjectivities
involved in fieldwork relationships when the "Other" and "getting inside" lose their force as the tropes that define the scene of fieldwork.

The essays of Part 2 have been included to show how specific ethnographic projects that I have undertaken during roughly the same span of time that I have been involved with critiques of anthropology and their implications indicate traces of and inspirations for the latter. While neither my work in Tonga (through the 1970s), nor my work on American dynastic fortunes and their legacies (from the late 1970s through the 1980s) was designed and conducted in terms of a multi-sited research imaginary, each reveals a groping toward it, and together they manifest an increasing propensity in this direction.

"Power on the Extreme Periphery . . . ," the last creative and speculative piece on my Tongan work, prefigures some of the critical spirit of the recent interest in the idea of transcultural flow and diaspora (see James Clifford's review, 1994, of the ways that this trope has functioned in the recent trends of ethnic, cultural, and postcolonial studies). This paper contains the first indication of the need for multi-sited methods and conceptions in anthropology as a response to contemporary trans-formations of the sorts of "peoples" it has traditionally made its sub-jects. In this paper a radically "internationalized" vision of Tongan soci-ety and culture is imagined such that the idea that the Tongan people belong only to the Tongan islands, with the notion that their culture is centered there, is called into question as the continuing frame in the anthropological tradition of the study of this "people." This work does, however, in its multi-sited suggestion retain the notion of a unified subject, albeit engaged in various identity quests and struggles in di-verse places, which my later work on dynastic fortunes does not.

The way that a multi-sited imaginary functions in this later work on dynastic fortunes indeed suggests the strong critical effect and poten-tial of such an imaginary in line with anthropology's long standing character as a mode of cultural critique by means of disrupting, "mak-ing strange," commonplace categories and perceptions. Dynastic for-tunes have mainly been the stories of families, partly because families have been perceived as natural subjects of ethnographic, or at least sociological, study, while fortunes have not. Once fortunes—money, as-sets, abstract values in everyday management—are understood as sites and objects of ethnographic study similar to the lives of the families tied to them, then the conventional ways of narrating the stories and histories of these kinds of old elites are called into question. In their place is a much more complicated and ethnographically rich field of study that raises new questions of fieldwork, ethics, analysis, and writ-ing. While I continued to do fieldwork and write largely within the framework of family relations, the way I thought about them was thor-oughly embedded in a multi-sited imaginary, involving not a unified subject, but subjects (fortunes and families) conventionally conceived as incommensurate.

The two other essays of Part 2 trace this evolving theme in my dynasty project. "The Problem of the Unseen World of Wealth for the Rich . . . " was written for a symposium on "Culture As Illusory Order," at the American Anthropological Association meetings. It tries to communicate a sense of the innovation brought about in my dynasty project by treating fortunes and families as dual, interrelated, but also independent sites of ethnographic inquiry by an analogy with the multi-sited imaginary encountered by anthropologists who study the cosmologies infusing everyday life of certain Melanesian peoples, in this case, of the Kaluli. In our own secular world, "unseen worlds" affecting local ethnographic subjects either could become necessary and connected sites for further parallel fieldwork, or else they are routinely finessed by constructs such as "the market," "capitalism," or by the use of an already constructed historical narrative.

"On Eccentricity," written for another American Anthropological Association symposium on "Rhetorics of Self-Making," reflects indirectly the concerns of the "The Uses of Complicity" paper of Part 1. It focuses on the subject position within dynastic families—that of the eccentric—that is keenly aware of the multiple authoring of dynastic selves, at the cost of what is considered normal *self*-awareness in a culture hypervaluing the individual. The eccentric is thus the one subjectivity in dynastic families that is wholly oriented to the complicities "elsewhere" which construct it. As such, the study of the eccentric in contexts of wealth, celebrity, and power is the study of one manifestation of the multi-sited imaginary embedded and operative in a particular form of social life itself.

The essays of Part 3 try to ground certain developments of recent intellectual history[6] in certain characteristics, practices, and styles of thought of corresponding professional cultures within academic institutions. "On Ideologies of Reflexivity . . ." looks at the politics of knowledge around the most common positions taken concerning the levels and kinds of reflexivity supported in social science writing and analysis, especially in ethnographic genres. What "postmodernism" has practically meant in the social sciences can be read, I argue, in terms of a field of tolerances for reflexive styles. In this essay I introduce the symptom of "messy" texts, and the aesthetic of "worlds apart" cultural criticism (or what I am calling here a multi-sited imaginary) that they indicate.

"Critical Cultural Studies as One Power/Knowledge Like, Among, and in Engagement with Others" detects a lack of confidence, a current worry among some practitioners about the relevance of critical textual scholarship on contemporary events and processes. It responds by an analysis (with a new journal on feminist economics in mind) of what would constitute effective critique and how the orientations of academic movements of cultural critique would have to change in orientation and in terms of whom they address in order to carry out such critique. In short, cultural studies scholars would have to reidentify themselves reflexively within spheres of dominant power so as to be able to talk intimately *to* and *with* power, however uncomfortably at first.

To demonstrate that such a bridging or conversation is at least possible among those who were formed by a distinctive generational experience (often cliched as "the sixties") and with similar class preoccupations but who chose different professional paths, I argue for an affinity between critical academics and the kind of cold warriors concerned with nuclear arms competition in terms of a certain shared modernist intellectual aesthetic that each has bent to their own interests. The tracing of such an affinity lends support to the possibility of conversation, or even a shared project of critique, within domains of dominant power. At any rate, taking cultural studies in this provocative direction might ease its anxieties about efficacy, whatever the attendant risks for its own traditional political self-definition. The multi-sited imaginary argued for in Part 1 is thus present in this paper in the facing up to and exploration of affinity as possibility by critical scholars in the U.S. in their reflexive understanding of their own relationship to dominant spheres of power.

Finally, "Sticking with Ethnography through Thick and Thin," prepared for the twenty-fifth anniversary symposium at the School of Social Science of the Institute for Advanced Study, focuses on the current generational predicament of cultural anthropology and tries for an ethnographic appreciation of a discipline itself in debate about how to do ethnography, what it is, and can yet be, for. This is the piece on which the understanding of the functions of a multi-sited research imaginary in the midst of generational transition and within a changing professional culture most depends.

Advice to Ethnographers-in-the-Making: Some Strategies for Redesigning the Research Imaginary of Fieldwork

Much of my effort in recent years has been devoted to the training of anthropology graduate students in dissertation research. This has occurred in a small program (taking in only four new students a year) noted for its association with the 1980s critiques of ethnography and for its "alternative" orientation where work is encouraged that proceeds critically and experimentally in relation to the discipline's mainstream methods and regulative ideals. We have several international students in the program, and a number of these are from diasporic communities (e.g., South Asians resident in Canada). We have a number of masters degree students from other graduate programs, in anthropology as well as other disciplines, who transfer to ours to pursue work that they and we feel might be better done in our departmental environment. Students arrive with research interests that reflect very much the interdisciplinary trends of the last decade—cultural studies, postcolonial studies, feminist studies, and the development of research by these movements in the arenas of media, popular culture, science and technology, institutional, corporate life, the rise of a global political economy, and the rapid transformation of civil societies in Europe and elsewhere.

The required entry course for new students—the pro-course—is a kind of "lab" for discussing new research protocols that are reshaping the fieldwork tradition in anthropology. Current work in this course has been inspired by our thinking about the emergent multi-sited framework in which fieldwork is now being conceived and conducted and the related changes in the regulative ideals by which relationships within the arena of fieldwork have been traditionally understood.

At least in U.S. anthropology today, there seems to be a major rethinking, not as yet well articulated, of the models of research practice, especially with regard to the nature and senses of collaboration, and of the conceptions of the objects of study around which research is designed, especially with regard to mobility or circulation as constitutive of cultural formations. What is lacking in discussions of anthropology's signature research practices is not so much more discussion of the experience of fieldwork under new conditions (indeed, the popularity of reflexive writing in recent years has made this kind of account pervasive), or even a critical perspective on the fieldwork idea (see Gupta and Ferguson 1997), but a sense of the changing presuppositions, or sensibilities—what I have called a research imaginary—that informs the way research ideas are formulated and actual fieldwork projects are conceived. This is a key area for discussion and development over a decade after the critique of ethnographic writing opened the current reassessment and readaptation of anthropology to its changing circumstances.

This level of consideration, crystallized as new strategies brought to the early conception of research, anticipates many of the issues that might arise later as to what the actual implications of such research would be for the conduct of fieldwork and what the resulting published ethnographies from such fieldwork would look like. However, I believe it is very important to operate at this level, somewhat betwixt and between fieldwork as a method and experience and the professional culture which promotes it, in order to address very specifically the concerns of the kinds of students we are now training, very much influenced by ideas outside the discipline of anthropology (e.g., in cultural studies, feminist studies, media studies, etc.), but which have had such a profound effect upon it in recent times.

The norms for producing standard or mainstream ethnography have changed considerably since the early 1980s, but even through such changes there are still habits and presumptions of work holding certain potentials in the development of critical research in anthropology back, and it is in questioning and opening up these strictures that the contemplation of a multi-sited research imaginary in teaching has been effective. Where the proposal for a multi-sited research imaginary intersects with the changing norms of professional culture is precisely in the predicament of students caught between the divergent characteristics of first and second projects that I focus on in the final essay of this volume.

Often drawn into anthropology by an interest in the second or later projects of their professors—projects that are in a sense governed by experimental norms which alter in various ways those of a standard training model of fieldwork research in anthropology—graduate students must negotiate with their teachers the standard model by bending and stretching it in designing career-making dissertation research projects that reflect new kinds of disciplinary interests for which the standard model is no longer a certain guide.

This predicament is being addressed with a variety of expressions, attitudes, and outcomes in every graduate department of anthropology. The multi-sited imaginary of research, developed in Part 1 in perhaps overly methodological terms, is currently my own way of addressing this student (and more broadly disciplinary) predicament in learning to be anthropologists through the choices to be made in the preparation and doing of dissertation research. It is this contemporary predicament of students and their professors that I have had in mind as I have produced the papers of Part 1 over the past decade. And it is in intervening in this key professionalizing process of a discipline in transition that has provided a major intention for making this collection now.

In the context of a multi-sited imaginary's function within the forming of graduate student research, I pose below some of the knotty issues that might be confronted by anyone formulating such research nowadays. In relation to each, I suggest how a multi-sited imaginary offers a challenge and potential opening in approaching the overall model of anthropology's research process, from the conception of fieldwork through to the production and reception of its results. Whether or not the operation of such an imaginary results consistently in multi-sited fieldwork and ethnography,[7] the provocation in itself of proposing a modified governing imaginary for ethnography does make a difference at least in addressing issues that rarely figure prominently in the choices that are made by ethnographers-in-the-making in their strategies of fieldwork and writing.

1. The Double Bind of Ethnography's Reception

There is an increasing need to contextualize *in equally ethnographic terms* focused, site-specific projects of fieldwork that address topics and problems shaped outside the traditional ethnographic archive developed in terms of geographic culture areas. The author/fieldworker did not bear the weight of this kind of contextualization in the past because, as several writers have shown (e.g., Appadurai's collection on "Voice and Place" published in *Cultural Anthropology*, 1988) there was a density of distinctive preexisting problem-defining discourse for fieldwork in any given culture area. The problems in terms of which one conceived one's ethnography were already given, so to speak. Ethnography in anthropology was thus designed to be only description, or description as a form of argumentation, within the well-regulated discourse regimes of culture areas.

All along, and especially in U.S. anthropology, there were studies that developed outside the traditional archive (e.g., budding urban anthropology), but before the 1980s they mainly followed the conventions of mainstream ethnography, and served more as cases of something than as full, ambitious, and contextualizing arguments about whatever was being described. Such studies of elites, cities, corporations, hospitals, and other institutions, were rather oddities within anthropology. They were generally admired for trying to do something different and showing the potential broader relevance of anthropological research, but were not much discussed because nothing like the density of disciplinary treatments existed for these studies as existed for a study embedded in a long-standing tradition of culture area discourse.

Outside anthropology, such studies might be taken as cases or supporting illustrations of something the significance of which would be defined by whatever other disciplines or experts appropriated ethnographic studies for their purposes. They could be taken as policy concerns, as often marginal illustrations for social scientists like political scientists and economists, or as ethnography standing in for the now suspect (but nonetheless desired) categories of the "primitive" and "exotic" for historians of art, literary scholars, and historians in general. In a sense, by their inability to make more ambitious argu-

ments within the frame of doing ethnography, the contributions of anthropologists outside of their own disciplinary archive have often been
circumstantially trivialized. They are always showing the generalized
"humanity" of life wherever it is lived and they are providing cases to
be lent significance and appropriated by the arguments of others.

This is still very much the situation even after the 1980s critiques of
ethnography which retained the basic conventions of the genre, but
did license dramatically the possibility of more variation about how
ethnography could be written as well as how fieldwork could be
thought about. Indeed, my problem with much contemporary histori-
cized, and historically sensitive ethnography is that its arguments and
significance are not produced or given within the frame of ethnographic work itself but by the contextualizing discourses and narratives
in which the ethnography comes to be embedded. Anthropologists are
more actively selecting framing contexts, theoretical associations, and
narratives for their ethnography, but they still mostly are not creating
them within the heart of the ethnographic process of fieldwork and
writing itself.

This situation is of course changing—but slowly—as more and more
research projects are defined and normalized outside the traditional
discourse realms of culture areas. In time, anthropology as a discipline
should have its own substantial scholarly discourse communities for
some of these topic areas. In the meantime, I would argue, the task of
making arguments, lending significance to the ethnographic project,
rests with the researcher, lest it merely be appropriated by and assimilated into the essentially non-ethnographically derived theoretical,
philosophical, and political agendas of more prominent others in academic and expert communities.

So what does this mean for the design of ethnographic research?
While there are many reasons for the current impulse toward multi-
sited research, I would argue that one of the most important reasons is
precisely this need for ethnography to contextualize itself—its significance, its arguments—in terms of the sensibility and special contribution of its own distinctive practice. The ethnography simply needs to
do more theoretical/argumentation work *within its own confines* than it
has done in a past of cultural area frameworks or of easy appropriations by others when it is not operating within those frameworks. Now
what does it mean to do this? Not, I think, to make ethnography the
frame to write essays or "do" theory, but to expand and innovate the
possibilities for making arguments through description, the delineating
of processes, the orchestrating and representation (or evocation) of
voice, etc.

For me, the development of multi-sited strategies for doing ethnography so as to discover and define more complex and surprising objects of study is literally one important way at present to expand the significance and power, while at the same time changing the form, of ethnographic knowledge. I am looking for a different, less stereotyped, and more significant place for the reception of ethnographically produced knowledge in a variety of academic and nonacademic forums. Viewed in this radical way, multi-sited research presents new challenges to both ways of writing ethnography and ways of pursuing fieldwork. In short, within a multi-sited research imaginary, tracing and describing the connections and relationships among sites previously thought incommensurate *is* ethnography's way of making arguments and providing its own contexts of significance.

What do multi-sited strategies mean practically at this point in time for students influenced by these new issues, but also definitely caught institutionally within the expectations of a disciplinary mainstream? With possible exceptions, the dissertation for the time being should take the form of a site-specific, intensively investigated and inhabited scene of fieldwork but framed and partially investigated by a multi-sited imaginary that provides the special context of significance and argument for the ethnography. Beyond the site there is still ethnography all the way up and down, rather than *only* the "system," or "history," or "grand historical narrative." Thus, in the shaping of first projects, I am suggesting that the question of framing context needs, even demands, more attention, and that while a multi-sited project may not be literally pursued at the dissertation level, every project should be imagined in this way (and critically against the usual borrowed, more programmed fill-ins for the contextualizing frame of ethnographic work). This kind of disciplinary and methodological independence is of the utmost importance now if the results of ethnography produced by anthropologists are ever to mean much. Who knows if the other sites in the frame of specific ethnography will ever be literally investigated by new anthropologists in post-dissertation work? But having this imaginary and some sense of its empirical validity is absolutely key to making more ambitious and powerful claims through the ethnographic sensibility.

2. The Problem of the Powerful Motivation of Personal Connection in Shaping Ethnography

The traditional assumption in planning ethnographic research is to make a subject of study something far from oneself. The necessary estrangement (or defamiliarization) of anthropological work is achieved by dramatically crossing cultural boundaries. Thus, traditionally, working in one's own society leads to a kind of second-class professional citizenship for the results (the well-known bias in U.S. anthropology against producing first fieldwork inside the U.S., among English-speakers). Also, ethnography that begins with the self is suspect as leading to a kind of digression from the proper subject of research—the Other. Self-reflection, in this mode, is useful only to recognize bias and the effect of subjectivity so as to neutralize it.

Of course, the critical hermeneutics so influential in recent years as well as the changing demographics of anthropologists toward including and recognizing more bicultural, "hybrid" identities among themselves have encouraged generating research in just the opposite ways. The extended exploration of existing affinities between the ethnographer and the subject of study is indeed one of the most powerful and interesting ways to motivate a research design. Self-indulgence might eventually become a problem, but fully exploring the personal dimensions of a project should not be cut off prematurely so as to deny projects sources of motivation and power. Working from very deeply probed affinities of varying sorts has often been the way in which the most interesting research proposals have been generated among students. The projection of these affinities from the realm of the more personal to the delineation of more generic social-cultural problems and issues is the key move which gives a project substance and force, and also more legitimacy in the mainstream tradition of social science writing.

The key move of course is in the distancing and the projection of a problematic that is first found and explored in the realm of the personal and in affinities with a particular subject matter to a more objectively defined subject of study. Otherwise, there really is the danger of ethnography becoming mere self-quests and of its vulnerability to the charges that have so frequently been laid against it in the interest of discrediting reflexive styles of analysis altogether. How to move from the personal or from the exploration of affinity to the proposal which speaks to other scholars and scholarly communities, as well as perhaps to a nonacademic public, is an important aspect of the evolution of any contemporary ethnographic research project.

In this move to shift the personal to the distanced "social," a multi-sited canvas or space of ethnographic research emerges almost naturally. The affinities themselves that motivate research, their exploration, and then projection, are all part of a process that inevitably leads to a multi-sited frame that should be treated ethnographically, whether the whole space is actually investigated or not (once again what becomes the focus and what becomes the context is a matter of decision and strategy in research design). Indeed, it has long been the case that

even in the traditional practice of ethnography, the self-conscious cen-
soring or eliminating of these connections early on as "irrelevant,"
"only personal," or "nonprofessional" has made the always present
multi-sited potential canvas of ethnography resolutely single-sited, so as
to be contextualized abstractly by history, political economy, or a traditional culture area's delimited field of recognition of what the problems for investigation are.

So students might proceed initially with what personally ties them to
an object of study, looking at these affinities in objective as well as
subjective ways, but ultimately this process should be translated into
one that does define a distanced, objectified realm of study that continues to be fed by the initial fascinations of connection, but now in a
subterranean way.

3. The Problem of Falling Easily into Naturalized Categories and Frames in Nontraditional Arenas of Research

Estrangement or defamiliarization remains the distinctive trigger of
ethnographic work, giving it the sense that there is something to be
figured out or discovered by fieldwork. What provides this estrangement now is not so much the literal crossing of cultural boundaries
and the entering of strange spaces (this is a working fiction that so-
called globalization makes more difficult anyhow) as the determined
effort to refuse the couching of one's work at its very beginning—in its
very conception—in naturalized, commonsense categories that is so
easy to do otherwise. Of course, ethnographers-in-the-making might be
studying political economies, art worlds, laboratories, cities, and the
like, but as one of my colleagues taunts his students—is that ALL that
you want to find out about? The subject is already bounded (and to
some extent, described) before the ethnography begins. If there is anything left to discover by ethnography it is relationships, connections,
and indeed cultures of connection, association, and circulation that
are completely missed through the use and naming of the object of
study in terms of categories "natural" to subjects' preexisting discourses
about them.

One of the premises, after all, of the 1980s critique was that ethnographers would no longer be able to define sites and objects of study
that had not already been written about and represented, and that they
could no longer constitute objects of study naively without explicit
strategies of engaging other, often competing modes of representation
about the same concerns and objects of study. While I don't believe,
then, that ethnography can be only the study of representations and
fields of overlapping and competing discourses, the most important

kind of reflexivity that enters into and changes the ethnographic form as it has traditionally developed is precisely that which seriously figures out ways to meld other traditions of representing particular subjects with the one—the anthropological one—that has promoted and produced fieldwork as a methodology for in turn generating a distinctive kind of writing and representation. Reflexivity about a contending field of representations in or around a particular site of ethnographic work stimulates radical rethinkings of research identities and relationships. The anthropologist becomes one kind of cultural producer among others, some of whom at least were traditionally identified as merely subjects or "informants."

While it is fine to warn about the unself-conscious use of naturalized categories in designing research and defining objects of study, how to do this in terms of techniques and alternative strategies of research is a more difficult matter. The danger is that naturalized categories will be replaced by merely invented, fanciful alternatives as a product of the imagination, or wishful thinking—the object of study will become too strange! Here again, the challenges of the multi-sited framing and contextualization of ethnographic research provide one means of alternative conceptualization in which something remains to be discovered, redefined, or found out that ultimately must be accountable to methodical experience in the world of participant-observation. The juxtapositions among sites embedded in multi-sited strategies of following leads and making connections tend to offset naturalizing categories and their bounding of the world common-sensically. A multi-sited imaginary really, then, creates the space of possibility and discovery in ethnography, and keeps this space open contextually for intensive fieldwork done in its constructed framing, the kind of site-specific fieldwork that many students will continue to do for their dissertation projects.

4. The Problem of the Current Ways in Which Ethnography Can Be "Set Up" By Theory or Even Overtheorized

This issue derives from the same general concern (of each of the above points, in their different emphases) that ethnography should not be overdetermined before it begins, that there should be something to be discovered, found out, in a world that in the literal (geographical) sense has been totally discovered already. Instead of the danger of too easily accepting naturalized categories, this time, the danger leading to the premature closing down of ethnography to possibility is the too rapid assimilation of the research project and its definition by theoretical terms that have been so influential from work over the past decade and more in interdisciplinary spaces, such as cultural studies, broadly conceived.

The anthropologist really does have to find something out she doesn't already know, and she has to do it in terms that ethnography permits in its own developed form of empiricism. Some contemporary ethnography is framed by the kind of theoretical concepts and sentiments that it can't possibly address in any cogent way. The problem of any particular ethnography is thus stated and thought in terms that ethnography itself, as a genre and method, is not traditionally designed to probe. Or else the particular ethnographer has not done the very difficult and uncertain work of translating the theoretical terms into a design of investigation through fieldwork. The result is the thinness that characterizes so much cultural studies ethnography, and for that matter, increasingly, anthropological ethnography as well. The space of potential discovery and increased understanding of processes and relationships in the world (which require a bedrock of very thick description indeed) is taken over by a discourse of purpose and commitment within a certain moral economy. While the latter is essential to any contemporary critical ethnography it cannot be developed at the expense of contributions to ethnographic knowledge that describe, interpret, and discover new relationships and processes embedded in the world.

Ethnographic projects that are heavily motivated by and cast in culture theory terms must be allowed to "breathe," especially in terms of their descriptive accounts of things, before the theory kicks in. Or else, alternatively, the difficult job of translation must be done before the fieldwork ever begins (I suppose I consider the latter to be much harder to do than the other way around). That is, the ethnographer should be able to figure out, describe, and explain very complex realities in fairly plain terms before clearly distinct theoretical framings, interests, and critiques of ordinary language as political also set in with full force. Otherwise, why bother with the arduous sweat of fieldwork?

I am arguing here for something very much like the integrity and center of gravity, so to speak, of old ethnographic discourse—where the standard of fieldwork quality is being able to inform someone of your own community (scholarly and otherwise) what is going in the frame of your project and fieldsite to the full extent of his or her curiosity. Anything less is obfuscation or covering by theoretical agility and artifice for insufficient involvement in the field and the materials that one generates from it.

This rather hard line arises from a sensitivity to the slippage in the density of even anthropological ethnography in recent years and the inability of disciplinary discussion to "police" this, so to speak, because of the fact that much of the most interesting work has been developed in new topical arenas on the margins of the old focus of discourses and debates over ethnography, and by implication, its quality, done in the framework of the culture area organization of its traditional archive.

I realize the counterarguments: for example, it is after all theory that has powered so much new thinking in anthropology, so how can you possibly artificially separate the context and terms of the stimulus to motivating and thinking about research from the terms in which research is actually pursued? But even if you could make this distinction, and operate in plainer terms (but not of course atheoretical or aideological terms either—just seemingly so) to figure out fieldwork and its materials with the idea of then assimilating them later to theory held in abeyance, why would you bother to do so? Would you have the energy or motivation to do so? Wouldn't this be the height of artificiality? True, but I still believe the effort must be made or the ability of ethnography to continue to do what it has always done especially well—thick description, to use the cliched Geertzian phrase—will be finally lost.

The multi-sited imaginary lends itself to this moderation of the tendency toward overtheorization in contemporary ethnography in that it focuses attention on the mapping of complex spaces into which fieldwork literally moves. It thus emphasizes the empirical challenge of just figuring out, demonstrating through description, and thus arguing for particular relationships and connections not at all obvious to the naturalized nominal categories of social space (#3 above) or the theoretical stimulations which might have initially inspired an idea for ethnographic inquiry. So much of recent culture theory focuses upon the complex construction of subjectivities with particular, but often caricatured, social milieus in mind. A resolute multi-sitedness in ethnographic terms tends to challenge and complicate in a positive way this hyperemphasis on situated subject positions by juxtaposition and dispersion through investigation in more complex social spaces than many recent varieties of poststructuralist theory on culture and identity have allowed.

5. The Problem of Ethnography's Vulnerability to a Closed, Overly Certain Moral Economy

As a corollary to the above issue about the overtheorization of ethnography, there is a tendency for contemporary ethnographies in their main arguments and orientations to explore the nuances and compass of the moral predicaments of their subjects. That is, ethnographies are mostly about subjects caught in the complexities of dominant regimes of power, and their critical thrust concerns questions of agency, feeling, and being within a certain moral economy in which explicit judgments are made about justice and virtue.

Whereas probing moral ambiguities and contradictions should be an often fearless goal of cultural critique, what I personally find missing in much cultural studies scholarship and genres such as ethnography influenced by it in anthropology is precisely an exploration of these uncomfortable ambiguities. While there is much sensitive and insightful probing of a subject's or group's position in contemporary cultural analysis, I find the moral compass or economy in which this analysis is probed all too certain. What's more, this effect of a given moral economy that seeks to redeem the subjugated against the powerful is enhanced in the case of anthropology where, regardless of the exact shift toward unconventional subjects and topics, there is a long-standing disciplinary orientation of sympathy and identification with the peoples that anthropologists have traditionally studied. The ambiguity of this normally clear orientation of anthropologists in relation to subjects[8] arose for me in the attempt to do ethnography of elites in Tonga and the U.S.,[9] and I believe it arises ever more often nowadays as ethnographers move away from the traditional model of the study of "peoples," toward multi-sited cultural formations that encompass processes across major fault-lines of the institutional exercise of power and its everyday life consequences.

There is certainly great potential of a multi-sited research imaginary to work against the moral certainties so important in shaping and directing critical arguments about culture in ethnography. It is not that moral judgments cannot be made in the abstract and that ethnographers are always operating in terms of certain definite political and ethical commitments—this is abundantly and richly communicated in contemporary ethnographies—but the open-ended problem for critical ethnography is to describe the ways that moral positions and norms take shape in diverse, broad, and conflicted spaces of social life. Since the demise of structuralist analysis of various kinds in anthropology, how very messy and ambiguous situated moral/ethical positions and possibilities are in relation to regimes of political economy in which subjects are embedded has less often been posed and probed by ethnography.[10]

What multi-sited strategies of research offer is an opportunity to dislocate the ethnographer from the strong traditional filiation to just one group of subjects among whom fieldwork is done and instead to place her within and between groups in direct, or even indirect and blind, opposition. This is, to be sure, not a very comfortable position for the ethnographer, in which "not taking sides" is not an option, and in which deception and betrayal are everpresent possibilities. In each case, some form of "circumstantial activism," as I suggest in the last papers of Part 1, is necessary to give better access to these more complicated ambiguities of fieldwork ethics. This is not simply a matter of soul-searching and personal decision, but requires new discussions concerning what the boundaries of ethnographic scholarship are and what it provides knowledge about. What is often taken for granted in terms of an encompassing moral ecomony for fieldwork is now actively probed and questioned along with other matters as the anthropologist moves among sites of fieldwork. The notion of complicity developed in the final paper of Part 1, as a positive, but morally ambiguous and difficult concept of fieldwork participation, is intended to open discussion about the uncertain moral economy of multi-sited strategies of research.

A Final Word . . .

While the exotic is in eclipse and there is no more of the literal world to discover, the sense of discovery in ethnographic research is still important and a key to why scholars engage in it. Certainly, there has always been much room for *self*-discovery in fieldwork, and this has only been reinforced by recent license to explore reflexive forms of analysis and writing. But this also has depended on being in the presence of and in interaction with a distinctive and literal "Other," a mise-en-scène that is attenuated by a multi-sited imaginary. So what remains to discover? Or in what sense does ethnography survive in terms of this trope? If it is the "making strange" or the act of defamiliarization that has given discovery its form in ethnography, then in a multi-sited imaginary of fieldwork, this operation is sustained in developing knowledge of the relationships and connections that extend beyond the frames that have held the traditional act of fieldwork in place. This is the contribution that a multi-sited imaginary makes in further opening possibility in the practice of ethnography, commensurate with its new interests and conditions of work.

Appendix to Introduction

THE EVOLUTION OF SANTIAGO VILLAVECES-IZQUIERDO'S
DISSERTATION RESEARCH ON ELITE RESPONSES TO VIOLENCE
IN CONTEMPORARY COLOMBIA

Note: The following brief account by Villaveces-Izquierdo, an anthropology graduate student at Rice University completing his degree, is included here to provide a concrete example of how a multi-sited imaginary emerges in the development of contemporary ethnography especially when it focuses on complex processes that are difficult to literally ground or trace in terms of lineal metaphors. While striking in its originality and ambition, this project wrestles with problems of designing ethnographic research that are by no means atypical nowadays.

Today, in the society of nations, Colombia is known for being both Latin America's oldest democracy and the western hemisphere's most violent country where democratic mechanisms coexist with increasingly restricted civil rights, authoritarian measures, and acute violence. Attempts to consolidate the nation-state, based on principles of national integration, have been blurred systematically by the elite's own needs for containing what they have historically understood as social disorder. Violence has been a founding problem throughout the history of Colombia, one that became endemically visible and decentered in Colombian modernity with the coming of the era known as *La Violencia* (1945–65). Today *La Violencia* is not only the country's most salient memory landmark, but also the events that spread long-standing political hatreds which triggered today's complex forms of violence. After 180 years of independence from Spain, Colombia is still caught in a transitional phase toward democracy.

In the late eighties several years of frustrating attempts to bring guerrillas and government into dialogue marked the Barco administration (1986–90). During this time I worked in the President's Office on programs to negotiate the demobilization and reintegration of guerrillas into civil society, and as a Colombian citizen I have, like others, experienced the quotidian effects of the constant awareness and news of various incidents of violence. In 1991 the opportunity to begin graduate work opened up the possibility of assessing anthropology as a means to understand something about this culture shaped by pervasive forms and acts of violence. My interest was not so much in doing an ethnography of the perpetrators, victims, or actual acts of violence themselves and their immediate consequences. Rather, I was interested initially in the impacts of violence on those who most expect to live free of it in terms of personal security, but of course cannot: that is, the lower and professional middle classes as well as the upper classes. I looked at how violence seeped into popular culture, media, advertising, images, architecture (with a distinctive "narco-style" reflecting the flamboyant taste and wealth of drug trafficking), and everyday speech and habits, as well as at the marketing of security (for homes, automobiles, etc.) to a culture that is increasingly fearful of the effects of violence and helplessly or complicitly indifferent to its causes. This initial phase of my thinking about research was exemplified in an interview I produced for the *Late Editions* series (in *Late Editions 4, Cultural Producers in Perilous States*, ed. by George E. Marcus, University of Chicago Press, 1996) with Doris Salcedo, a Colombian artist, well known for her installations dealing with the traces and effects in everyday life of the atmosphere of violence.

It was difficult to determine a site-specific ethnographic access to my inquiry thus far, so as I planned an extended period of fieldwork in Bogotá, I shifted my interest to those institutional sites in Colombian state and society in which the daily work of particular professionals was taken up with responses to violence—understanding it and doing something about it within particular manifestations and institutional constraints. Not only do these professionals come from the Colombian middle- and upper-class culture of fear and indifference in which I had already been interested, but their work defines locations for sustained fieldwork participation and observation. Further, probing the more active responses of elites to violence would allow me to assess actual constraints and untapped possibilities in those sites where there are a certain mandate and empowerment to define the pervasive violence of Colombia as a social problem.

As proposed for funding, my project focused on legal institutions. My aim was to explore the use and abuse of Colombia's remarkable "state of siege" legislation before and after the new Constitution of 1991, as the state's most expedient mechanism for the containment and management of endemic violence. With this working framework, I attained funding and set off for a period of fieldwork to last from 1994 through 1996.

Upon arriving in Colombia in August 1994, I found myself visiting and participating in associations familiar from my past: the Universidad de los Andes, from which I had graduated in economics in 1986; the Instituto Colombiano de Antropología (ICAN); and the Centro para la Investigación y Educación Popular (CINEP), a Jesuit NGO and the main human rights research organization in the country. Such associations and institutions are cross-cut and permeated by very messy networks of personal association and circulation. A mainstay of past social science inquiry has rested on mapping and defining the characteristics of such networks as a basic contribution of research. My own questions were elsewhere, and the tracing of networks was only interesting to me as a way to locate and define the background of sites where the main activity and possibility was to act upon social violence as a function of state office, profession, and expertise. How was I to find my way through this labyrinth?

As I began to make contacts that would inform me about the Constitutional Court, where the most important decisions and debates about the state of siege legislation were taking place, I met a highly reputed psychoanalyst, a disciple of Erich Fromm, who was once a political activist and a perceptive witness to changes in Colombia over a long period. We began a series of wide-ranging and open-ended coversations that continued through my entire period of fieldwork (a record of these is published in Santiago Villaveces and Jose Gutiérrez, *Una Travesía Freudiana Cruzando Colombia.* Bogotá, 1996: Spriridon). Oblique to the direct pathway of inquiry, this site—meta-site, actually—was perhaps the most important of my fieldwork. It was the "control" upon my movements among the networks, a context in which interpretations could be shaped and reflected upon, as they were being thought. Many fieldwork projects, I imagine, have such a muse, but he or she is located off the map of the work (perhaps evident only in the Acknowledgments).

It became very clear to me that neither networks nor one particular site—even one as important as the Constitutional Court—would be sufficient to address the more diffuse elite discussions about violence and their locations in institutions. Sites of focus were needed so as to provide some sort of comparative lever on how issues of violence were formulated and hopes for action were expressed. I returned to Houston in July 1995, to discuss my research with my supervisors, and in a meeting at a cafe, I drew a sketch on a napkin of a visual representation of the complex spaces and connections that defined the "universe" of my fieldwork thus far.

This sketch decisively posed the problem of a multi-sited strategy for bounding this project. I finally settled on the juxtaposition of two sites where different institutional openings and foreclosures were operating upon opportunities for active response to violence. One was the arena of the Constitutional Court, which I had initiated fieldwork to research. The other was that of the expert specialization and enterprise of violentology, the self-defined and often political state supported intellectual effort of the public sphere to address all aspects of violence in Colombian society. These were by no means the most obvious nor the only sites in which elite response to violence could be probed in a focused way—there is the media, journalism, the practice of criminal law, and most interesting of all, the recent effort of doctors to medicalize the problem of violence and define it as a public health issue through epidemiological study (the latter is actually a transnational site since the movement to define violence as a matter of public health is truly global in scope).

While my field of study is open-ended and I may very well add sites in the future, I needed to strategically bound my dissertation. To me, the comparative, juxtaposed movement of my fieldwork back and forth between the Constitutional jurists and the violentologists made the most sense, even though as sites for ethnographic study they are quite incommensurate. But I did not choose them for their structural similarities, or even for how they define networks of elites, but for the ways in which each in its particular social manifestation and embeddedness defines possibilities for opening new public debates and terms of action in the consideration of the myriad forms and deep past of violence in Colombia.

Only ethnography that deals with the entire field by moving through clear design and choice in and between sites has potential as a potent means for defining this unruly field of intellectual and institutional life in Colombia's still very restricted democracy. The Constitutional Court and the academic violentologists can be viewed in juxtaposed relation to one another as spaces, or even experiments, where alternative and action are, if only realized in very constrained ways, at least possibilities. This is why I have made them *together* the medium of my ethnography in progress.

Notes

1. I am grateful to the person who recently encouraged me to collect some of my essays of the last decade. I had thought of doing so myself, but because of a certain ambivalence about the current "essay mode of production" flourishing in anthropology and more broadly in the interdisciplinary arena stimulated by intellectual trends in the study of culture over the past decade and more, I probably would not have gotten around to it on my own. Aside from this exercise of making an assemblage having proved generative in revealing connections that I had not appreciated before, I also have come to like the idea of participating intellectually in the fin-de-siècle in this way. There is something very cogent about anthropology's reflexive (or transitional) predicament in trying to come to terms with a sense of the contemporary that presents itself in a different way than the past as well as in indulging in a mode of academic production into which a good deal might be read about the state of cultural studies, broadly conceived, at the end of the twentieth century. (See the *Late Editions* series of annuals which I have edited since the early 1990s for another venue in which I and the participants in this project have tried to make something of the fin-de-siècle construction.) If it weren't for the suggestion that nudged me forward now, this act of assemblage (for example, if I had not gotten around to it until, say, 2001) would never have enjoyed, at least in my mind, this contextualization within a construction of self-consciously heightened sense of historic temporality. To me, the sense of possibility, hope, and emergence as well as exhaustion—in short, of transition—fits much more the

mood of fin-de-siècle (fin-de-millenium is much too grand given the relative youth of anthropology and its prospects), than the beginning of a new century. The reflexive conception of the moment suited for these essays, and much of anthropology at present, is one that is forward looking, but very much of the twentieth century rather than the twenty-first, still immersed in its habitual technologies of form giving, but with the expectation of immense changes in media on the very near horizon.

2. Both lines of thought juxtaposed and reflected upon in relation to one another in this volume were present in my contributions to *Writing Culture*. In my essay "Contemporary Problems of Ethnography in the Modern World System," the multi-sited (then "multi-locale") possibility was considered as an alternative to the encompassment (and submission) of ethnography within the classic, highly predictable, and morally certain metanarratives of history and political economy from which it has come to derive its meanings. As an Afterword to this volume, I also wrote a brief piece on ethnographic writing in the context of the anthropologist's career process. It seemed to me from the outset that the fortunes of any intellectual critiques of anthropology would be intimately entwined with the institutional forms and practices that shape anthropologists as well as the character of generational transitions that are affecting the professional culture of the discipline. Only with the juxtaposed essays of this volume have I tried to make more explicit the complex relationships between a changing research imaginary and its embedding in a changing professional culture.

3. This memoir in progress has been informed by observations and participation in a variety of conferences, in the U.S. and elsewhere, over the years. To take one very recent example, I attended in late April 1997, a conference reflecting on fieldwork at the Institute for Cultural Anthropology at the University of Frankfurt am Main. While this conference had a predominantly European flavor, the deep assumptions which shaped most of the presentations I found to be fairly universal among anthropologists, especially when it comes to analyzing and reflecting upon their emblematic practice. Most of the presenters were senior scholars, middle-aged, mostly male, and mostly white, although of diverse nationalities. While there were a number of interesting and provocative arguments made about aspects of contemporary fieldwork, there was an unstated consensus that ran through the papers about the traditional virtues and contributions of fieldwork itself as an activity—the best of liberal, humanistic values about openness and humility in negotiating the cross-cultural boundaries and relationships of the field. The audience, heavily composed of students from the Institute and elsewhere, was much more diverse in gender and ethnicity than the presenters and certainly contrasted with them in generational identification. Someone from the audience made the following provocative comments: none of the papers allowed for the idea that personnel producing fieldwork might change markedly over time, and this would make quite a difference in how fieldwork might be talked about—and in what precise terms it might continue to be valued as a professional ethos—simply, that who was doing fieldwork at the time of Malinowski or of Boas is different from who was doing it after World War II and is different from who is doing it now, or might

do it in the near future. Further, that many of the most valuable lessons of fieldwork of earlier periods—that instilled liberal values of openness, humility, etc. and defined its unarticulated ethos for certain generations—may now be learned in other venues (feminism, postcolonial studies) and even before one enters anthropology as a profession, so that what fieldwork meant as a powerful intellectual program to one generation might be very different for a later generation of different backgrounds. This seemed to me to be a very indirect, polite way of the audience (or certain segments of it) to communicate sympathetically that despite cogent arguments and insights of the presenters, they did not really speak specifically to them. That while they share the basic value of doing fieldwork with their seniors, what this experience means to them must be different from the unstated values of professional fellowship which shaped the papers they were hearing. What lay behind the indirection I could only guess. From informal conversations with some of the students in the audience, I saw that they shared something of an international interdisciplinary intellectual culture with their counterparts in the U.S. In any case, I have witnessed numerous such moments of social and psychodrama within the academic conference arena over the years, in diverse places. Encounters like this have been my food for thought, so to speak, reflected in the papers on changing professional culture included in this volume.

4. Or whatever the long interdisciplinary trend focused on cultural analysis might yet become.

5. For example, the emergence of "messy" texts as a symptom in the essay on ideologies of reflexivity; the need for cultural studies to reidentify itself and talk to power while focusing on subaltern and popular culture subjects in the essay on critical cultural studies as one power/knowledge among and in relation to others; and again, the identification of fragmented texts and the collected essay genre as a marker of change in professional culture in the last essay.

6. That is, the waves of critical thought carried to the disciplines over the past two decades by feminism, postmodernism, postcolonial studies, and cultural studies.

7. Indeed, outcomes are often messy and highly variant in terms of what the imaginary might be thought to imply about practice.

8. There are many fieldwork accounts which show just how unclear this orientation can be, how psychologically and emotionally complex it is, but still, there is no question that in professional culture, however objective some studies might be, or however ambivalent expressions of reflexivity in anthropological writing might be, the identification of one with one's subjects and their virtues is still overwhelming.

9. In studying elites in the 1970s and 1980s, I was never happy with the idea of an ethnography of elites expressed as "studying up" (Nader 1969), which carried the connotation of compensating for the preponderant interest in anthropology in studying the dominated, but also of "getting the goods"—the ethnographic "goods"—on elites, by probing the interior dynamics of how power shapes their lives and is produced by them so that they can be opposed. I didn't think that anthropologists were temperamentally suited to be so clearly oppositional at the outset in relation to whom they studied, and further to be

interesting, at least to me, studies of elites had to be about more than just proving a broadly understood moral postulate about their nature. In fact, I found the study of elites to be much more complicated and ambiguous than this, and indeed their study throws one immediately into multi-sited spaces and the sort of circumstantial activism that I have posed. The most interesting results of elite research are the unsuspected relationships, connections, and affinities that their ethnographic study reveals, not the seemingly eternal verities of modernist theories about how they are positioned and what they are responsible for in global histories of relations of domination. Regardless of strong moral positions and commitments of the ethnographer in the abstract, studies of elites will rarely confirm who the "good" and bad" guys are, but more likely pose the ambiguity and messiness of any moral position mapped onto social life across communities of difference. This is the territory that a multi-sited imaginary insures ethnography will be exploring, with whatever degrees of success or confidence.

10. There is rarely anything as complex in terms of moral ambiguities probed in ethnography as very occasionally occurs in journalism and on television dramas. My favorite example—I believe portrayed on *L.A. Law* or *Law and Order* some years back—concerns the adjudication of a legal case in which concentration camp survivors are opposing the use of crucial data derived from experiments on prisoners by Nazi doctors in contemporary research on a disease that disables children. This blocks together in situated contradiction good and evil in the most extreme way. It provides a striking instance of the sort of ambiguous issues that, while they are resolved under the authority of courts, remain unresolved problems for extended cultural analysis in the space of multi-sited ethnographic imaginary. Maybe the extremity of the example is unusual, but its juxtaposition and sense of an ambiguous moral economy is not, for ethnography pursued within a multi-sited imaginary.

References

Appadurai Arjun, ed. 1988. *Place and Voice in Anthropological Theory.* Theme Issue of *Cultural Anthropology.* 3(1).j.

Clifford, James, and George E. Marcus, eds. 1986. *Writing Culture: The Poetics and Politics of Ethnography.* Berkeley: University of California Press.

Clifford, James. 1994. "Diasporas." in *Further Inflections: Toward Ethnographies of the Future,* ed. by Susan Harding and Fred Myers. Theme Issue of *Cultural Anthropology.* 9(3): 302–38.

Gupta, Akhil, and James Ferguson, eds. 1997. *Anthropological Locations: Boundaries and Grounds of a Field Science.* Berkeley: University of California Press.

Marcus, George E. 1986. "Contemporary Problems of Ethnography in the Modern World System." in *Writing Culture,* ed. by J. Clifford and G. E. Marcus, pp. 165–93. Berkeley: University of California Press.

Marcus, George E., ed. 1993. *Perilous States: Conversations on Culture, Nation, and*

Politics. Late Editions 1. Chicago: University of Chicago Press. (The first of a series of eight annuals, ending in the year 2000.)

Marcus, George E., and Dick Cushman. 1982. "Ethnographies as Texts." *Annual Review of Anthropology.* 11:25–69.

Marcus, George E., and Michael M. J. Fischer. 1986. *Anthropology as Cultural Critique: An Experimental Moment in the Human Sciences.* Chicago: University of Chicago Press.

Nader, Laura. 1969. "Up the Anthropologist." in *Reinventing Anthropology,* ed. by Dell Hymes. New York: Pantheon Books.

Part One

AN EVOLVING PROPOSAL FOR MULTI-SITED
RESEARCH

One

Imagining the Whole

ETHNOGRAPHY'S CONTEMPORARY EFFORTS
TO SITUATE ITSELF (1989)

THE GROUNDING ACT of fiction in any project of ethnographic writing is the construction of a whole that guarantees the facticity of "fact." As Robert Thornton has noted (1988:287):

> Reference to some ulterior entity is always implicit in holism: we merely choose between the moral imperative of society, the "spirit" of history, the textile-like "text" which is no text in particular, or the "nature" of Man. Like the imaginary "frictionless space" in Newtonian mechanics, these ulterior images of wholes are not directly accessible to either the author's nor his subject's experience. They can only exist in the imaginations of the author, her informants, and her readers. This is the "essential fiction" of the ethnographic text.

The most common construction of holism in contemporary realist ethnography, as we will explore, is the situating of the ethnographic subject and scene as a knowable, fully probed micro-world with reference to an encompassing macro-world—"the system"—which, presumably, is not knowable or describable in the same terms that the local world of an ethnographic subject can be. Most often, this fiction of the whole, which also limits very definitely the range of kinds of stories that ethnography can tell about contemporary worlds, global or local, is treated cursorily with mere references to "the state," "the economy," or more specifically the "world system," or "capitalism." Yet, in demonstrating the distinct and plural manifestations of this ulterior whole— the system—when explored as forms of cultural life, the ethnographer cannot help but to import into the closely watched life of his knowable community of subjects unexamined assumptions and premises about the way the larger world really is. Such assumptions are essential both to giving his account closure and lending it an explanatory dimension. However slightly developed or imagined, then, as a direct concern of contemporary ethnographic writing, the fiction of the whole does indeed exercise a powerful control over the narrative in which an ethnographer frames a local world.

This consideration brings me to the central question I wish to raise in this essay: can we continue to let the conceptualizations, catchwords even, of other traditions or levels of study in social theory stand for the whole in our ethnographies, especially given the across-the-board questioning of basic frameworks of description in the human sciences that Mike Fischer and I (1986) labelled a crisis of representation? Even some of our best contemporary ethnography is written within a fiction of the whole that relies on gross constructs of state and economy that are relatively insensitive to the ways that those working in traditions of macro-system description, the Marxists or even the latter-day heirs of Parsons, have been revising their own classic frameworks of social theory. Writing about modern predicaments of ethnographic subjects in terms of mid- or early twentieth century, or even nineteenth century, visions and conceptual vocabularies of the world system, vitiates the powerful function of ethnography to represent the world with a certain currency. Thus, it also lessens the capacity of ethnography, in future perspective, to constitute a historical document in the making, keenly sensitive to its own times.

As such, I wish to let the following line of argumentation dominate the rest of this essay. As part of a so-called contemporary crisis of representation, work in political economy and other disciplines dedicated to macro-modelling and the definition of systems is moving in a less totalistic, more pluralistic direction—one more open to decentralized, mutable ideas of structure. This is a direction more open, in short, to the demonstration of global cultural diversity which has been a major, if not the major, self-conscious goal of contemporary ethnography. This movement of convergence on the part of those concerned with the structure of macro or world systems—particularly the new, more labile envisionings of late capitalism within the traditional stage-framework of Marxist theory (see Lash and Urry, 1987)—creates new opportunities for innovations in ethnographic writing to break out of old narrative constraints by constituting a much more complex object for ethnographic study and representation. In a later part of this paper I want to envision such a complexification of the ethnographic subject, stimulated by a reimagining of the holistic frame for ethnography that is more sensitive to changes in macro-views of systems that themselves have been shaped by the same crisis of representation that has affected ethnography. For now, it is enough to say that the corresponding change in ethnographic research and writing that I have in mind is a shift away from the ethnography that is so centrally place- and local-world determined toward an ethnography that emphasizes a link-up with the more pluralistically sensitive systems perspectives. I want to consider an individual project of ethnography whose main ambition is to represent something of the operation of the system itself rather than to demonstrate continually and habitually in the spirit of pluralism the power of local culture over global forces of apparent homogenization. The point is to reconceptualize through ethnography such forces themselves, to efface the macro-micro dichotomy itself as a framing rhetoric for ethnography that seriously limits ethnography's possibilities and applications in the context of so-called postmodern conditions of knowledge.

I want to work up to an elaboration of this line of argument through a set of discussions that I will present less in the holistic trope of a polished essay, than through a set of modular notes of varying length. While I hope these notes will have an order of progression and coherency that I intend, I do not see them as part of any ulterior whole itself except the one I am making up as I go along.

Note 1: On holism as the central rhetorical and structuring convention classic functionalist ethnographies.

In perhaps the most interesting discussion of holism as it has operated in the standard anthropological ethnography, Robert Thornton (1988:287) argues that:

> . . . [the] imagination of wholes is a rhetorical imperative for ethnography since it is the image of wholeness that gives the ethnography a sense of fulfilling closure that other genres accomplish by different rhetorical means. Actually narrative has very little to do with structuring the classic ethnography, except where the experience of fieldwork is alluded to. Rather, the distinctive trope of holism in ethnography has been classification, that is, chapter and verse much like the bible has established its textual effect of totality.

As Thornton says further (1988:288), ethnography is:

> . . . [a] genre in which the description of the economy exists side by side with the personal confession, the myth, and the well-worn fireside tale. It attempts to lead the reader to believe that the myth or the personal confession has a definite relation to the way the economy works. It attempts to establish the reality of the connections it describes. The vast apparent gap between the person who confesses and the economy that works must be bridged.

This bridge was achieved by the segmentation of everyday life into supposedly universal categories such as religion, economics, politics, ecology and kinship. The classificatory organization of the text, lent a systematic scheme of relationships by the application of abstract part-whole imagery of functionalist theory, allowed the physical text itself to stand for the wholeness of the social reality of which it was a representation.

The particular fiction of the social whole achieved through a rhetoric of classification, while it remains venerated and practiced in the pursuance of the classical sort of ethnographic project that can still circumscribe an isolated people as its subject matter, has otherwise thoroughly been called into question. The arbitrariness of modes of ethnographic classification, or rather its specific disciplinary and literary foundations as a mode of representation, has been explicitly critiqued, and further, ethnographers find few peoples who can be plausibly fictionalized as societies or forms of life whole unto themselves. The possibilities of writing ethnography as narrative have considerably increased with the displacement from dominance of the older classification rhetoric, and the foundational concern that the ethnography remain holistic has given way to various senses in which there is a desire among writers and readers of ethnographies that the latter be able to say more than they traditionally have and that they should contrive new fictions of the whole in which to ground their facts. A shift to which I now turn.

Note 2: The fate of the commitment to ethnographic holism in a moment of critique and experimentation.

If there is one broad contemporary impulse to change past conventions of ethnographic writing—to break out of generally acknowledged genre constraints—it can be characterized as the desire for ethnographies "to say more" than they have. This in turn is a response to multiple critiques of anthropological practices that have appeared over the past two decades, and that come down to complaints about the inadequacies of ethnographic accounts by various omissions or absences despite the anthropological spirit of holism. To unpack the different senses in which this "saying more" is being explored, I would argue, is to define a range of experimental strategies presently in play. I will outline four such strategies, and spend the remainder of the paper on the fourth.[1]

1. *Saying more by "letting others say it."* This strategy is informed by recent textual theories in literary criticism that challenge the authority of the writer and more broadly the construct in discourses of the unified agent, integral subject, or the autonomous self. Such influences include the work of French post-structuralists—the semiotics of Barthes, the notion of discourse in Foucault, the attack on a metaphysics of presence by Derrida—as well as Bakhtin's notion of polyphony, and feminist criticism. For ethnography in particular, the effect is to critique the dominating authority of the ethnographic writer in a text that is actually composed by many voices/perspectives out of fieldwork, and to seek alternatives to monologic authority given form by the writer, figured as scientist and sojourner. Thus while benefitting from recent trends in literary theory, this strategy is really trying to articulate a particular kind of *ethics* of anthropological representation in response to the specific past of ethnographic research and in facing up to the

changing conditions of fieldwork in which subjects are far more militantly self-conscious about the historic contexts of anthropology.

Much of the existing experimental literature in anthropology—variously labelled by the characteristics of dialogic, reflexive, or hermeneutic concerns—is encompassed within this strategy and what motivates it. Likewise, much of the discussion of ethnographic rhetoric so far has been limited to this one sort of experimental strategy. Of all the above influences, Bakhtin probably has had the most appeal for Anglo-American ethnographers in pursuing this strategy. While insisting upon the multiple voices or texts that in fact compose any particular singular voice that asserts authority in writing, Bakhtin does not radically challenge the integrity or ethics of the act of representation itself. Rather, as in his study of Dostoyevsky's *Poetics* (1983), he exposes (and approves of) the craft and technique of polyphonic representation. In this vision of polyphony as a counterfeiting craft, he is thus usable rather than undermining for ethnographers. He undermines monologic authority to be sure, while not subverting ethnographic knowing. Finally, he celebrates in his vision of carnival the kind of diversity that ethnography has sought but which has been masked by past genre conventions. This strategy of experimentation in ethnography, which has already been well labelled as dialogic, has generated a literature of collaborative works, confessional texts reflecting on the conditions of fieldwork discourses, and works with a heightened attention to the character and content of the multitude of distinct discourses (voices?) that compose any project of ethnographic research. The key recurrent problem in pursuing this strategy is that of Plato's Phaedrus—a sense of corruption involved in the inscription of the oral in the production of ethnography.

2. *Saying more by juxtaposing multiple levels and styles of analysis.* This strategy is very methodology oriented, and is located securely within the traditional epistemological concerns of social science. Its urge toward analytical completeness as its version of the classical anthropological goal of holism recognizes the limitations of any one level of analysis, despite claims to completeness, as well as the intractability of levels to neat transcendent synthesis. It hopes to substitute a pragmatic holism that juxtaposes several alternative analytical accounts of the same subject or phenomenon. It is pragmatic in that it recognizes that you can't *really* say it all; all analyses, no matter how totalistic their rhetorics, are partial. Rather, you can try for a comprehensive display of levels of analysis, of epistemological angles, so to speak. In the past, such ethnographic strategies might have juxtaposed the levels of social structure, culture, and psychology. Perhaps the one classic work in anthropology that best exemplifies this strategy is Gregory Bateson's *Naven*

(1936) which is composed of successive encompassings of incomplete but self-contained levels of analysis—different juxtaposed versions that comment on each other. Bateson is clearly bored by the initial sociological account of the Iatmul, but it is a necessary prelude to the more original discussions of ethos.

Nowadays the strategy might be to juxtapose structuralist analysis, historical analysis, and the hermeneutic/dialogic mode as different takes on a common object of study. This strategy is not however neutral among levels displayed by juxtapositions—there is indeed a subversive critical element. You write it one way, then by marginal commentaries, building on one another, you write it in other alternative ways.

For example, a beginning and a very conventional account of social structure would then nest more interesting levels of analysis that to some degree complement, and to some degree contest, the terms of the preceding social structural account. Each preceding account liberates the one that follows until you can write about a subject in an unconventional way. Thus holism and "saying more" is in the combinatory strategy of nesting levels of analysis. This evokes for me the style of Jacques Derrida, who writes on the margins of, or in reaction to, an object which is presumed to be constructed in a certain way before it can be deconstructed (in philosophical discourse, one can rely on others to construct the object of critique which opens one's own perspective, but in ethnography, obliged to describe or at least evoke a whole world separate in time and space, the writer must do all the work herself of traversing possible levels of analysis). This strategy thus addresses the problem in ethnography of having to prepare so much ground conventionally (or else risk intelligibility) that the power of an alternative favored analysis is diminished. By the nesting of alternatives, this strategy finds a powerful marginal space for novelty.

3. *Say more by drawing out the implicit critique of Western thought and society that is embedded in most ethnographies.* This strategy seeks to juxtapose two objects which can mutually and critically comment on one another. This is the classic mode of anthropological cultural criticism, such as that developed in the ethnography of Margaret Mead, and the issue in experimentation is to establish a dialectical relationship between the Western practice and the other cultural one in which both are progressively transformed in the text's movement. What is to be assiduously avoided by this dialectic is the caricaturing of either the Western practice (which happens in most ethnographic works with its critical agenda masked) or the other cultural one (which happens in texts like Mead's where the critical purpose is overt and the cultural other, e.g., the Samoans, is pulled out of context as an instrument of critique). This strategy works from an explicitly developed anthro-

pological counter-discourse, presented as a work of enlightenment by anthropology to its own culture. The idea is to more fully relativize Western practice against the "other" practice and vice versa, without distorting the ethnographic contexts in which both have been understood. There is no single work that fully realizes this strategy of juxtaposition, but some recent works incompletely incorporate elements of such a strategy (see, for example, Kapferer, 1988).

4. *Saying more by "saying it all."* This strategy is a reaction against charges of political and theoretical naiveté levelled at past ethnography. Its goal is to salvage some version of the holism for which traditional ethnographic accounts have strived, while fuming past simplistic and hardly realizable notions of total description into a more sophisticated problematic of representation. Rather than the encyclopedic or categorical holism of past accounts (a chapter on politics, one on economics, one on kinship, one on religion, etc.), or the structural holism of cultural systems grasped as integrated totalities, this strategy strives for a holism that is sensitive to both local meanings and historical political economy or world system processes. It evokes the sort of holistic social realism of nineteenth-century literature that Raymond Williams has described (1981).

The aim is to represent a whole local world and simultaneously a world system, by attempts either to represent an intensively studied locale penetrated by larger systems, or to represent larger systems in human terms by revealing as intersubjective processes the multiple centers of activity that constitute the systems, conventionally labelled the market, capitalism, or the state. In anthropology, this strategy is currently evidenced in ethnographies like the recent works of Jean Comaroff (1985) and Michael Taussig (1987), among others, which try to bring together the traditions of political economy and interpretative/ symbolic analysis. However, this strategy could probably gain some valuable moves from the practice of contemporary literary journalism which tries to encompass multiple locales of action while still capturing what Raymond Williams has called structures of feeling. *Common Ground: A Turbulent Decade in the Lives of Three American Families* by J. Anthony Lukas (1985) comes to mind, for example, as a stunning example of such a journalistic return to a kind of Dickensian or Balzacian realism from which an effort to reshape the long-standing aim of holism in ethnography could learn much. Ethnography is not of course journalism, and what is gained in coverage might be at the cost of analytic acuity. Another cost is that ethnography, focused on the locale of fieldwork, might succumb to relying on "canned" visions of what the world historical system is like (e.g., relying too heavily on Marxist views of capitalism), rather than taking the appropriately ethnographic view that macro system terms of analysis should be radically rethought from the ground up.

Social realism has long been considered to be outmoded in the reign of twentieth-century modernist styles of cognition as well as the development of statistical portraiture and computing technology, but for this very reason, an effective revival of such totalistic classic realism lends it a critical or counter-discourse function at present. The future challenge for this strategy is to achieve within the limited narrative space of ethnography the scope of realist representation while absorbing the lessons of modernism and acknowledging the present hegemonic valuation in the West of statistical and computational means of describing social "wholes." This experimental strategy for ethnography might be called new old realism.

New old realism is thus the conservative end of the current trend of experimentation and critique of ethnography in that, while taking very seriously the arguments about the limits of representation and therefore of any conventional commitment to holism, it nonetheless wants to sustain that commitment in novel ways, primarily by complexifying the definition and construction of the realities treated by ethnography. We now turn to such attempts in projects where the whole in the ethnographic account is carried by a fiction of an encompassing, largely homogenous world historical, political, economic, and social system that is plurally resisted and accommodated by particular and culturally distinct local worlds. The conservation of this distinctiveness in complex ways is the point of such ethnography, if not ethnography in general, these days.

Note 3: New old realism grounds for the moment the dominant micro-macro narrative structure of ethnography in place-focused "resistance and accommodation" studies.

With the demise of the classification trope, including the cement of functionalist theoretical practice which gave it explanatory coherence, ethnography had to have an alternative mode of closure, on which its status as a moral discourse or tale depends, as well as a different mode of explanation. The positing of internal coherence and integrity of a form of life, through the holism of classificatory rhetoric, would no longer do. The fiction of the ulterior whole, previously just off stage, so to speak, of the ethnographic focus on any local realm of knowledge has moved to center stage in the macro-micro world narrative structure of new old realism, and in so doing, has come to bear the weight of giving explanatory and moral context to ethnographic accounts. For example, the recent trend to bring anthropology and history closer together by grafting focused ethnographic descriptions onto the narrative of social history (see Behar 1986), exemplifies this need to reframe an ethnography which can no longer be satisfied with autonomous, completely internal accounts of culture. History (or rather world historical process) in one or another of its grand theoretical versions lends broader moral and explanatory meaning to the local cultural events and acts represented within the circumscribed sites of ethnographic focus, such as villages, neighborhoods, and knowable communities of all kinds.

Yet adopting this macro-micro world narrative structure as an enlightened successor to the classification trope as the dominant mode of holistic rhetoric in the current strategies of new old realism in ethnographic writing leads to a different set of problems and binds. These are well illustrated in certain of the essays in *Writing Culture* (Clifford and Marcus, 1986). For example, Jim Clifford and Paul Rabinow have both been prominent in calling into question the traditional tropes and rhetorics of ethnographic realism by exposing anthropologists to recent bodies of theory that persuasively demonstrate the limits of any form or act of representation. Yet, both feel themselves obliged in different ways to deal defensively with those who would characterize their loosely identified modernist or postmodernist positions as being overly textualist, as making realist writing impossible, and thus paralyzing ethnography. Both anticipate this objection by affirming some version of the macro-micro narrative structure of new old realism. As Clifford states near the end of the volume's introduction (p. 25): "To place this volume in a historical conjuncture, as I have tried to do here, is to reveal the moving ground on which it stands, and to do so without benefit of a master narrative of historical development that can offer a coherent direction, or future, for ethnography." Aware of the precariousness of this position (can you have your macro perspective, or in Thornton's terms, an ulterior fiction of the whole that guarantees the factity of the ethnographic fact, without a master narrative?), Clifford adds this clarifying footnote (p. 24):

> My notion of historicism owes a great deal to the recent work of Frederic Jameson. I am not, however, persuaded by the master narrative (a global sequence of modes of production) he invokes from time to time as an alternative to postmodern fragmentation (the sense that history is composed of various local narratives). The partiality I have been urging in this introduction always presupposes a local historical predicament. This historicist partiality is not the unsituated partiality and flux with which Rabinow taxes a somewhat rigidly defined postmodernism.

Yet, if Clifford is unable to privilege a master narrative as Jameson is, then, given the important role that such an ulterior fiction of the whole plays in any focused ethnographic description, how can the local historical predicament, presupposed by Clifford, be written about at all? This is of course Clifford's challenge to those who write ethnography in the shadow of the critique of ethnographic rhetoric he has forged.

For his part, Rabinow is the interior critic of the volume in which he participates and especially of Clifford himself. As a leading interpreter of Foucault, Rabinow argues for the whole that embeds ethnography and that ethnography can explore (as in Rabinow's current project on French colonial discourse) to be envisioned in terms of Foucault's notion of power in which, as in Rabinow's title, representations are social facts. Representations and how they become powerful as social facts become synonymous with world historical processes of political economy themselves. Yet, Rabinow, like Clifford, feels compelled to affirm a macro-micro world structure for his thinking that is hard to express as a narrative device for ethnography. Instead, he does not even try to do so. He enshrouds this structure, not in ethnography, but in the position of critical cosmopolitanism from which ethnographic research and writing should be approached (p. 257).

As with Clifford's specification of partiality, this is very good as provocation, as a statement of position appropriate to late twentieth-century conditions of global and local knowledge, but what guidance do these provocations give the more hardheaded (hardhearted?) old new realists who are less bothered by the limits of representation (although they can no longer be unaffected by them) and strive to construct more complex realities to write about, to experiment with more sophisticated strategies that merge local narratives of the particular with global narratives that encompass the macro-interdependencies of which Rabinow speaks? The answer, I think, is very little. Instead we have to turn to the best macro-micro structured ethnographies that have been produced, and examine their narrative and rhetorical structures in some detail. This was the aim of my contribution in *Writing Culture*, a critique of Paul Willis's *Learning to Labour* (1981), which I considered to be, and still consider to be, the richest vehicle for examining the macro-micro rhetoric of holism in new old realism. I want to establish that Willis's book is both an exemplar and a pioneer of what I will call resistance and accommodation studies. The "big picture" for these studies is eloquently stated in a recent article by Charles Bright and Michael Geyer, "For a Unified History of the World in the Twentieth Century" (1987:69):

> The problem is to understand the embattled efforts to establish order on a globe that has become one, yet is also becoming more self-consciously diverse. The central themes of this world history cohere around the ever more

radical disjuncture between global integration and local autonomy. The problem of world history is no longer the evolution and devolution of world systems, but the tense, ongoing interaction of forces promoting global integration and forces recreating local autonomy. This is not a struggle for or against global integration itself, but rather a struggle over the terms of that integration. . . . The world has moved apart even as it has been pulled together, as efforts to convert domination into order have engendered evasion, resistance and struggles to regain autonomy. This struggle for autonomy— the assertion of local and particular claims over global and general ones— does not involve opting out of the world or resorting to autarky. It is rather an effort to establish the terms for self-determining and self-controlled participation in the process of global integration and the struggle for planetary order.

This might be considered the manifesto for the spate of resistance and accommodation studies in anthropology like Jean Comaroff's *Body of Power, Spirit of Resistance: The Culture and History of a South African People* (1985), Michael Taussig's *The Devil and Commodity Fetishism in South America* (1980), and his more recent *Shamanism, Colonialism and the Wild Man* (1987), and many others.[2] The new old realist ethnography has specialized in the manifestation of local struggle with the world system to different degrees off-stage. The terms resistance and accommodation adequately summarize the complex determinations of identity and cultural meaning that these ethnographies explore.

Now to return to Willis as an exemplar of such place-focused resistance and accommodation ethnography, who is of interest here not only because his *Learning to Labour* fully reveals the considerable value of such a study within the macro-micro narrative structure outlined provocatively by Clifford and Rabinow, and more programmatically by Bright and Geyer, but also because, in its sophisticated asides that reflect on problems of its own production as a text, this volume reveals the considerable limitations of such ethnography.

The great strength of Willis's strategically situated study of a dozen nonconformist working-class lads in an English middle school is that he argues persuasively for the necessary understanding of macro-structural process in micro cultural terms (1981:122)—"In order to have a satisfying explanation we need to see what the symbolic power of structural determination is within the mediating realm of the human and cultural . . . we can say that macro determinants need to pass through the cultural milieu to reproduce themselves at all"—and in his close analysis of the lads' discourse he provides a set of concepts, such as differentiation, penetration, and limitation, which allows the ethnographer to explore empirically such labels as resistance and accommodation.

The corresponding weakness of Willis's study is that in confining his ethnography to a very limited number of subjects in such a focused, albeit strategic, setting (strategic in that it is precisely in the school setting rather than the others—the shop floor, the home, the street, the dance hall, or the bar—that working-class thought is fundamentally shaped), he lets a rather canned fiction of the whole—a personified, monolithic capitalism rather than a historically nuanced and diverse notion of capitalism—carry the weight of explanation and closure in his account. His is not really an ethnography of a macrostructure but merely an ethnography of its local determinations, mediated by the human and the cultural, as he says. The world of capitalist culture in which the lads live is thus the essential classic world of such capitalism rather than the state of this culture in the 1960s, 1970s, or 1980s (British capitalism being quite different in each of these decades). Also, the middle-class kids and the conformist working-class lads are presumably agents just as Willis's subjects are; they in their own ways resist and accommodate, as do bureaucrats, teachers, and managers. What is commendable about Willis's book is that he realizes all this, but he nonetheless accepts the limitations of ethnography as usually practiced—its intensive look at a few place-focused subjects. As he says (1981:207),

> Since my main focus was on the culture of the lads, ear'oles necessarily became something of a dramatic foil for their activity and creativity. . . . Nevertheless, the general case I am arguing is that in different ways, all social agents have a hand collectively in constructing their own destiny, doing so in a way which is not simply determined from outside and which often enjoys the labyrinthine complexity of a cultural form. But this cannot be said all at once! And if the ethnographic act of giving life to one particular cultural form seems to take life from others, to make others look anemic, then this should not be taken to mean that social theory is true only for the former . . .

In a later discussion, I want to take Willis up on this limitation that he sets for ethnography, by arguing that the macro-micro frame can be collapsed in the single ethnographic project (rather than waiting for numerous separate comparative ethnographic projects, as Willis suggests, to give full broader life to the holistic culture of capitalism, since each would be written according to the same rhetorical limitations as this one) and that the structure or macro-system itself can be addressed by the inclusion of multiple connected local determinations in a single ethnography. Rather than a strategic single site ethnography, written against a canned view of what the system is, I would argue for a multi-locale ethnography whose purpose is to fundamentally revise in the same human and cultural terms, that Willis calls for, our view of the macro-structure itself. The question is whether the ethnographic text can bear such complexity—this is a key question for experimentation and innovation.

Accepting the limitation of ethnography, and thus relying on a canned notion of capitalism as the ulterior fiction of the whole in his account, Willis is left with the irony of unintended consequences to explain how the system works (see Marcus 1986, 182–183). To me, unintended consequences are the unsatisfactory result of ethnography accepting a limitation about what it can say about macro-structures except in strategically chosen local determinations which Willis's study exemplifies. While unintended consequences undoubtedly do and would play a role in discussing the effects of any closely observed and situated acts in a complex society, the blanket positing of them I see as a failure of ethnography to be more resolutely concerned about the fiction of the whole in which it sets its place-focused discussions. One way beyond repetitive resistance and accommodation studies I believe is the multi-locale systems directed ethnography to which I have alluded. It is the sort of account that Willis sees clearly but excuses himself from attempting. I will in the final note of this paper try to say more about such experiments that blur the macro-micro dichotomy in trying to represent both place and system in multiple perspective.

However, an interlude is necessary to examine certain changes or shifts in the theoretical construction of major frameworks for discussing such world historical macro-structures as capitalism. The possibility for experimenting beyond the place-focused, macro-micro structured resistance and accommodation ethnography toward a multi-locale, system-directed one depends on such changes in the fiction of ulterior wholes in terms of which such ethnography has been written. The limitation of this ethnography is precisely that it has relied more on canned visions of capitalism rather than on changes in the macro-models which, if incorporated in the ulterior fiction of the whole, would offer new opportunities and ambitions for ethnographic projects of research and writing. The question then is, what sorts of ethnography might be suggested by changes in the conception of macro-structures? We now turn to look at one such major change in the conception of capitalism in Western societies.

Note 4: The vision of an end to organized capitalism as the basis of a new rhetoric of holism for macro-micro ethnography.

There have been numerous recent attempts to reconceptualize macro narratives in response to a contemporary crisis of representation, a sense that the macro views of industrial society and the world system created in the nineteenth century are severely out of line with contemporary realities, at least from the point of view of Western nation-states. These attempts are not so much efforts to do away with master narratives (in fact most are attempts to conserve them), as to open them up and make them more sensitive to the diverse contexts in which they are relevant; they are a recognition of a historic present moment, the characteristics of which are emergent and not wholly subsumable within existing liberal and Marxist frameworks for the study of capitalism. I have recently come upon what I think is an exemplary effort in this stream of volumes which try to modify, open up, or deconstruct macro visions of global order—the volume *The End of Organized Capitalism* (1987) by the two British sociologists Scott Lash and John Urry. I want to use this work here to illustrate how the substitution of a particular and very contemporary view of the state of capitalism, the ulterior whole most commonly built into macro-micro ethnography, in the place of the standard generic view of capitalism, stimulates thinking about how the macro-micro structure of ethnography itself might be transformed.

There are two general things to note about this study before dealing specifically with it. First, it in a sense plays out the master narrative issue raised by Jim Clifford in his comment on Frederic Jameson's commitment to sustaining the Marxist stage vision of capitalism. Lash and Urry are committed to sustaining the stages of capitalism view as a privileged master narrative, but they also clearly understand that it cannot be sustained in the traditional way, if only because a focus on the working class and its fate can no longer explain much of the contemporary dynamism and turmoil in Western political economies. They lean toward privileging a macro narrative against which all others are understood, but the narrative they describe is in itself open to diversity, uncertainty, processes of disorder, and the play of local, pluralistic contexts. Indeed, their work is characteristic of the best contemporary Marxist work in its willingness to maximize the amount of play and indeterminacy in the classic framework. It is this openness to plural/ diverse representations of macro processes that creates a place, even an essential place, in their framework for ethnographic knowledge. But is it the same kind of ethnographic account that the resistance and accommodation, place-focused studies have developed? This is a key question to which we will return.

Second, Lash and Urry deal only with the Western democracies in their study, so that what they say is outside the specific realm in which much anthropological ethnography has been done—how capitalism plays out in former colonial and neo-colonial areas of the world. Nonetheless, Lash and Urry manage to define global processes, which may have different resonances in Asia or Africa, but which at base are just as relevant there as to the Western states. But to avoid a disguised Euro-centrism, we must assume that as a potential ulterior whole for stimu-lating a different sort of macro-micro ethnography, their vision of disor-ganized capitalism would serve best and most directly for Western oriented ethnography. Yet, as we will see, one of their most radical notions that has great implications for ethnography is that place, re-gionalism, and urbanism have become much less important in the study of global political economy than processes that are everywhere at once, so to speak, that simultaneously operate across specific settings and places. So, while the focus of the study is the West, Lash and Urry's conceptual innovations belie the idea that our usual means of classify-ing social phenomena by territory or place are any longer adequate.

Now for a brief summary of the grounding ideas of their volume. In sustaining a master narrative of capitalism, Lash and Urry define three historic stages of development. The first two, liberal and organized cap-italism, are progressive as to increased coherent organization and accu-mulation of capital, while the third is degenerative, or as they label it, disorganized. Capitalism is not dying; it is just harder to grasp in an imagery of ever larger and more coherent systems. They develop four-teen points, which define the conditions of disorganized capitalism (1987:5–7). Let me quote the key ones:

1. The growth of a world market combined with the increasing scale of industrial, banking and commercial enterprises means that national markets have become less regulated by nationally based corporations. From the point of view of national markets there has been an effective deconcentration of capital. Such deconcentration has been aided by the general decline of tariffs and the encouragement by states to in-crease the scale of external activity of large corporations. In many countries there is a growing separation of banks from industry.

2. The continued expansion of the number of white-collar workers and particularly of a distinctive service class, which is an effect of orga-nized capitalism, becomes an increasingly significant element which then disorganizes modern capitalism. This results both from the devel-opment of an educationally based stratification system which fosters individual achievement and mobility and growth of new social move-ments which increasingly draw energy and personnel away from class politics.

3. Decline in the absolute and relative size of the core working class that is composed of manual workers in manufacturing industry as economies are de-industrialized.

4. Decline in the importance and effectiveness of national-level col-lective bargaining procedures in industrial relations and the growth of

company and plant level bargaining. This accompanies an important shift from Taylorist to flexible forms of work organization.

5. Increasing independence of large monopolies from direct control and regulation by individual nation-states; the breakdown of most neo-corporatist forms of state regulation of wage bargaining, planning, etc., and increasing contradiction between the state and capital (e.g., fiscal crises); development of universalistic welfare state legislation and subsequent challenges from left and right to the centralized welfare state.

6. The spread of capitalism into most Third World countries, which has involved increased competition in many of the basic extractive manufacturing industries and the export of jobs of part of the First World proletariat. This in turn has shifted the industrial, occupational structure of First World economies towards service industry and occupations.

8. An increase in cultural fragmentation and pluralism, resulting both from the commodification of leisure and development of new political, cultural forms since the 1960s. The decodification of some existing cultural forms. The related reductions in time-space distinction (e.g., the global village) likewise undermine the construction of unproblematic national subjects.

11. The overlapping effect of new forms of the spatial division of labor has weakened the degree to which industries are concentrated within different regions. To a marked extent there are no longer regional economies in which social and political relations are formed or shaped by a handful of central extractive/manufacturing industries.

13. Industrial cities begin to decline in size and in their domination of regions. This is reflected in the industrial and population collapse of so-called inner cities, the increase in population of smaller towns, and more generally of semi-rural areas, etc. Cities also become less centrally implicated in the circuits of capital and become progressively reduced to the status of alternative pools of labor power.

14. The appearance and mass distribution of a cultural-ideological configuration of postmodernism: this affects high culture, popular culture, and the symbols and discourses of everyday life.

In a sense, Lash and Urry's definition of the conditions of disorganized capitalism is done as a negative image since the key mode of class analysis so central to the traditional Marxist narrative of capitalism, among others, has become deconstructed. What takes its place? Nothing yet—the situation this vision lays out begs for an ethnography whose purpose is new concepts for a different sort of macro narrative that realizes its dependence on the understanding of multiple plural process to complete its grand view of the world.

Three points in the preceding listing are crucial as challenges to current macro-micro ethnography in the shaping of a macro-oriented, systems inflected ethnography written according to a fiction of the whole as disorganized capitalism. One, Lash and Urry indicate that major processes are no longer distinctly place-focused. The implication is that place-focused, single site ethnography provides very partial views of social processes with which it might centrally be concerned; that is, such ethnography can no longer be in explanatory, or even narrative, control of the subject matter it wants to encompass by description.

Two, the rise and proliferation of so-called service classes plays a large part in Lash and Urry's comparative analyses of the historic entries of the United States, Germany, France, England, and Sweden into the conditions of organized capitalism. Such classes cannot be descriptively harnessed by the analytic power of the class concept as it now exists. The ethnographic exploration of the social and cultural worlds of so-called service classes is a key task for ethnography and a major challenge to its existing strategies of description. Just substitute service classes for Willis's working class, and one can understand how little help from existing social theory this sort of ethnography has to count on.

Three, Lash and Urry raise the issue of postmodernism, not just as a form of high culture, or academic artifice, but as the conditions of everyday life. They indeed end their book with a discussion of postmodernist culture, and claim that given the processes of disorganization they describe, issues of identity and cultural production become the issues of political economy. Two important characteristics of this culture are (p. 14):

1. Postmodernism is about the transgression of boundaries—between what is inside and what is outside of a cultural text, between reality and representation, between the cultural and the social, and between high culture and popular culture.

2. If communications in liberal capitalism are largely through conversation, and in organized capitalism through the printed word, disorganized capitalism postmodernist communications are through images, sounds and impulses, the surface connections of styles and pastiche.

They go on to say (pp. 14–15):

not all cultural forms in disorganized capitalism are postmodernist but only that such forms take on an added weight and have an elective affinity with disorganized capitalism. We also claim that there are important postmodernist characteristics of not only high and popular culture but of the discourse, styles, and symbols of everyday life. We do not claim that postmodernist cul-

ture is necessarily liberating or a culture of resistance, but that it can, as
could modernism, provide cultural resources for either dominant or subordi-
nant collective actors.

There is something importantly classless about postmodernism. Postmodernism finds an audience when the boundaries which structure
our identities break down; that is, during personal experiences of liminality during which identity is unstable. Middle-class youth and the
professions in the service class are a potential audience for postmodern-
:ist culture and potential sources of resistance to domination in disorganized capitalism. This partly explains their overwhelming presence in
the so-called new social movements. The point here is that much of
such popular culture, whoever consumes it, is largely classless in content and form, and the radical anti-hierarchical values and practices,
the anti-authoritarian populism it can engender are equally not particularly marked by class characteristics.

If social action always involves an intermingling of presence and absence, modern culture permits an extraordinarily heightened presence-
availability of social situations, events, myths, and image which cohere
around and construct diverse subjects. With the sea change in modern
society in which large organizations, workplaces, and cities are of di-
minishing significance for each individual, the processes of forming,
fixing, and reproducing subjects are increasingly cultural, formed in
diverse ways out of a myriad of myths and images, of consumer products, of available lifestyles not at all based on where one lives or whom
one knows, that is, on those who are immediately present. In this last
statement, Lash and Urry offer a substantial challenge to ethnography
to redefine its object so as to capture these pervasive postmodernist
expressions of place and community.

What future Lash and Urry's work holds out for ethnography is a
macro view which in its formation demands micro or ethnographic
views. It is essentially a macro narrative built from ethnographic knowledge, but not particularly of the ethnography of the local, that is the
coherent internal local culture that in a particular place plays out capitalist, world system structure. Rather, it calls for a collapsing of the
macro-micro distinction itself; a particular kind of ethnography that is
places-, rather than *place-focused*. An ethnography of complex connections, itself, becomes the means of producing a narrative that is both
macro and micro, and neither one particularly. Some sort of ethnographic practice of research and writing that portrays chunks, cross-
sections, bits (an appropriate label for this kind of circumscription of
the ethnography does not yet exist) in its simultaneity and intimacy is
central to fulfilling the kind of representation of an emergent world of

order and disorder that Lash and Urry forge out of the old Marxist master narrative of capitalism. In the following concluding note I will try to specify a little further what kind of ethnographic text might be evolved if it were written against Lash and Urry's particular fiction of the whole—one that denies its separateness from the particularity of ethnography, but is not satisfied with the place-focused situating of the ethnographic project. In Bahktin's terms, what's needed is a shift in the chronotope of ethnography—that is, the space-time in which ethnographic narratives can occur—from a place, to places, simultaneously and complexly connected, by intended and unintended consequences.

Note 5: Multiplace, systems directed ethnography: effacing the macro-micro narrative structure.

There are a number of different strategies for creating an object for an ethnography that is written according to the holistic fiction of a world of disorganized capital, or in cultural shorthand, postmodernism. For example, Ulf Hannerz has been producing a number of papers which attempt to define a construct of world, nether than local culture. As he says in one paper (n.d.), "Cosmopolitans and Locals in World Culture":

> There is now a world culture, but we had better make sure that we understand what this means. It is marked by an organization of diversity rather than by a replication of uniformity. No total homogenization of systems of meaning and expression has occurred, nor does it appear likely that there will be one any time soon. But this world has become one network of social relationships, and between its different regions there is a flow of meanings as well as of people and goods.

Hannerz thus tries to capture the most illusive, cosmopolitan dimensions of contemporary cultural process. Much of what he opens up for ethnography is the study of popular culture, but while his definition of the space of cultural process is eloquent and clear, it is difficult to know how this conceptualization relates to strategies of ethnographic research and writing.

In reconceptualizing ethnography itself, I take a more traditionalist approach to innovation. I think the place-focus of the ethnography should be preserved, but the ethnographic text, and the project behind it, has to do more than it has. Thus, my repeated preference for an ethnography that while it encompasses local conditions, is aimed at representing system or pieces of system. It undertakes a cultural deconstruction, so to speak, of rationalized, institutionalized life—that is, the study of the macro-interdependencies that Hannerz and Rabinow focus upon plus the insight from the holistic view of Lash and Urry that these macro-interdependencies under disorganized capitalism are a matter of studying complexly interconnected local or micro worlds, all at once.

For the study of such phenomena as markets, media, social movements, wealth, and crises, rather than villages, social structures, neighborhoods, and the like, Fischer and I argued in *Anthropology as Cultural Critique* for a multi-locale ethnography. The idea is that any cultural identity or activity is constructed by multiple agents in varying contexts, or places, and that ethnography must be strategically conceived to represent this sort of multiplicity, and to specify both intended and unintended consequences in the network of complex connections within a system of places. Actually, this kind of ethnographic project is not as abstract or programmatic as it might seem, since it reflects how research I was conducting on American dynastic families actually evolved—the study of the relationships between wealth and persons over time necessarily required me to move beyond the households and communities of the rich to the diffuse contexts of social and cultural activity that produce them (see Marcus 1988, 1989). It was along the lines of these complex and diffuse relationships that something like a postmodern object for ethnography could be represented while still preserving many of the techniques and conventions of ethnographic work.

In conclusion, I want to point out three characteristics of special interest in the development of multi-locale ethnography:

1. The particular feature of a whole that multi-locale ethnography tries to fictionalize is that of the effect of simultaneity. One wants to demonstrate how action in connected contexts occurring at the same time has implications for and direct effects on each other. Focus on an event, such as a scandal or stock market crisis, creates the opportunity for a narrative framework which emphasizes the simultaneity of action in multiple locales. This feature of the multi-locale ethnography thus concerns itself with the complex relationships between settings of activity and addresses the key issue of unintended consequences in a much more elaborate, if not precise, way than does the resistance and accommodation ethnography.

2. The multi-locale ethnography embodies within itself a comparative dimension, through which, quite independent of the connections linking locales, the latter might be juxtaposed or artificially engaged with one another by the analyst to explore what sort of mutual critical commentary they make upon each other. In some cases, what might be considered incomparable becomes comparable through the analyst's artifice. Activities and local sites of knowledge blind to each other, might through the analyst's efforts be brought into engagement with

one another to produce new insights. The point then is that multi-locale ethnographics can reveal new opportunities for critical comparative juxtaposition, that otherwise might not have made sense.

3. Finally, when looking for complex connections between locales as a special project of ethnography, what sort of ethnographic knowledge does one now especially want about these settings? That is, does the effort at multi-locale ethnography encourage or emphasize distinctive lines of inquiry within the places that such ethnography covers? I would argue that the particular kind of local knowledge or culture that this kind of ethnography does probe is the register of critical consciousness in any domain of discourse and action as the expression of counter-discourses. In other words, and in Raymond Williams's terms (1977), the ethnographer is particularly after what is emergent in discourse and action aside from what is obviously dominant. This is precisely what Willis was probing in the talk of his working-class lads—the limits and depth of their cultural insight into the workings of capitalist society through the labor process. The problem of course is that Willis's work was a cut-off multi-locale ethnography, restricted to the usual place-focused ethnographic narrative so that critical consciousness in one setting could not be compared with the development of such consciousness in other settings to which the school was systematically related.

Aside from the emergence and development of critical consciousness, the other element of local culture in which the multi-locale ethnography might be particularly interested is the conservation of traditional concepts, ideas, and the like through postmodernist processes of pastiche. If Lash and Urry are correct that postmodernism is not just a matter of art, albeit popular art, representing life, then one ought to be able to register ethnographically the play of postmodernist processes like pastiche in everyday life settings themselves. This presents a special problem for anthropology which in its ethnography here or abroad has had a definite (often nostalgic) interest in conserving the past—in demonstrating that arguments for modernity and change aside, fundamental cultural phenomena like kinship, ritual, etc., traditionally associated with stable community life, maintain a flexible and not always apparent stable presence even in the world of capitalism where, as eloquently and presciently stated by Marx and Engels (quoted in Lash and Urry, 1987:312–13): "All fixed, fast-frozen relations are all swept away, all new formed ones become antiquated before they can ossify. All that is solid melts into air, all that is holy is profaned."

Up to the present anthropology has been quite successful through ethnography in contradicting this vision: the notion of culture that anthropology has used in fact ideologically resists such a characterization of the world. The issue is, can this view of culture, sustained through simple place-focused ethnography still be sustained? A new kind of narrative content seems necessary to handle the many contexts of local knowledge in which anthropologists are increasingly interested. I would argue that the stability of certain phenomena, grounded in a rooted local culture with boundaries and memory, no longer can be written about in the same way.

Pastiche allows for the thorough mixing of modes, meanings, styles. What remains rooted, or of momentary stability, are the processes and relations which connect locales, the sorts of factors, in other words, which shape pastiche, in any locale. Take for example, my concern with dynastic families, and the complex of ideas that define something as traditional and primordial sounding as dynasty itself. What I found was that in the servicing of dynastic families and wealth, the notion of dynasty as a cultural figure disseminated among diverse contexts such as lawyers', stockbrokers', journalists', and therapists' offices. The ideal or idea of dynasty exists across all of these settings and settles in as a cultural object of variable intensity and longevity, but it is not stable nor the characteristic of a particular rooted community. Spatially uprooted, mobile cultural phenomena like "dynasty," then are what ethnography needs to explore to fully conceptualize new ways of thinking about contemporary conditions. Old concepts are conserved but in ways that are unexpected in the frame of ethnography's notion of culture rooted in the idea of community and communality.

Multi-locale ethnography requires providing this kind of postmodern cultural analysis of the internal life of the locales or places it considers. What constitutes identity and how it is constructed with some sense of credibility and commitment on such moving ground remains an orienting question for the continuing tradition of ethnographic place focus within a multi-locale text.

Notes

1. I have intentionally omitted discussion of the contemporary experimentation with ethnography in conventional literary genres that provocatively blurs the boundaries between fiction and nonfiction. Here I refer to the poetry of Stanley Diamond and Paul Friedrich, among others, as well as the fiction of writers like Michael Jackson, John O. Stewart, and Barbara Tedlock. I suggest that such experimentation deserves a very different kind of treatment than the modes of experimental work discussed in this essay, which more narrowly and selectively circumscribe a range of new strategies in keeping with basic assumptions and conventions in the past making of ethnographic texts.

2. What Comaroff and Taussig, among others, are prominently attempting in very recent Anglo-American anthropology actually has a considerable precedent, especially among European ethnographers. See, for example, Fabian's collection (1979) and the references in Geschiere (1988) to the work of J. F. Bayart, G. Dupré, and P. P. Rey.

References

Bakhtin, Mikhail
  1983 *Problems of Dostoevsky's Poetics.* Minneapolis: University of Minnesota Press.
Bateson, Gregory
  1936 *Naven: A Survey of the Problems Suggested by a Composite Picture of the Culture of a New Guinea Tribe Drawn from Three Points of View.* Cambridge: Cambridge University Press.
Behar, Ruth
  1986 *Santa Maria del Norte: The Presence of the Past in a Spanish Village.* Princeton: Princeton University Press.
Bright, Charles and Michael Geyer
  1987 For a Unified History of the World in the Twentieth Century, in *Radical History Review* 39:69–92.
Clifford, James
  1986 Introduction, in *Writing Culture: The Poetics and Politics of Ethnography,* eds. J. Clifford and G. Marcus. Berkeley: University of California Press.
Comaroff, Jean
  1985 *Body of Power, Spirit of Resistance: The Culture and History of a South African People.* Chicago: University of Chicago Press.
Fabian, Johannes
  1979 Beyond Charisma: Religious Movements as Discourse, in *Social Research,* special issue 46:1.
Geschiere, Peter
  1988 Sorcery and the State, in *Critique of Anthropology* 8 (1): 35–63.
Hannerz, Ulf
  1987 *Cosmopolitans and Locals in World Culture.* Unpublished manuscript, University of Stockholm.
Kapferer, Bruce
  1988 *Legends of People, Myths of State: Violence, Intolerance, and Political Culture in Sri Lanka and Australia.* Washington, D.C.: Smithsonian Institution Press.
Lash, Scott and John Urry
  1987 *The End of Organized Capitalism.* Madison: University of Wisconsin Press.
Lukas, J. Anthony
  1985 *Common Ground: A Turbulent Decade in the Lives of Three American Families.* New York: Knopf.

Marcus, George E.
  1986   Contemporary Problems of Ethnography in the Modern World System, in *Writing Culture: The Poetics and Politics of Ethnography*, op. cit.
Marcus, George E.
  1988   The Constructive Uses of Deconstruction in the Study of Notable American Families, in *Anthropological Quarterly* 61:3–16.
Marcus, George E.
  1989   The Problem of the Unseen World of Wealth for the Rich: Toward an Ethnography of Complex Connections, in *Ethos* 17:110–119.
Marcus, George E. and Michael Fischer
  1986   *Anthropology as Cultural Critique: An Experimental Moment in the Human Sciences.* Chicago: University of Chicago Press.
Rabinow, Paul
  1986   Representations are Social Facts, in *Writing Culture: The Poetics and Politics of Ethnography*, op. cit.
Taussig, Michael
  1980   *The Devil and Commodity Fetishism in South America.* Chapel Hill: University of North Carolina Press.
Taussig, Michael
  1987   *Shamanism, Colonialism and the Wild Man: A Study in Terror and Healing.* Chicago: University of Chicago Press.
Thornton, Robert
  1988   The Rhetoric of Ethnographic Holism, in *Cultural Anthropology* 3 (3):285–303.
Williams, Raymond
  1981   *Politics and Letters: Interviews with the New Left Review.* London: Verso.
Williams, Raymond
  1977   *Marxism and Literature.* Oxford: Oxford University Press.
Willis, Paul
  1981   *Learning to Labour: How Working Class Kids Get Working Class Jobs.* New York: Columbia University Press.

Two

Requirements for Ethnographies of Late-Twentieth-Century Modernity Worldwide (1991)

THE FOLLOWING PASSAGE from a recent paper by Charles Bright and Michael Geyer, "For a Unified History of the World in the Twentieth Century" (1987: 69–70), is a typical statement of a problematic current within the interdisciplinary space that is often labelled in the U.S. and Britain as cultural studies:[1]

> The problem of world history appears in a new light. At its core is no longer the evolution and devolution of world systems, but the tense, ongoing interaction of forces promoting global integration and forces recreating local autonomy. This is not a struggle for or against global integration itself, but rather a struggle over the terms of that integration. The struggle is by no means finished, and its path is no longer foreordained by the dynamics of western expansion that initiated global integration. The world has moved apart even as it has been pulled together, *as efforts to convert domination into order have engendered evasion, resistance and struggles to regain autonomy. This struggle for autonomy—the assertion of local and particular claims over global and general ones—does not involve opting out of the world or resorting to autarky.* It is rather an effort to establish the terms of self-determining and self-controlled participation in the processes of global integration and the struggle for planetary order.
>
> *At the center of this study is the question of who, or what, controls and defines the identity of individuals, social groups, nations and cultures.* This is as much a political as an intellectual formulation, for it involves a critical reassessment of the practice of globalism. (*emphases mine*)

The paradoxical, even vertiginous, equality of the above passage's manifesto-like formulations asks the scholar of world history to keep similarity and difference, the global and the local, in mind simultaneously, requiring of him or her the ability to see "everything everywhere" as the key to perceiving diversity also. Indeed, it recalls the cognitive framework with which classic aesthetic modernists revolted against realism in art and literature, and signals to me the penetration, at long last, of this critical framework into the modes of representation that the social sciences and history have employed to construct their subjects and explain them. This is occurring just as aesthetic modernism in art and literature has been suffering a moment of exhaustion in the continuing efforts to define a postmodernism.[2] Marshall Berman, in *All That Is Solid Melts into Air* (1982), has creatively redeemed the power of classic modernism to speak to contemporary history and culture, against the so-called postmodern condition. In Berman's words (1982: 14):

> Modern irony animates so many great works of art and thought over the past century; at the same time, it infuses millions of ordinary people's everyday lives. This book aims to bring these works and these lives together, to restore the spiritual wealth of modernist culture to the modern man and woman in the street to show how, for all of us, modernism is realism.

The vision of social life with which a nineteenth-century avant-garde tried to tax the progress-orientated narratives of bourgeois life in European industrial society has now become, or at least has come to be appreciated as, the empirically describable conditions of modernity, not only in consumer societies in the West, but for vast areas of an increasingly transcultural globe. This is perhaps the one area where the current attempts to recast the framing of description and analysis in the social sciences and history inspired by modernist challenges to the assumptions of realist narrative intersect with the parallel effort in the arts to define a postmodernism: postmodernism distinguishes itself from modernism on the perception that there can no longer be avant-gardes for the cultural productions of classic modernism. Ironic statement, parody, spectacle, ruptures, and shock effects now are produced for large, even popular culture "reception" classes which exhibit a sensibility for, or at least a recognition of, such productions. Such "reception" classes include, of course, academics and scholars, among whom are those social scientists and historians who understand the social lives of their subjects (who also understand their own lives) in terms akin to the classic avant-garde experimenters, and who as analysts and describers of culture and society seek techniques of representation from the same source. Thus, while Berman, like others who study the legacy of modernist expression in contemporary life, departs from the postmodernist project in literature and the arts, his ground for defending the relevance of classic modernism is the common insight with postmodernism that the conditions of life worldwide are fundamentally and increasingly self-consciously modernist. However, what is apparently a predicament for the artist in this recognition is an opportunity for the social scientist and historian.

In the Bright and Geyer passage, the modernist problem in historical and social scientific research is foregrounded specifically as one of identity formation, "the question of who, or what controls and defines the identity of individuals, social groups, nations and cultures." And

with this formulation, we also come to a salient 1980s trend in ethnographic research and writing within anthropology, on which I want
to focus this essay. In *Anthropology as Cultural Critique* (1986), Mike
Fischer and I paralleled Bright and Geyer in our documentation of a
diverse and complex trend in contemporary ethnographic research
which attempts to synthesize, through the current play of strategies by
which ethnographies are constructed,[3] major theoretical interests in
the description of culture at the level of experience, or shared categories of experience (the prominence of studies of the "self"). The trend
also has equivalent concerns with how the conventional ethnographic
studies of locales, regions, communities, and diverse peoples generally
fit into the formation of a world-historical political economy (viz. the
major anthropological statement by Eric Wolf (1982) of the influential
metanarrative about world-historical political economy introduced by
Wallerstein, after Braudel, in the early 1970s). By the mid-1980s, these
cross-cutting interests in culture as lived *local* experience and the understanding of the latter in *global* perspective have come specifically to
be about how collective and individual identities are negotiated in the
various places that anthropologists have traditionally, and now not so
traditionally, conducted fieldwork. Such ethnography bears the burden
of explaining how in the conventional local contexts and sites familiar
to ethnographic research paradoxical diversity emerges in the saliently
transcultural world that Bright and Geyer envision. Thus, in the face of
global creolization processes, there is renewed interest among anthropologists in such topics as ethnicity, race, nationality, and colonialism.
While such primordial phenomena as traditions, communities, kinship
systems, rituals, and power structures continue to be documented, they
can no longer in and of themselves serve as the grounding tropes
which organize ethnographic description and explanation. The most
venturesome works in the trend of ethnographies are profoundly concerned with the shaping and transformation of identities (of one's subjects, of their social systems, of the nation-states with which they are
associated, of the ethnographer and the ethnographic project itself).
These are the most radically questioning of analytic and descriptive
frameworks which rest on, and privilege, a particular "solidity that does
not melt into the air"—that is, exclusive identities, emergent from an
authoritative cultural structure, which can always be discovered and
modelled. The modernist problematics of ethnography, outlined in the
next section, instead emerge from a systematic *disqualification* of
the various structuring devices on which ethnographic realism has
depended.

   That the problem of collective and individual identity has itself become the identity at the moment of this leading trend of ethnography
is worthy of comment.[4] The very notion of identity, after all, has been a

rather generic one in the history of Western social theory. At moments
such as this, when change and its character as a process become the
predominant theoretical and empirical concern of social scientists, how
identities at different levels of organization take shape also seems to
become the goal of study. But the treatment of identity formation, for
example, in ethnographies written under the reign of the development
and modernization paradigm of the 1950s and 1960s is far different
from what might be seen as their 1980s heirs, the ethnographies of
identity processes under a theoretical regime focused on modernity, a
term with quite different implications than modernization. The differences are probably as much political as intellectual. The regime of
modernization dealt in progressive stage frameworks, based on Western
experience and applied to the rest of the world. Under this regime,
change was of course disruptive to identity—personal, communal, or
national—but there was a clear valuation on the re-establishment
through whatever process of the coherence and stability of identity.
The "homeless mind" was clearly a condition of change, but was profoundly unsettling to the theorist/analyst and had to be resolved in
community or its possibility, in the reinvention of tradition in which
one could have faith, or in the notion that history, however complex
events may be, operates by something akin to laws. The theoretical
conception of this process depended on arguing between dualities
such as traditional-modern, rural-urban, *Gemeinschaft-Gesellschaft* and
the like—the form that the intellectual capital of nineteenth-century
social theory commonly took in translation and deployment in twentieth-century Anglo-American social science.

The regime of modernity globalizes specific histories of the modern
and encompasses the dualities of modernization theories and their creation as kinds of ideologies and discourses that are themselves products of the modern. The study of the modern or modernity requires a
different frame of reference and this recognition is what has occupied
so much of social theory in the twentieth century, in itself a project of
self-identity that is not yet completed, or perhaps is uncompletable.
Thus identity processes in modernity concern a "homeless mind" that
cannot be permanently resolved as coherent or as a stable formation in
theory or in social life itself. However, its changing permutations, expressions, and multiple determinations indeed can be systematically
studied and documented as the ethnography of identity formation anywhere, but only in terms of a different set of strategies for the writing
of ethnography, to which we now turn.

Referring once again to the Bright and Geyer passage, we find that
the key question of identity formation is pursued through a specific
conceptual rhetoric of "resistance and accommodation"; as they say,

"efforts to convert domination into order have engendered evasion, resistance and struggles to regain autonomy. This struggle for autonomy . . . does not involve opting out of the world or resorting to autarky." Distinguishing the elements of resistance and accommodation in the formation of collective or personal identities at the site of any ethnographic project has become the almost slogan-like analytic formula for addressing the paradoxical modernist vision of "everything everywhere, yet everywhere different" (see Marcus n.d.).

The resistance and accommodation formula, however, can be explored with more or less radical departures from the conventional framing assumptions of realist ethnography. In its more conservative use, this formula negotiates the simultaneity of cultural homogenization and diversification in any locale through preserving the foundational framing power of such notions as community, subculture, tradition, and structure. Local identity emerges as a compromise between a mix of elements of resistance to incorporation into a larger whole and of elements of accommodation to this larger order. The irony of unintended consequences is often brought into play in ethnographies to account for the articulation of such parsed elements of identity formation to each other in a local setting and, in turn, for their combined articulation of a small, local world to a larger order. (See my analysis (1986) of Paul Willis, *Learning to Labour*, for an account of how a very sophisticated use of the resistance and accommodation strategy operates along conservative, realist lines.)

Resistance and accommodation ethnographies often do privilege some form of stable community, or cultural structure, over any logic of enduring contradiction. The two poles of the strategy most importantly serve to position traditional studies in a satisfactory ideological way in the face of the modernist problematic as stated in the Bright and Geyer passage. On the one hand, admitting accommodation avoids the nostalgia for the whole, for the community, and more broadly avoids the allegory of the pastoral which, as Jim Clifford has shown (1986b) has organized so much ethnography as narrative. On the other hand, admitting resistance avoids the "iron-cage" pessimism of the totally administered world vision of modernity in the Frankfurt School critical theory of Theodor Adorno or in the theory of power and knowledge in the later work of Michel Foucault. However, what is really avoided or refused in the more conventional or conservative resistance and accommodation ethnographies is an exploration of the uncompromising sense of paradox in the intertwining of diversity and homogeneity that will not allow an easy parsing of these two terms.

In the following section, I will briefly and schematically lay out a set of requirements for shifting the chronotope of ethnography, to use

Bakhtin's concept, toward modernist assumptions about the organization of contemporary social reality. This will involve both changing certain parameters in the way that ethnographic subjects are analytically
constructed as subjects and altering the nature of the theoretical intervention that the ethnographer deploys in the text he or she creates.
This duality of alteration encompassing both the observer and the observed is fully consistent with the simultaneous levels on which modernist perspectives work—the writer shares conditions of modernity,
and at least some identities, with his or her subjects, and no text can be
developed without some registering of this.

Thus, three requirements will deal with the construction of the subjects of ethnography through problematizing the construction of the
spatial, of the temporal, and of perspective or voice in realist ethnography. And three requirements will concern strategies for establishing the
analytic presence of the ethnographer in his or her text: the dialogic
appropriation of analytic concepts, bifocality, and the critical juxtapositions of possibilities. These requirements are by no means exhaustive,
nor are there necessarily any existing ethnographies that satisfactorily
enact any or all of them. I am particularly interested in how a distinctly
modernist text is created in each work where it is shown how distinctive
identities are created from turbulence, fragments, intercultural reference, and the localized intensification of global possibilities and associations.

Requirements

Remaking the Observed

PROBLEMATIZING THE SPATIAL: A BREAK WITH THE TROPE OF COMMUNITY
IN REALIST ETHNOGRAPHY

The concept of community in the classic sense of shared values, shared
identity, and thus shared culture has been mapped literally onto lo-
cality to define one basic frame of reference orientating ethnography.
The connotations of solidity and homogeneity attaching to the notion
of community, whether concentrated in a locale or dispersed, has been
replaced in the framework of modernity by the idea that the situated
production of identity—of a person, of a group, or even a whole society—does not depend alone, or even always primarily, on the observable, concentrated activities within a particular locale or a diaspora.
The identity of anyone or any group is produced simultaneously in
many different locales of activity by many different agents for many
different purposes. One's identity where one lives, among one's neigh-

bors, friends, relatives, or co-strangers, is only one social context, and perhaps not the most important one in which it is shaped. For a modernist approach to identity in ethnography, it is this process of dispersed identity in many different places of differing character that must be grasped. Of course, such a requirement presents new and some very difficult problems of research method and textual representation in ethnography. To capture the formation of identity (multiple identities, really) at a particular moment in the biography of a person or the history of a group of people through a configuration of very differing sites or locales of activity recognizes the powerful integrating (rationalizing) drives of the state and economy in modernity. It also takes account of constant technological innovations to power these drives, and the resulting dispersals of the subject—person or group—in multiple overlapping fragments of identity that are also characteristic of modernity (see Marcus 1989). There are a number of questions for study in this so to speak parallel processing, of identity at many sites. Which identities coalesce and under what circumstances? Which become defining or dominant and for how long? How does the play of unintended consequences affect the outcome in the coalescence of a salient identity in this space of the multiple construction and dispersed control of a person's or group's identities? And what is the nature of the politics by which identity at and across any site is controlled, perhaps most importantly at the site where identity in a literal sense is the embodiment of a particular human actor or group? Cultural difference or diversity arises here not from some local struggle for identity, but as a function of a complex process among all the sites in which the identity of someone or a group anywhere is defined in simultaneity. It is the burden of the modernist ethnography to capture distinctive identity formations in all their migrations and dispersions. This multi-locale, dispersed identity vision thus reconfigures and complexifies the spatial plane on which ethnography has conceptually operated.

PROBLEMATIZING THE TEMPORAL: A BREAK WITH THE TROPE OF HISTORY IN REALIST ETHNOGRAPHY

The break is not with historical consciousness, or a pervasive sense of the past in any site or set of sites probed by ethnography, but rather with historical determination as the primary explanatory context for any ethnographic present. Realist ethnography has become dependent on, to some degree has been revived by, its incorporation within existing Western historical metanarratives. There is a lively effort these days, in contradistinction to the classic period in the development of ethnography in Anglo-American anthropology, to tie the site of ethnographic close observation to a stream of history within which it can be explained by reference to origins, not in the generic sense of earlier anthropology, but in the framework of historical narrative. Modernist ethnography is not so sanguine about the alliance between conventional social history and ethnography. The past that is present in any site is built up from memory, the fundamental medium of ethnohistory. In modernist ethnography, collective and individual memory in its multiple traces and expressions is indeed the crucible for the local self-recognition of an identity. While this significance of memory as the linking medium and process relating history and identity formation is well recognized by contemporary ethnographers, analytic and methodological thinking about it is as yet very undeveloped. It is another diffuse phenomenon of the conditions of modernity which nonetheless encompasses the possibility of comprehending the processes of diversity that derive not from rooted traditions or community life, but from their emergence amid other associations in collective and individual memory. The difficulty of descriptively grasping memory as a social or collective process in modernity is not unrelated to the inadequacy of the trope of the community to conceptualize the spatial plane of ethnography, as noted in the last section. In the electronic information age there is an erosion of the public/private distinction in everyday life (on which community is constructed in Western narratives) as well as displacement of the long-term memory function of orality and storytelling (again a condition of life in community as traditionally conceived). This makes the understanding and description of any straightforward "art of memory" especially problematic in modernity. Collective memory is more likely to be passed through individual memory and autobiography embedded in the diffuse communication between generations than in any spectacles or performances in public arenas, the power of which relies on ironic references to the present or what is emergent, rather than on exhortations of varying subtlety to remember. Collective representations are thus most effectively filtered through personal representations. With this insight, the modernist ethnography transforms the conventional realist concern with history as it infuses, expresses, and even determines social identities in a locale into a study that is synonymous with addressing the construction of personal and collective identity itself. It is probably in the production of autobiography, as this genre has returned to prominence, with a salient focus on ethnicity (see Fischer 1986), that the sort of historical experiences carried in memory and shaping contemporary social movements can best be appreciated.

The return of an ethnographic present, but a very different ethnographic present from the one that largely ignored history in the classic functionalist anthropology of traditional, tribal society, is thus a challenge to the construction of the temporal setting for modernist ethnography. This is a present that is defined not by historical narrative either, but by memory, its own distinctive narratives and traces. This art of memory is synonymous with the fragmented process of identity formation in any locale—one whose distinctly social forms are difficult to grasp or even see ethnographically—and that thus sets another problematic to be explored in the production of modernist works.

PROBLEMATIZING PERSPECTIVE/VOICE: A BREAK WITH THE TROPE OF
STRUCTURE IN REALIST ETHNOGRAPHY

Ethnography has opened to the understanding of perspective as "voice," just as the distinctly visual, controlling metaphor of structure has come into question. The trope of structure—that is, either social structure on the surface derived from patterns of observed behaviors, or structures as underlying systematic meanings or codes that organize language and social discourses—may well continue to be indispensable in rendering descriptions of the subject matter even of modernist ethnography. Nevertheless, the analytic weight or heft of an account shifts to a concern with perspective as voice, as embedded discourse within the framing and conduct of a project of ethnographic enquiry.

In part, this came about as a result of questioning the adequacy of structural analysis of whatever kind to model the complexity of intracultural diversity. A Wittgensteinian family of resemblances problem confronted the ethnographer who would represent reality as organized by the operation of cultural models or codes (usually one key or central model) and the more or less orderly transformations of their components. Controlling for context and the empirical recording of actual montage flows of association in data on discourse have challenged the adequacy of structural or semiotic models to account for associations that resist assimilation to a model of limited dimensions.

In part, the modernist alternative in voice, accepting the montage of polyphony as the problem of simultaneous representation and analysis, probably has had as much to do with the changing ethics of the ethnographic enterprise as with a dissatisfaction concerning the structural analysis of cultural phenomena. These changes are rooted in a marked sensitivity to the dialogic, oral roots of all anthropological knowledge, transformed and obscured by the complex processes of writing which dominate ethnographic projects from field to text, and of the differential power relationships that shape the ultimate media and modes of representing knowledge. Here, I merely want to comment on this shift in terms of the analytic difference in the way modernist ethnography creates its chronotope regardless of one's assessment of the possibilities for success in representing ethically as well as authoritatively voice and its diversity.

In the mode of cultural analysis that Raymond Williams developed (1977), a structure of feeling (the use of structure is quite idiosyncratic) would be the goal of ethnography, focused on what is emergent in a setting from the interaction of well-defined dominant and residual formations with that which is not quite articulable to subjects or to the analyst. (Such formations could be systems of social relations in the British sense of structure, but they also refer to possible and established modes of discourse.) Making it more sayable/visible is one of the critical functions of ethnography. The modernist ethnography in this vein, recognizing such properties of discourses as dominance, residualness, and emergence (or possibility), would map the relationships of these properties in any site of enquiry not by immediate structural appropriations of discourse formations, but by exposing, to the extent possible, the quality of voices by means of metalinguistic categories (such as narrative, trope, etc.). Voices are not seen as products of local structures, based on community and tradition, alone, or as privileged sources of perspective, but rather as products of the complex sets of associations and experiences which compose them. To enact this refocusing of ethnography from structure to voice/discourse involves different conceptions of the relationship of the observer to the observed, to which we now turn.

Remaking the Observer

It should not be lost on one that while a more complex appreciation of the dynamics of identity formation is the object of the modernist strategies of remaking the observed, the parallel strategies of remaking the observer are no less directed toward the dynamics of identity formation of the anthropologist in relation to his or her practice of ethnography.

THE APPROPRIATION THROUGH DIALOGUE OF A TEXT'S CONCEPTUAL APPARATUS

The realist ethnography has often been built around the intensive exegesis of a key indigenous symbol or concept pulled from its contexts of discourse to be reinserted in them, but according to the dictates of the ethnographer's authoritative analytic scheme. Much in recent cultural ethnography has depended on this central organizing and analytic technique so common in ethnographic accounts. On the quality and thoroughness of such exegesis often depends the professional assessment of the value of a particular ethnographic work.

In one sense, exegesis at the center of ethnography is a gesture toward recognizing and privileging indigenous concepts over anthropology's own. Most importantly, such targeted concepts come to act as synedoche for identity—they stand for a system of meanings but also for the identity of a people in the anthropological literature and sometimes beyond it. Keying an account to particular concepts, myths, or symbols thus tends to impose an identity upon a people as a contribution (or curse) of anthropology.

One alteration of the modernist ethnography is to remake this exercise into a fully dialogic one in which exegesis is foregrounded in the ethnography and frame of analysis as arising from at least the dual voices party to dialogue. In this basic process of cultural translation— one of the favored metaphors for characterizing the interpretive task in ethnography—the purpose is not so much to change indigenous concepts (that is the responsibility of the anthropologist's interlocutors) as to alter the anthropologist's own. In no ethnography of which I am aware (maybe Maurice Leenhardt's *Do Kamo*, but then the whole project of ethnography is redefined in his work) does the central exegetical task lead to the re-creation of concepts in the apparatus of social theoretic discourse. For example, in the face of the apparent exhaustion of our concepts to map late-twentieth-century realities, Fredric Jameson in an interview responds thus to a comment (1987: 37):

Q: It is obvious, nevertheless, that postmodernist discourse makes it difficult to say things about the whole.

FJ: One of the ways of describing this is as a modification in the very nature of the cultural sphere: a loss of autonomy of culture, a case of culture falling into the world. As you say, this makes it much more difficult to speak of cultural systems and to evaluate them in isolation. A whole new theoretical problem is posed. Thinking at once negatively and positively about it is a beginning, but what we need is a new vocabulary. The languages that have been useful in talking about culture and politics in the past don't really seem adequate to this historical moment.

From where might this vocabulary come, for the sake of Western social theory and cognition? Maybe from a modernist reshaping of the translation of concepts at the core of realist ethnographies. Perhaps moments of exegesis, of definitions in context, would be replaced by the exposure of moments of dialogue and their use in the ethnographer's revision of familiar concepts that define the analytic limits of his or her own work, and of anthropological discourse more generally. Such a move would open the realm of discussion of ethnographies to organic intellectuals (to use Gramsci's term) and readerships among one's subjects, wherever this is now feasible.

Modernist exegesis, distinctively tied to a recognition of its dialogic character, becomes a thoroughly reflexive operation. While one explores the changing identity processes within an ethnographic setting, the identity of one's own concepts changes. The process of constructing an analysis thus can take on and parallel aspects of the process it describes. The key challenge here is whether an identity can ever be explained by a reference discourse when several discourses are in play, not the least of which is the ethnographer's in dialogue with specific other subjects. There are several resolutions in the way this activity might be represented textually, but the modernist innovation is that the identity of the ethnographer's framework should not remain intact, "solid," if the subject's is "melting into air." This leads to a consideration of the bifocal character of any project of ethnographic research, a character that is heightened by the modernist sense of the real—that the globe generally and intimately is becoming more integrated and that this paradoxically is not leading to an easily comprehensible totality, but to an increasing diversity of connections among phenomena once thought disparate and worlds apart.

BIFOCALITY

Looking at least two ways, an embedded comparative dimension, has always been a more or less implicit aspect of every ethnographic project. In the evolving global modernity of the twentieth century in which anthropology has been pursued almost from its professional inception, the coevalness of the ethnographer with the Other as subject has for the most part been denied (Fabian 1983). There is indeed a history in ethnography of a developing critical juxtaposition, made explicit between one's own world and that of the Other as subject, but the construct of separate, distant worlds in analytically making such juxtapositions has been sustained. Only in the periodic internal critique of anthropology's relationship to Western colonialism has the thoroughly blurred historic relationship of the anthropologist's own society and practices to the subject's under colonial domination been argued.

Now that Western modernity is being reconceptualized as a global and thoroughly transcultural phenomenon the explicit treatment of bifocality in ethnographic accounts is becoming more explicit and openly transgressive of the us-them, distanced worlds in which it was previously constructed. In other words, the identity of the anthropologist and his or her world by whatever complex chain of connection and association is likely to be profoundly related to that of any particular world he or she is studying. However, only the modernist remaking of the observed, outlined in the previous section, makes possible this revision of the bifocal character of ethnography. For example, the multilocality of identity processes across various levels of conventional divisions of social organization—the pathway of the transcultural—creates a mutuality of implication for identity processes occurring in any ethnographic site. The chain of preexisting historic or contemporary connection between the ethnographer and her or his subjects may be a long or short one, thus making bifocality an issue of judgement and a circumstance even of the personal, autobiographical reasons for pursuit of a particular project, but its discovery and recognition remains a defining feature of the current modernist sensibility in ethnography. The mere demonstration of such connections and affinities, the juxtaposition of two identity predicaments precipitated by the ethnographer's project, itself stands as a critical statement against conventional efforts to sustain distanced worlds and their separate determinations, despite the modernist insight about global integration through paths that are transcultural as well as technological, political, and economic in nature.

CRITICAL JUXTAPOSITIONS AND CONTEMPLATION OF ALTERNATIVE
POSSIBILITIES

The function of the modernist ethnography is primarily one of cultural critique, of one's disciplinary apparatus through an intellectual alliance with the subject, or of one's society that in the increasing condition of global integration is always bifocally related in transcultural process and historical perspective (or rather retrospective) to the site of ethnographic attention. The cultural critique is also directed to conditions within the site of ethnographic focus—the local world which it treats. Given the general commitment of modernist ethnographies to explore the full range of possibilities for identities and their complex expressions through voice in any setting, such exploration is a key form of cultural critique also. This move is indeed the distinct and committed voice of the ethnographer in his or her text, and it operates from the critical attitude that things as they are need not have been or need not be the way they are, given the alternatives detectable within the situations—there are always more possibilities, other identities, etc., than those that have come to be enacted. Exploring through juxtapositions all actual and possible outcomes is itself a method of cultural critique which moves against the grain of the given situation and its definition in dominant identities which might otherwise be mistaken as authoritative models from which all variation is derived. The modernist treatment of reality allows, rather, for the traces of the roads not taken or the possibilities not explored. Indeed, this kind of critical thought experiment incorporated within ethnography, in which juxtaposed actualities and possibilities are put analytically in dialogue with one another, might be thought to border on the utopian or the nostalgic if it were not dependent, first of all, on a documentation that these traces do have a life of their own, so to speak, and are integral to the processes that form identities, including the ones that appear defining or dominant. Such clarification of possibilities against the objective, defining conditions within the limits of the discourses "that matter" in any setting, is the one critical intervention and contribution that the ethnographer can make that is uniquely his or her own.

In line with the preceding sets of requirements for modernist ethnography, what the diverse kinds of contemporary works that might be identified as such share is an experimental attitude. This is brought to bear in writing and analysis precisely at those points or moments when one is compelled to explain how structure articulates with the particular cultural experiences encompassed in the account (including the reflexive ones made explicit by the author); how the global articulates with the local; or, as the problematic is currently and commonly expressed, how identities are formed in the simultaneity of relationship between levels of social life and organization (that is, the coevalness, to use Fabian's term (1983), of the state, the economy, international media and popular culture, the region, the locale, the transcultural context, the ethnographer's world and his subjects' *all at once*).

What makes the operations in such works different from, and more daring than say, the work of Anthony Giddens, a theorist who is also very much concerned with the same general problem, is that at the just noted points of articulation they do without, or are open to the possibility of doing without, an imagery of structure to see their accounts through. While understanding the play of structures and unintended consequences in the shaping of any domain or site of social life, they do not need a linking theory of structure as a determination of process, as does Giddens in his resolution of the problem of structure and action in "structuration." It is precisely at this theoretic point in their accounts that the relationship between world and experience, text and reality, structure and action remains uncompromisingly problematic in a way that allows no given or traditional social theoretic solutions to impose order on what is not orderly.[5] Here, then, at the site of articulation where the global and the local are entwined, without grounding reference to a determining culture or history that went before, resides the main experimental problem of modernist ethnography. Here also is the possibility of treating what have been the deepest sorts of issues in traditional social theory as problems of form in which conceptual artifice and descriptive imagination face the facts of ethnographic minutiae.

Exemplars

Nowadays, there is a constant stream of ethnographic works appearing that might each in its own particular way be appreciated as an exemplar of one or more of the modernist strategies developed in this essay. Most do not advertise themselves as experiments or as having an experimental purpose. Rather, they exhibit aspects or dimensions, more or less well developed, that enact a shift toward modernist ethnography as I have depicted it. Such works are interesting here because of this enactment, regardless of how successful they might be judged, or how good they might be otherwise assessed by the conventional standards according to which ethnographies are currently and soberly evaluated (see Marcus and Cushman 1982).

Other contemporary works are interesting for their mere acknowledgment or recognition of alternative possibilities for developing their projects, aside from the ones that they actually pursue. These acknowledgments are usually to be found in the reflexive "spaces" that are increasingly reserved in contemporary ethnographies—in footnotes, anecdotal asides, prefaces, appendices, epilogues, and the like. Paul Willis's *Learning to Labour* (1976), for example, is an early and pioneering example of such a work in the current tendency toward modernist ethnography. This study of the genesis and taxing of working-class identity among a group of nonconformist boys in an English grammar school setting is highly conventional in its rhetoric and development (ethnography is a method of gathering and constituting data on which analysis is then performed), but it is also keenly sensitive and self-critical as to what is elided and finessed by its manner of construction. On its margins (in footnotes, asides, and the afterword), there is a sort of "negative image" of the text which I would see as a prologue to a more experimental effort. For example even as he focuses exclusively on a particular situated group of boys at school, Willis makes it clear that the genesis of class culture should encompass several settings of activity, and that the resistance to capitalist culture as manifested in school experience among the nonconformist boys should be juxtaposed to the same process occurring among other students with a different class identity emerging. He recognizes the challenge, then, of giving up the overly place-focused nature of conventional ethnography without actually taking it up.

So, fitting the requirements that I outlined to exemplars discovered in contemporary ethnography is not so much a classificatory exercise that cannot, in any case, be accomplished mechanically or with any sort of precision, but is rather a framework for coherently documenting, interpreting, and arguing about the diverse range of moves in the construction of works that markedly depart from the traditional objectivist and realist project of ethnography at the core of anthropological practice. Thus, the requirements I have posed are as much a way of reading novelty in contemporary ethnographies as a plea for rethinking the ways that they might be written.

If at the time of writing this paper I were to choose a selection of exemplary texts to discuss, these might be Fischer and Abedi's *Debating Muslims: Cultural Dialogue in Postmodernity and Tradition* (1990), Herzfeld's *Anthropology through the Looking Glass: Critical Ethnography in the Margins of Europe* (1987), Kapferer's *Legends of People, Myths of State: Violence, Intolerance and Political Culture in Sri Lanka and Australia* (1988), Latour's *Pasteurization of France* (1988), Rabinow's *French Modern: Norms and Forms of the Social Environment* (1989), Siegel's *Solo in the New Order: Language and Hierarchy in an Indonesian Town* (1986), and Taussig's *Shamanism, Colonialism, and the Wild Man: A Study in Terror and Healing* (1987). I hope that readers might be stimulated to have a look at these texts to judge for themselves the plausibility of classifying them each as enactments of one or more of the modernist strategies that I have proposed. Even more, I hope that this exercise might suggest to readers other even more appropriate and more complexly realized exemplars from among the works with which they are familiar.

Concluding Notes

Different Senses of Contextualization and Comparison in Modernist Ethnography

Ethnography, realist or modernist, provides interpretation and explanation by strategies of contextualizing the problematic phenomena focused upon. Once we see how something exists embedded in a set of relationships we understand it. The realist ethnography contextualizes with reference to a totality in the form of a literal situated community and/or a semiotic code as cultural structure. The referent of contextualization for the modernist ethnography, which denies itself any conventional concept of totality, are fragments that are arranged and ordered textually by the design of the ethnographer. The rationale or argument for this design is often the most compelling dimension of the modernist work. The whole that is more than the sum of the parts of such ethnographies is always in question, while the parts are systematically related to each other by a revealed logic of connections.

Because modernist texts are not built upon the idea of little worlds in and of themselves—of community or an autonomous and spatially discrete locus of social activity—they, unlike realist ethnographies are aware of and often explicitly incorporate in analytic designs the comparative dimensions which are inherent in their conception. A realist ethnography is usually developed as a potential case for controlled comparison in a geographic areal perspective, where the comparative synthesis of cases is a discrete, specialized task. In contrast, comparison is inherent to analysis and argumentation within modernist ethnographies because they study processes that cross-cut time frames and spatial zones in quite uncontrolled ways (from the conventional areal perspective). In the modernist revisions of both the temporal and spatial dimensions that we discussed in the section on remaking the observed, comparative juxtaposition of quite disparate but related fragments of the past in memory and of situated sites of social activity in space is a key technique of analysis in these works. Also, as noted in the discussion of the remaking of the observer, modernist ethnographies tend to foreground the comparative bifocality that is inherent in all ethnography but remains submerged in most. And in pursuing a thought experiment of critical intervention, the modernist ethnography also, by juxtapositions, compares the various discourses and identity constructs that are present (dominant, residual, possible, and emergent) in any site of study. So, there are at least three senses of comparative analysis embedded within the single project of modernist ethnography, and they differ markedly from the projects of comparative analysis which are external to any realist ethnography and in which the latter may eventually be integrated.

A Constructive Use of Deconstruction in Modernist Ethnography

The general notion of deconstruction derived from the work of Derrida that has come down to us now through various commentaries and applications as a shared intellectual capital is particularly useful in the modernist design for the ethnographic study of identity formation, since empirically this process seems to exhibit basic characteristics of a deconstructive critical process in action. Constructed and migrating through a grid of sites that constitute fragments rather than a community of any sort, an identity is a disseminating phenomenon that has a life of its own beyond the simple literal sense of inhering in particular human agents at a particular site and time. Its meanings are always deferred in any one text/site to other possible loci of its production through the diverse range of mental associations and references with which any human actor can creatively operate, literally through the contingencies of events, and sometimes through an explicit politics for or against the establishment of identities in particular places. In the modernist vision, deconstructive process stands for the human condition itself and is an elaborated restatement of the famous modernist sentiment in Marx—all that is solid melts into air.

However, the potentiality for the endless play of signs exists, and could be pursued by the analyst, for whatever critical purposes, even after certain human subjects would will it to stop. (A Derridean, for example, might want to show that the idea that an identity can be fixed through the will is a self deception, however convenient or satisfying, by playfully continuing the demonstration of dissemination without end.) Yet, identities do seem to stabilize, do resist the modernist condition of migration and dissemination in situations of both great tragedy (racial violence) and liberation (nationalism out of colonialism). To document the stabilizations of identity in any domain or across them in an essentially deconstructive world is a primary task of all ethnography. The modernist ethnography only asserts that such resistance in the struggle to establish identity does not rest on some nostalgic bedrock of tradition or community, but arises inventively out of the same deconstructive conditions that threaten to pull it apart or destabilize what has been achieved.

The Treatment of Power and Ethics in Modernist Ethnography

In the elaborate and programmatic discussions of this essay about the design of modernist ethnography there has been little direct reference to power, class struggle, inequality, and the suffering that has moved history. But modernist strategies focused on problems of describing identity formation in any contemporary site(s) of ethnographic research are indeed so obviously directed toward looking at processes of contestation, struggle, etc., among discourses arising from objective political and economic circumstances that this could go without saying. Far from ignoring "objective conditions" such as processes of coercion, the play of interests, and class formation, the focus of modernist ethnography on the experiential and access to it through language in context is a direct engagement with and exploration of such conditions—without, however, the usual obeisances to the given social scientific frameworks for their discussion. The modernist strategies for ethnography articulate with Foucaultian and Gramscian ideas about the playing out of power relations in cultural cognitions, ideologies, and discourses (apprehended as voices here). In relation to the concerns of political economy with the operations of states, markets, and productive capacity, they seek to display critically the voices/alternatives present at any site of political contest, and to define the politics and the alternatives addressed and not addressed by it in a cultural frame. The great promise of such ethnography is indeed the possibility of changing the terms in which we think objectively and conventionally about power through exposure to cultural discourses.

But while modernist ethnography operates fully cognizant of the history of the political and economic circumstances in which identities have been formed, it is not built explicitly around the trope of power, but rather of ethics, that is, the complex moral relationship of the observer to the observed, of the relevance of the observed's situation to the situation of the observer's own society, and ultimately the exploration of the critical purpose of contemporary ethnographic analysis. These ethical concerns are never resolved in any ethnography, and they expose the kinds of contradictions embedded in the doing of ethnographic research and writing that make the ethnographer vulnerable to a diverting critique of his or her own ethics. But the risk of some readers not seeing anything in this but narcissism and hand-wringing is well worth taking, since the shaping of modernist strategies through a kind of ethical awareness (about the distinctive grounds of knowledge generated through ethnography) is essential to pursuing the traditional ends of ethnographic realism in the late twentieth century. This is what the modernist remaking of the observer and observed in ethnography stands for.

Notes

1. Other formulations of the same general problematic that I have recently come across or been reminded of are, for example, Ahmad 1987: 22–25; Clifford 1986a: 24; Rabinow 1986: 258; and Jameson 1987: 40.

2. Thus, to my mind, the tendency to label the current ongoing critique of anthropology as the "postmodern turn" or "postmodern" anthropology is misguided. True, the nature of contemporary artistic production and the debates about it have powerfully fed the appetite for controversy in the humanities and

the human sciences in the United States during the past decade, but the critique of ethnography and the experiments that follow from it can in no way be closely identified with aesthetic postmodernism. The provocations of the latter have merely created the conditions for appreciating the worth among some anthropologists in research and writing strategies of aspects of classic modernism rethought and revived for their continuing, rather traditional purposes.

3. This play has been facilitated by a rhetorical, literary-style critique of ethnography perhaps best represented in the volume that Jim Clifford and I edited, *Writing Culture* (1986). In my view, the main value of this critique is that it has made possible the exploration of new problems and even methods in anthropology by allowing for the possibility of alternative frameworks and terms in which its traditional problem areas could be rethought. This has been the most important contribution, thus far, of the so-called literary turn in anthropology, which some have unfairly charged with leading to hermeticism and narcissism, among other academic disorders. Whatever one might think of the use of the textual metaphor in the actual interpretation of ethnographic materials, or of reflexivity as an analytic strategy, the contribution of the textual critique of ethnography itself can hardly be denied.

4. The renewed and focused interest in local determinations of identity (and, by extension, in the traditional topic areas of ethnicity, race, and nationality) is just one of a number of areas of social scientific study which are being rethought through assimilation for its own purposes of aspects of the current debate over modernism/postmodernism. Identity formation is the one that most proximately affects the traditional subject-matter and methods of anthropology. Other social scientific arenas which are being especially influenced by attempts to describe a contemporary modern/postmodern world are urban and regional planning; the emergence of global post-Fordist production processes and political economy; the media and mass cultural productions; and the so-called crisis of "foundations" in the intellectual work of experts and academics generally (for a survey of such applications, see the special double issue of the journal *Theory, Culture and Society*, 1988, on postmodernism).

5. Of course, Victor Turner's influential notions of anti-structure and liminality (1969) are related to the "space of experimentation" that I am delineating here. Indeed, Turner is ancestral to the contemporary spirit of experimentation, but the "anti-structure" tendency in modernist ethnography is significantly different from the similar notion in Turner's work. Turner did not attempt to theoretically do without or dissolve the idea of structure. Liminality fitted easily into a broader scheme of order and derived its definition in relation to it. Modernist anti-structure has a much more uneasy relation to concepts of order, and is more radically deconstructive of the latter. In contemporary experiments, order is not so easily disambiguated in theory and concept from deconstructive process (or disorder). It is in relentlessly sustaining an ambiguity about such distinctions that modernist ethnography clearly distinguishes itself from Turner's liminality, which has its own sphere, and assumes a contrast with structure.

References

Ahmad, Aijaz 1987: "Jameson's rhetoric of Otherness and the 'National Allegory,'" *Social Text* (Fall), 3–25.

Berman, Marshall 1982: *All That Is Solid Melts into Air: The Experience of Modernity.* New York: Simon & Schuster; 1983: London: Verso; 1988 (2d ed.): Harmondsworth: Penguin.

Bright, Charles, and Geyer, Michael 1987: "For a unified history of the world in the twentieth century," *Radical History Review,* 39, 69–91.

Clifford, James 1986a: Introduction, in Clifford and Marcus 1986.

Clifford, James 1986b: "On ethnographic allegory," in Clifford and Marcus 1986.

Clifford, James, and Marcus, George E. (eds.) 1986: *Writing Culture: The Poetics and Politics of Ethnography.* Berkeley: University of California Press.

Fabian, Johannes 1983: *Time and the Other: How Anthropology Makes Its Object.* New York: Columbia University Press.

Fischer, Michael 1986: "Ethnicity and the post-modern arts of memory," in Clifford and Marcus 1986.

Fischer, Michael, and Abedi, Mehdi 1990: *Debating Muslims: Cultural Dialogue in Postmodernity and Tradition.* Madison: University of Wisconsin Press.

Herzfeld, Michael 1987: *Anthropology through the Looking-glass: Critical Ethnography in the Margins of Europe.* Cambridge: Cambridge University Press.

Jameson, Fredric 1987: "Regarding postmodernism—a conversation with Fredric Jameson," *Social Text* (Fall), 29–54.

Kapferer, Bruce 1988: *Legends of People, Myths of State: Violence, Intolerance and Political Culture in Sri Lanka and Australia.* Washington, D.C.: Smithsonian Institution Press.

Latour, Bruno 1988: *The Pasteurization of France.* Cambridge, Mass.: Harvard University Press.

Marcus, George E. 1986: "Contemporary problems of ethnography in the modern world system," in Clifford and Marcus 1986.

Marcus, George E. 1989: "The problem of the unseen world of wealth for the rich: toward an ethnography of complex connections," *Ethos,* 17, 110–19.

Marcus, George E. n.d.: "Imagining the whole: ethnography's contemporary effort to situate itself," *Critique of Anthropology* (forthcoming).

Marcus, George E., and Cushman, Dick 1982: "Ethnographies as texts," in *Annual Review of Anthropology,* vol. 2, 25–89. Palo Alto, Calif.: Annual Reviews, Inc.

Marcus, George E., and Fischer, Michael 1986: *Anthropology as Cultural Critique: An Experimental Moment in the Human Sciences.* Chicago: University of Chicago Press.

Rabinow, Paul 1986: "Representations are social facts: modernity and postmodernity in anthropology," in Clifford and Marcus 1986.

Rabinow, Paul 1989: *French Modern: Norms and Forms of the Social Environment.* Cambridge, Mass.: MIT Press.

Siegel, James T. 1986: *Solo in the New Order: Language and Hierarchy in an Indonesian Town.* Princeton: Princeton University Press.

Taussig, Michael 1987: *Shamanism, Colonialism, and the Wild Man: A Study in Terror and Healing.* Chicago: University of Chicago Press.

Theory, Culture and Society 1988: "Postmodernism." Special double issue, 5/2–3.

Turner, Victor 1969: *The Ritual Process.* Chicago: Aldine.

Williams, Raymond 1977: *Marxism and Literature.* New York: Oxford University Press.

Willis, Paul 1976: *Learning to Labour: How Working Class Kids Get Working Class Jobs.* New York: Columbia University Press.

Wolf, Eric 1982: *Europe and the People without History.* Berkeley: University of California Press.

Three

Ethnography in/of the World System

THE EMERGENCE OF MULTI-SITED ETHNOGRAPHY (1995)

Introduction

In the mid-1980s, I specified two modes in which ethnographic re-search was embedding itself within the context of a historic and con-temporary world system of capitalist political economy (56, 57). The most common mode preserves the intensively-focused-upon single site of ethnographic observation and participation while developing by other means and methods the world system context. Examples of these other methods include working in archives and adapting the work of macrotheorists and other kinds of scholars as a mode of contextualiz-ing portraiture in terms of which the predicaments of local subjects are described and analyzed. In this mode, a vital literature continues to appear on the historic (colonial) and contemporary incorporation of peoples as working classes or on the apparent reduction of local cul-tures by the macro-processes associated with capitalist political econ-omy in the many forms it has taken (e.g., 10, 11, 31, 70, 74, 100). Such ethnography has produced refined examinations of resistance and ac-commodation—a concern with the dynamics of encapsulation, focused on the relationships, language, and objects of encounter and response from the perspectives of local and cosmopolitan groups and persons who, although in different relative power positions, experience a pro-cess of being mutually displaced from what has counted as culture for each of them. This mode has shown that the heart of contemporary ethnographic analysis is not in the reclamation of some previous cul-tural state or its subtle preservation despite changes, but rather in the new cultural forms to which changes in colonial subaltern situations have given rise.

The other, much less common mode of ethnographic research self-consciously embedded in a world system, now often associated with the wave of intellectual capital labeled postmodern, moves out from the single sites and local situations of conventional ethnographic research designs to examine the circulation of cultural meanings, objects, and identities in diffuse time-space. This mode defines for itself an object of study that cannot be accounted for ethnographically by remaining focused on a single site of intensive investigation. It develops instead a strategy or design of research that acknowledges macrotheoretical concepts and narratives of the world system but does not rely on them for the contextual architecture framing a set of subjects. This mobile ethnography takes unexpected trajectories in tracing a cultural formation across and within multiple sites of activity that destabilize the distinction, for example, between lifeworld and system (49), by which much ethnography has been conceived. Just as this mode investigates and ethnographically constructs the lifeworlds of variously situated subjects, it also ethnographically constructs aspects of the system itself through the associations and connections it suggests among sites.

This second, still emergent mode of ethnography, upon which I focus in this essay, may begin in the world system, but because of the way it evolves its object of study, this mode comes circumstantially to be of the world system as well. In particular, I focus on the various mapping strategies evident in this mode of ethnography and on the challenges that it poses for the assumptions and expectations embedded in the ethnographic method itself. Of course, the intellectual capital of so-called postmodernism has provided ideas and concepts for the emergence of multi-sited ethnography, but more importantly it arises in response to empirical changes in the world and therefore to transformed locations of cultural production (see especially 47). Empirically following the thread of cultural process itself impels the move toward multi-sited ethnography.

Research in anthropology that has embedded ethnographic subjects of study within contexts of a world system, historical political economies of colonialism, market regimes, state formation, and nation-building has developed explicitly within genres of Marxist anthropology (e.g., 16), anthropology and political economy (e.g., 79), and anthropology and history (e.g., 11, 79). Although some contemporary exemplars of multi-sited ethnography have developed within these traditional genres, many of the most striking examples have emerged in arenas of work that have not been identified with these typically world system–based contexts. These studies arise instead from anthropology's participation in a number of interdisciplinary (in fact, ideologically antidisciplinary) arenas that have evolved since the 1980s, such as media studies, feminist studies, science and technology studies, various strands of cultural studies, and the theory, culture, and society group (see 23, 50). Precisely because such interdisciplinary arenas do not share a clearly bounded object of study, distinct disciplinary perspectives that participate in them tend to be challenged. For ethnography this means that the world system is not the theoretically constituted holistic frame that gives context to the contemporary study of peoples or local subjects closely observed by ethnographers, but it becomes, in a piecemeal way, integral to and embedded in discontinuous, multi-sited objects of study. Cultural logics so much sought after in anthropology are always multiply produced, and any ethnographic account of these logics finds that they are at least partly constituted within sites of the so-called system (i.e., modern interlocking institutions of media, markets, states, industries, universities—the worlds of elites, experts, and middle classes). Strategies of quite literally following connections, associations, and putative relationships are thus at the very heart of designing multi-sited ethnographic research.

Shifts in macro-perspectives of the world system since the 1970s have accommodated well the trends of ethnography described here. Wallerstein's world system initiative (97) revived historically embedded social science generally. It provided a grand systemic narrative of world history that invited itself to be filled in and debated through the production of regional and micro-geographic social histories and ethnographies. In 1982, Wolf (101) provided an articulation of the specifically anthropological version of the grand world system narrative, which preserved, albeit on a comparative scale, the model of the ethnographic research project as single-site probing of local situations and peoples.

Successor views of the world system in the 1980s were pushed both by new sets of intellectual influences that operated against working within the frame of closed, though dynamic, systems narratives of macro-social processes and by the reflective awareness throughout the academy of massive changes afoot in the post–World War II international regimes of political economy. For those across disciplines interested in placing their specific projects of research in the unfolding of new arrangements for which past historical narratives were not fully adequate, a firm sense of a world system framework was replaced by various accounts of dissolution and fragmentation, as well as new processes—captured in concepts like post-Fordism (48), time-space compression (48), flexible specialization (48), the end of organized capitalism (51), and most recently, globalization (23, 44, 84) and transnationalism (39a,b)—none of which could be fully understood in terms of earlier macromodels of the capitalist world system. Even from within the heart of neoclassical economics, there are eloquent (and not altogether pessimistic) statements about the contemporary predicament of the loss of a firm systemic grasp of contemporary political economy. For example, as Robert Solow, the MIT Nobel laureate, said in 1991, "There is not some glorious theoretical synthesis of capitalism that you can write down in a book and follow. You have to grope your way" (86a). What does such groping mean for the ethnographer?

For ethnographers interested in contemporary local changes in culture and society, single-sited research can no longer be easily located in a world system perspective. This perspective has become fragmented, indeed, "local" at its very core. With the collapse, then, of the easy distinction between system and lifeworld (49) as the mode for situating and designing ethnographic research on the contemporary world, the only alternatives have been to use various successor works of scholarship on global changes in political economy as the framing for single-site studies that are fully defined and contextualized in terms of those mostly nonethnographic works, or to pursue the more open-ended and speculative course of constructing subjects by simultaneously constructing the discontinuous contexts in which they act and are acted upon. The distinction between lifeworlds of subjects and the system does not hold, and the point of ethnography within the purview of its always local, close-up perspective is to discover new paths of connection and association by which traditional ethnographic concerns with agency, symbols, and everyday practices can continue to be expressed on a differently configured spatial canvas (see 56).

At stake here are conventional views and commitments to ethnographic method, which in recent times have not been discussed very much in methodological terms. Rather, novelty in method has been embedded in a discourse of reflexive self-presentation in contemporary ethnography in which the emphasis is on ethics, commitment, and activism. The pure, scaffold-like methodological implication of the way that multi-sited ethnography is devised in more committed language might seem to be mechanical and smack of older forms of positivism and of the disengaged positioning characteristic of value-free social science. The selection of space and sites of investigation emerge inseparably from the highly politicized way that the problem of investigation and then writing is cognized. Still, for conventional ethnography as it has been practiced in anthropology, the most interesting issues concerning emergent multi-site studies are most clearly understood in methodological terms (see especially 54a), so I have adopted such a methodological focus in this essay. In the final section, however, I consider the reflexive activist persona through which this mode of ethnographic research actually articulates and designs methodological questions and research designs.

Methodological Anxieties

Among anthropologists, the move toward multi-sited ethnography might give rise to three sets of methodological anxieties: a concern about testing the limits of ethnography, a concern about attenuating the power of fieldwork, and a concern about the loss of the subaltern.

Testing the Limits of Ethnography

Ethnography is predicated upon attention to the everyday, an intimate knowledge of face-to-face communities and groups. The idea that ethnography might expand from its committed localism to represent a system much better apprehended by abstract models and aggregate statistics seems antithetical to its very nature and thus beyond its limits. Although multi-sited ethnography is an exercise in mapping terrain, its goal is not holistic representation, an ethnographic portrayal of the world system as a totality. Rather, it claims that any ethnography of a cultural formation in the world system is also an ethnography of the system, and therefore cannot be understood only in terms of the conventional single-site mise-en-scène of ethnographic research, assuming indeed it is the cultural formation, produced in several different locales, rather than the conditions of a particular set of subjects that is the object of study. For ethnography, then, there is no global in the local-global contrast now so frequently evoked. The global is an emergent dimension of arguing about the connection among sites in a multi-sited ethnography. Thus, the multi-sited ethnography is content to stipulate some sort of total world system as long as the terms of any particular macro-construct of that system are not allowed to stand for the context of ethnographic work that becomes opportunistically constituted by the path or trajectory it takes in its design of sites.

Attenuating the Power of Fieldwork

The issue then arises of whether multi-sited ethnography is possible without attenuating the kinds of knowledges and competencies that are expected from fieldwork. In other words, is multi-site fieldwork practical? One response is that the field broadly conceived and encompassed in the fieldwork experience of most standard ethnographic projects indeed already crosses many potentially related sites of work, but as research evolves, principles of selection operate to bound the effective field in line with long-standing disciplinary perceptions about what the object of study should be. Thus, fieldwork as traditionally perceived and practiced is already itself potentially multi-sited.

Furthermore, standard cultural history (e.g., 7, 38a) is very much multi-sited, but unlike in anthropology, this feature of research is unproblematic. This undoubtedly has something to so with the fragmentary, reconstructive nature of historical method, in which the composition and probing of the relationships of dispersed materials are basic. It is perhaps anthropologists' appreciation of the difficulty of doing intensive ethnography at any site and the satisfaction that comes from such work in the past when it is done well that would give them pause when the ethnographer becomes mobile and still claims to have done good fieldwork.

Indeed, something of the mystique and reality of conventional fieldwork is lost in the move toward multi-sited ethnography. But not all sites are treated by a uniform set of fieldwork practices of the same intensity. Multi-sited ethnographies inevitably are the product of knowledge bases of varying intensities and qualities. To do ethnographic research, for example, on the social grounds that produce a particular discourse of policy requires different practices and opportunities than does fieldwork among the situated communities such policy affects (see especially 22). To bring these sites into the same frame of study and to posit their relationships on the basis of firsthand ethnographic research in both is the important contribution of this kind of ethnography, regardless of the variability of the quality and accessibility of that research at different sites.

Many factors thus control for the quality of fieldwork in multi-sited research. The point is that in such research a certain valorized conception of fieldwork and what it offers wherever it is conducted threatens to be qualified, displaced, or decentered in the conduct of multi-sited ethnography. Still, what is not lost but remains essential to multi-sited research is the function of translation from one cultural idiom or language to another. This function is enhanced since it is no longer practiced in the primary, dualistic "them-us" frame of conventional ethnography but requires considerably more nuancing and shading as the practice of translation connects the several sites that the research explores along unexpected and even dissonant fractures of social location. Indeed, the persuasiveness of the broader field that any such ethnography maps and constructs is in its capacity to make connections through translations and tracings among distinctive discourses from site to site.

In this enhanced challenge of translation, literal language learning remains as important as it has been in preparing for traditional fieldwork. Just as "knowing the language" guarantees the integrity of traditional fieldwork and gives the bounded field—e.g., a people, an ethnic group, a community—its most important coherence as a culture, this skill is as important in multi-sited fieldwork and with even more exactitude. It is perhaps no accident that exemplars thus far of multi-sited fieldwork have been developed in monolingual (largely Anglo-American) contexts in which fine-grained knowledge of the language is unproblematic for native English speakers. Yet, if such ethnography is to flourish in arenas that anthropology has defined as emblematic interests, it will soon have to become as multilingual as it is multi-sited. In this sense, it conforms to (and often exceeds) the most exacting and substantive demands of traditional fieldwork.

The Loss of the Subaltern

It is not just any situated subjects that ethnography concerned with the world system focuses upon, but in this context, it habitually focuses upon subaltern subjects, those positioned by systemic domination (ultimately traceable to capitalist and colonialist political economy in its variety of forms). Although multi-sited ethnography may not necessarily forsake the perspective of the subaltern, it is bound to shift the focus of attention to other domains of cultural production and ultimately to challenge this frequently privileged positioning of ethnographic perspective. In the frame of science studies, Haraway is eloquent on this point: "A commitment to mobile positioning and to passionate detachment is dependent on the impossibility of innocent 'identity' politics and epistemologies as strategies for seeing from the standpoints of the subjugated in order to see well. One cannot 'be' either a cell or molecule—or a woman, colonized person, labourer, and so on—if one intends to see and see from these positions critically . . ." (46:192).

In yielding the ethnographic centering on the subaltern point of view, one is also decentering the resistance and accommodation framework that has organized a considerable body of valuable research (see 82) for the sake of a reconfigured space of multiple sites of cultural production in which questions of resistance, although not forgotten, are often subordinated to different sorts of questions about the shape of systemic processes themselves and complicities with these processes among variously positioned subjects.

So, it is a mistake to understand multi-sited ethnography, as it sometimes has been, as merely adding perspectives peripherally to the usual subaltern focus—e.g., adding perspectives on elites and institutions, or "studying up" (68) for mere completeness. Rather, this kind of ethnography maps a new object of study in which previous situating narratives like that of resistance and accommodation become qualified by expanding what is ethnographically "in the picture" of research both as it evolves in the field and as it is eventually written up.

Nor is multi-sited ethnography merely a different kind of controlled comparison, long a part of anthropological practice, as it has also sometimes been understood, although it does represent a revival of comparative study in anthropology. Conventional controlled comparison in anthropology is indeed multi-sited, but it operates on a linear spatial plane, whether the context is a region, a broader culture area, or the world system (see, e.g., 31, 85); comparisons are generated for homogeneously conceived conceptual units (e.g., peoples, communities, locales), and such comparisons usually are developed from distinctly bounded periods or separate projects of fieldwork.

In projects of multi-sited ethnographic research, de facto comparative dimensions develop instead as a function of the fractured, discontinuous plane of movement and discovery among sites as one maps an object of study and needs to posit logics of relationship, translation, and association among these sites. Thus, in multi-sited ethnography, comparison emerges from putting questions to an emergent object of study whose contours, sites, and relationships are not known beforehand, but are themselves a contribution of making an account that has different, complexly connected real-world sites of investigation. The object of study is ultimately mobile and multiply situated, so any ethnography of such an object will have a comparative dimension that is integral to it, in the form of juxtapositions of phenomena that conventionally have appeared to be (or conceptually have been kept) "worlds apart." Comparison reenters the very act of ethnographic specification by a research design of juxtapositions in which the global is collapsed into and made an integral part of parallel, related local situations rather than something monolithic or external to them. This move toward comparison embedded in the multi-sited ethnography stimulates accounts of cultures composed in a landscape for which there is as yet no developed theoretical conception or descriptive model.

Interdisciplinary Arenas and New Objects of Study

There are several inspirations for multi-sited ethnography within the high theoretical capital associated with postmodernism: One might think, for example, of Foucault's power/knowledge and heterotopia (18), Deleuze & Guattari's rhizome (13), Derrida's dissemination (15), and Lyotard's juxtaposition by "blocking together" (78). These concepts anticipate many of the contemporary social and cultural conditions with which ethnographers and other scholars are trying to come to terms in shaping their objects of study in the absence of reliable holistic models of macroprocess for contextualizing referents of research, such as "the world system," "capitalism," "the state," "the nation," etc. However, such high theoretical capital usually is not the most proximate source for the terms by which multi-sited ethnographic research is thought through and conceived. Instead, multi-sited ethnography is intellectually constructed in terms of the specific constructions and discourses appearing within a number of highly self-conscious interdisciplinary arenas that use the diverse high theoretical capital that inspires postmodernism to reconfigure the conditions for the study of contemporary cultures and societies. This section briefly samples three such milieus in which objects of study have been evoked appropriate for composite, multi-method, mobile works of scholarship, including specifically multi-sited ethnography.

Unfortunately, there are many more concepts and visions for doing multi-sited ethnography than there are achieved exemplars (see next section). There is no doubt, however, that within the various interdisciplinary arenas, the following concepts for reconfigured objects of study come not from detached theoretical exercises, but from vital and active research efforts in progress, the forms of whose written and published results are yet to be established fully.

Media studies has been one important arena in which multi-sited ethnographic research has emerged. Distinct genres of research have appeared on production (especially in television and film industries), on the one hand, and on the reception of such productions, on the other. These two functions have been encompassed and related to each other within the frame of individual projects of research, thus making even more complex the trajectory of modes of ethnographic research that had already tended to be multi-sited in their construction of objects of study (77).

In anthropology, there has been a shift from older interests in ethnographic film toward a more encompassing terrain for the study of indigenous media (Ginsburg's writings have been key in this shift [35–37]). This change has been stimulated by ethnographic study and participation in contemporary indigenous peoples' movements within and across nation-states. The control of means of mass communication and the activist role of indigenous peoples as media producers in these movements have reconfigured the space in which the ethnography of many of anthropology's traditional subjects can effectively be done; they also have made this space inherently multi-sited (see, e.g., 96). The above-noted merging of production and reception sites in media studies has reinforced this tendency in the design of ethnographic research on specifically indigenous media.

The social and cultural study of science and technology is another major arena in which genres of multi-sited ethnographic research have established their importance. Theorists such as Latour (52, 53) and Haraway (45, 46) have been crucially important in pushing the ethnographic dimensions of this field beyond pioneering lab studies to more complex (and multi-sited) social and cultural time-spaces. Haraway's cyborg (45) has been an especially influential construct in stimulating field researchers to think unconventionally about the juxtaposed sites that constitute their objects of study (17).

In anthropological work within the field of cultural studies of science and technology, the tendency toward multi-sited research is most prevalent in the following topical areas: the study of issues concerning reproduction and reproductive technologies (originating in an important domain of feminist research in medical anthropology) (38); epidemiological studies in medical anthropology (4a); studies of new modes of electronic communication such as the Internet (see, e.g., 19, 61); and studies concerned with environmentalism and toxic disasters (e.g., 54, 88, 102). Another area is the study of the emergence of biotechnology and "big" science projects like the human genome project (of particular interest here is Rabinow's [76] work on the discovery and commodification of the polymerase chain reaction, especially related to the multi-sited style of his earlier work on French modernity [75]). The title of a recent survey of biotechnology, *Gene Dreams, Wall Street, Academia, and the Rise of Biotechnology* (93), captures the methodological tendency toward multi-sited objects of study.

Amid the diffuse inspirations and influences of the broad interdisciplinary arena of cultural studies in the United States, the collection edited by Grossberg et al. (41) surveys the possibilities and limits of this remarkable remaking of the early and equally diffuse discussions of postmodernism during the 1970s and 1980s. Within this diffuse area of cultural studies, the Public Culture project deserves special mention because it addresses the long-standing concerns of anthropology and area studies. It was originated by Arjun Appadurai and Carol Breckenridge and developed through the independent Center for Transnational Cultural Studies in Chicago (8), with the journal *Public Culture* as its major publication. This project has constituted a major point of intersection for many diverse strands of cultural studies, broadly conceived around issues of the rethinking of ideas of culture (especially questions of trans- and cross-cultural production) in the face of contemporary world system changes. Appadurai's widely read paper (4) on the global cultural economy has provided a complex multi-sited vision for research in this transnational domain that defies older practices of "locating" culture(s) in place(s).

Theoretically rethinking concepts of space and place in ethnographic research (43, 47), for which the work of cultural geographers and sociologists (30, 86) has been a reinforcing inspiration, has stimulated the opening of established genres of anthropological research to multi-sited constructions of ethnographic research designs. For example, migration studies have become part of a much richer body of work on mobile and contingently settled populations, across borders, in exile, and in diasporas (e.g., 9, 33, 71). This work, concerned theoretically with the construction of identities in global-local frames, merges with the methods and spaces constructed by media studies (e.g., 1, 69).

Development studies are similarly being reconceived. Important critiques by Ferguson (25) and Escobar (20) of older development agencies and paradigms have been followed by a much more diverse sense of the field in which any study of development must now be evolved. For example, Escobar's study of a region in Colombia (21) draws the intersections among social movements, older development approaches, and the powerful global environmentalist doctrine of biodiversity. Again, redrawing the boundaries of topics of study here inevitably causes overlap with the terrains being established by other interdisciplinary arenas such as media studies and science and technology studies. But the most interesting and specific manifestations of these reconfigurations of perspective in overlapping interdisciplinary arenas are in the modes of constructing multi-sited spaces of investigation within individual projects of research, to which we now turn.

Modes of Construction

Powerful conceptual visions of multi-sited spaces for ethnographic research that have been especially influential in anthropology, such as Haraway's construct of the cyborg (45) and Appadurai's idea of the global cultural economy with its variety of "scapes" (4), do not also function as guides for designing the research that would exemplify and fulfill such visions. This requires a more literal discussion of methodological issues, such as how to construct the multi-sited space through which the ethnographer traverses.

Such explicitly methodological discussions are rare. An interesting exception is Strathern's (89) highly theoretical discussion of rethinking problems of relationality and connectivity in light of influential ideas within science and technology studies deriving from chaos theory (39) as well as from Haraway's notion of the cyborg. Despite the abstract character of Strathern's work, she remains close to issues of how ethnographic research is to be designed.

Multi-sited research is designed around chains, paths, threads, conjunctions, or juxtapositions of locations in which the ethnographer establishes some form of literal, physical presence, with an explicit, posited logic of association or connection among sites that in fact defines the argument of the ethnography. Indeed, such multi-sited ethnography is a revival of a sophisticated practice of constructivism, one of the most interesting and fertile practices of representation and investigation by the Russian avant-garde of momentous social change just before and after their revolution. Constructivists viewed the artist as an engineer whose task was to construct useful objects, much like a factory worker, while actively participating in the building of a new society. Film-making, especially the work of Vertov (e.g., "The Man with the Movie Camera"), was one of the most creative and de facto ethnographic media through which constructivism (72) was produced. From a methodological perspective, Vertov's work is an excellent inspiration for multi-sited ethnography.

Multi-sited ethnographies define their objects of study through several different modes or techniques. These techniques might be understood as practices of construction through (preplanned or opportunistic) movement and of tracing within different settings of a complex cultural phenomenon given an initial, baseline conceptual identity that turns out to be contingent and malleable as one traces it.

Follow the People

This technique is perhaps the most obvious and conventional mode of materializing a multi-sited ethnography. Malinowski's *Argonauts of the Western Pacific* is the archetypal account (55). The exchange or circulation of objects or the extension in space of particular cultural complexes such as ritual cycles and pilgrimages may be rationales for such ethnography, but the procedure is to follow and stay with the movements of a particular group of initial subjects. Migration studies are perhaps the most common contemporary research genre of this basic mode of multi-sited ethnography. Within this genre, a recent paper by Rouse (80) (but see also the statement by Gupta & Ferguson [42] as well as their edited collection [43]) is notable and often cited for moving migration studies (e.g., 40) into the terrain of diaspora studies, which has arisen as one of the key genres of cultural studies. Rouse follows his Mexican subjects across borders and sites in the conventional mode of migration studies, but in the spirit of contemporary, self-consciously multi-sited ethnography, he materializes a new object of study, a sense of a diasporic world independent of the mere movement of subjects from one place to another.

Willis's study (99), and Foley's study (29) of a school in Texas, inspired by the former, is a foreshortened version of "following the people" in that their strategic significance as single-site research with multiple sites evoked is their "off-stage" knowledge, so to speak, of what happens to their subjects in the other sites. The sense of "system" in their work arises from the connection between ethnographic portraits of their subjects and the posited relationship of these portraits to the fates of these same subjects in other locations.

Follow the Thing

This mode of constructing the multi-sited space of research involves tracing the circulation through different contexts of a manifestly material object of study (at least as initially conceived), such as commodities, gifts, money, works of art, and intellectual property. This is perhaps the most common approach to the ethnographic study of processes in the capitalist world system. Indeed, this technique is at the heart of Wallerstein's method for fine-grained study of process in the world system (97:4):

> The concept of commodity chain is central to our understanding of the processes of the capitalist world-economy. . . . Take any consumable product, say clothing. It is manufactured. The manufacturing process minimally involves material inputs, machinery, and labor. Material inputs are either manufactured or produced in some way. Machinery is manufactured. And labor must be recruited either locally or by immigration, and must be fed. . . . We may continue to trace each "box" further back in terms of its material inputs, machinery, land, labor. The totality constitutes a commodity chain.

Wallerstein's commodity chain is hardly laid out with a specifically ethnographic sensibility, but it is clearly a blueprint appropriate for multi-sited research.

In anthropology, Mintz's culture history of sugar (66) is an exemplar of the "follow the thing" technique, but also within a conventional political economy framework that depends on a master historical narrative of the workings of colonialism and capitalism. However, the most important and influential statement of this technique for multi-sited research on the circulation of things is Appadurai's introduction to his collection, *The Social Life of Things* (3, see also 12). In tracing the shifting status of things as commodities, gifts, and resources in their circulations through different contexts, Appadurai presumes very little about the governance of a controlling narrative of macroprocess in capitalist political economy but allows the sense of system to emerge ethnographically and speculatively by following paths of circulation. Although there are no ethnographies in the genre traditionally associated with studies of contemporary capitalist political economy that literally take a thing-oriented approach, an impressive ethnographic literature on consumption and commodities has appeared, which if not multi-sited in actual research design, is produced in the speculative, open-ended spirit of tracing things in and through contexts (see especially 65, 98).

The most explicit experimentation with multi-sited research using this technique seems to have emerged in studies of contemporary worlds of art and aesthetics (see especially 63). Notable examples include Myers's study (67) of the circulation of Pintupi acrylic paintings in Western art worlds, Savigliano's study of tango (81a), Steiner's study (87) of the transit of African curios into Western art markets, along with Taylor and Barbash's film (92) based on Steiner's study, Silverman's study of taste in Reagan's America (83) across three intensively explored sites, Feld's mapping (24) of "world music" and "world beat," and Bright's study of Chicano low riders (5a, 5b).

Finally, among some of the most influential, self-consciously multi-sited work in the arena of science and technology studies, the "follow the thing" mode of constructing the space of investigation has been prominent. Latour's work (52, 53) exemplifies this mode, albeit less so than does Haraway's, which has as much a metaphorical as a material sense of the things she traces. Latour's study (53) of the triumph of Pasteur's biology in France provocatively places, with a claim of equivalence, microbes, machines, and humans in various locations on the same plane or map of investigation.

Follow the Metaphor

When the thing traced is within the realm of discourse and modes of thought, then the circulation of signs, symbols, and metaphors guides the design of ethnography. This mode involves trying to trace the social correlates and groundings of associations that are most clearly alive in language use and print or visual media. Haraway's influential studies work primarily through this mode of constructing the object of study. In anthropology, the most fully achieved multi-sited ethnography in this mode (and in a sense, the most fully achieved and rationalized multi-site ethnography, whatever mode of construction, thus far) is Martin's *Flexible Bodies: Tracking Immunity in American Culture From the*

Days of Polio to the Age of AIDS (64). Her initial interest is in ways of thinking about the body's immune system at various locations in American society—in the mass media, "on the street," in the treatment of AIDS, among alternative practitioners, and among scientists. She is interested in the variety of distinct discourses and registers concerning the immune system and in the ethnographic characteristics of their social locations. She uses a variety of methods and modes of participation for each location she probes—some in more depth than others.

Martin notes a pivotal point in her research: "One of the clearest moments of 'implosion' in my fieldwork, when elements from different research contexts seemed to collapse into one another with great force, occurred in a graduate course I was taking in immunology . . ." (64:91). With an ear for metaphor, Martin makes the association between the trope of flexibility so prominent in scientific conceptions of the immune system and the regime of flexible specialization so salient in late-twentieth-century capitalism. She is then led to a fascinating exploration of complexity theory in which the trope of flexibility seems to be most systematically thought out, to theories and practices of corporate management, and to new ideologies of work and how they are inculcated in training programs in which she participates. Her provocative argument about an emergent from of post-Darwinist subjectivity in the United States depends for its persuasiveness on the multi-sited ethnographic space she has tracked by working through discovered metaphorical associations. This mode of constructing multi-sited research is thus especially potent for suturing locations of cultural production that had not been obviously connected and, consequently, for creating empirically argued new envisionings of social landscapes.

Follow the Plot, Story, or Allegory

There are stories or narratives told in the frame of single-site fieldwork that might themselves serve as a heuristic for the fieldworker constructing multi-sited ethnographic research. This has been a routine technique in the disciplinary history of Levi-Straussian myth analysis within so-called traditional societies. In the framework of modernity, the character of the stories that people tell as myth in their everyday situations is not as important to fieldworkers tracking processes and associations within the world system as is their own situated sense of social landscapes. Reading for the plot and then testing this against the reality of ethnographic investigation that constructs its sites according to a compelling narrative is an interesting, virtually untried mode of constructing multi-sited research. However, Brooks's reading for the plot (6) in classic Freudian case studies as a way of developing innovative re-envisionings of relationships in Victorian society is suggestive of the way that plots in ethnographically found stories and narratives might be used to diversify the space of an object of study in fieldwork (58).

Perhaps the one genre of work where this technique is now being used is the renewed interest among anthropologists and others in social memory. Boyarin's recent collection (5) on the remapping of memory concerns social struggles over alternative visions about the definition of collective reality. Processes of remembering and forgetting produce precisely those kinds of narratives, plots, and allegories that threaten to reconfigure in often disturbing ways versions (myths, in fact) that serve state and institutional orders. In this way, such narratives and plots are a rich source of connections, associations, and suggested relationships for shaping multi-sited objects of research.

Follow the Life or Biography

The life history, a particularly favored form of ethnographic data in recent years, is a special case of following the plot. How to produce and develop life histories as ethnography has been the subject of much reflection, but the use of biographical narrative as a means of designing multi-sited research rarely has been considered. Fischer has produced one of the few discussions (26) of the use of life history in this way, and his work with Abedi (28) is a partial implementation of a strategy of developing more systematic analysis, generalized from the story of a particular individual's life (see also his recent work [27] on scientists' autobiographies as documents that suggest more general ways to materialize rich and diverse cultural formations within the history and practices of various sciences).

Life histories reveal juxtapositions of social contexts through a succession of narrated individual experiences that may be obscured in the structural study of processes as such. They are potential guides to the delineation of ethnographic spaces within systems shaped by categorical distinctions that may make these spaces otherwise invisible. These spaces are not necessarily subaltern spaces (although they may be most clearly revealed in subaltern life histories), but they are shaped by unexpected or novel associations among sites and social contexts suggested by life history accounts.

Follow the Conflict

Finally, following the parties to conflicts defines another mode for generating a multi-sited terrain in ethnographic research. In small-scale societies, this has been an established technique ("the extended case method") in the anthropology of law. In the more complex public spheres of contemporary societies, this technique is a much more central, organizing principle for multi-sited ethnography. Beyond the context of the anthropology of law, most notable contested issues in contemporary society involve simultaneously spheres of everyday life, legal institutions, and mass media. Ethnographic study of these issues thus requires multi-sited construction, perhaps more obviously than do any of the other above modes. The collections edited by Sarat and Kearns (81) and the Amherst Seminar on Law and Society (2) are excellent samplings of work that is inherently multi-sited. Ginsburg's study (34) of the abortion controversy in a small community and Gaines's study (32) of conflict over the legal status of cultural productions as copyrighted exemplify how law- and media-focused topics of ethnographic research ramify quickly into multi-sited terrains of investigation.

The Strategically Situated (Single-Site) Ethnography

As with Paul Willis's now classic study (99) of English working-class boys at school, some ethnography may not move around literally but may nonetheless embed itself in a multi-sited context. This is different than assuming or constructing a world system context.

The sense of the system beyond the particular site of research remains contingent and not assumed. Indeed, what goes on within a particular locale in which research is conducted is often calibrated with its implication for what goes on in another related locale, or other locales, even though the other locales may not be within the frame of the research design or resulting ethnography (e.g., in Willis's work the particular kind of interest that he develops in the boys at school, on which he focuses solely, is guided by his knowledge of what happens to them on the factory floor).

This strategically situated ethnography might be thought of as a foreshortened multi-sited project and should be distinguished from the single-site ethnography that examines its local subjects' articulations primarily as subalterns to a dominating capitalist or colonial system. The strategically situated ethnography attempts to understand something broadly about the system in ethnographic terms as much as it does its local subjects: It is only local circumstantially, thus situating itself in a context or field quite differently than does other single-site ethnography.

The consideration of this foreshortened version of the multi-sited project gives us the opportunity to ask what sorts of local knowledges are distinctively probed within the sites of any multi-sited ethnography.

If not the resistance and accommodation frame alone for studying subjects' articulation to larger systems, then what? The key question is perhaps: What among locally probed subjects is iconic with or parallel to
the identifiably similar or same phenomenon within the idioms and
terms of another related or "worlds apart" site? Answering this question
involves the work of comparative translation and tracing among sites,
which I suggested were basic to the methodology of multi-sited ethnography. Within a single site, the crucial issue concerns the detectable
system-awareness in the everyday consciousness and actions of subjects'
lives. This is not an abstract theoretical awareness such as a social scientist might seek, but a sensed, partially articulated awareness of specific
other sites and agents to which particular subjects have (not always
tangible) relationships. In Willis's study, it is how much the boys manifest in their talk a "knowingness" about the very specific system and set
of relations in which they are caught as labor. In the more fractured,
discontinuous sites of Martin's study (64), it is lay notions "on the
street," so to speak, of the body's immune system, compared to notions
of the immune system in the lab, compared to ideas of flexibility in the
corporate boardroom. In my study of the dynastic rich (62), it is how
the abstract management of wealth elsewhere subtly enters the daily
lives of prominent families. In the vision of the novelist DeLillo (14), it
is getting at the "white noise" in any setting that makes the ethnographic probing of either multi-sited or strategically situated research
distinctive.

In iconically identifying a cultural phenomenon in one site that is
reproduced elsewhere, a number of conceptual discussions are guides
to how to see or ethnographically probe a "sensibility" for the system
among situated subjects. Taussig's essays (90) under the governing notion of the "nervous system" are suggestive here, as is his ethnographically embedded investigation (91) of Benjamin's "mimetic faculty."
Pietz's (73) discussion of Marx's notion of fetishism in the theory of
capitalism makes this important concept usable as another way of
thinking about the system-sensitive dimensions of the everyday articulated thoughts and actions of ethnographic subjects. Studies of the
phenomenology of the ethnographically situated awareness among
subjects of doubled or multiply constructed selfhood in contexts of
new forms of electronic communication (95) and the inheritance of
great wealth (62) provide clues to the ethnographic registering of a
multi-sited sensibility within any particular site. Tsing's recent ethnography (94) might also be understood as a bold attempt to establish a
new way of seeing the broader registers of rich materials arising from
fieldwork in an out-of-the-way place. Finally, a primary goal of the *Late
Editions* series of annuals (59–61) is to expose, under different themes,

the varieties of *fin-de-siècle* consciousness and sensibilities embedded in different sites as they are articulated by interlocutors in experiments with the interview or conversation format, employed by anthropologists and other scholars who return to sites of previous work.

The most important form of local knowledge in which the multi-sited ethnographer is interested is that which parallels the ethnographer's own interest—in mapping itself. Sorting out the relationships of the local to the global is a salient and pervasive form of local knowledge that remains to be recognized and discovered in the embedded idioms and discourses of any contemporary site that can be defined by its relationship to the world system. In this cognitive and intellectual identification between the investigator and variously situated subjects in the emergent field of multi-sited research, reflexivity is most powerfully defined as a dimension of method, serving to displace or recontextualize the sort of literal methodological discussion that I have provided above. Haraway's discussion of positioning (46) is perhaps the most eloquent statement of the reflexive context and significance of multi-sited research. In contemporary multi-sited research projects moving between public and private spheres of activity, from official to subaltern contexts, the ethnographer is bound to encounter discourses that overlap with his or her own. In any contemporary field of work, there are always others within who know (or want to know) what the ethnographer knows, albeit from a different subject position, or who want to know what the ethnographer wants to know. Such ambivalent identifications, or perceived identifications, immediately locate the ethnographer within the terrain being mapped and reconfigure any kind of methodological discussion that presumes a perspective from above or "nowhere."

In practice, multi-sited fieldwork is thus always conducted with a keen awareness of being within the landscape, and as the landscape changes across sites, the identity of the ethnographer requires renegotiation. Only in the writing of ethnography, as an effect of a particular mode of publication itself, is the privilege and authority of the anthropologist unambiguously reassumed, even when the publication gives an account of the changing identities of the fieldworker in the multi-sited field.

The virtue of Haraway's discussion of positioning is that it argues persuasively for the objectivity (rather than the often presumed subjectivism) that arises from such a scrupulous, methodological practice of reflexivity. However, the qualification or effacement of the traditional privileged self-identification as ethnographer that seems inevitable in multi-sited research in favor of a constantly mobile, recalibrating practice of positioning in terms of the ethnographer's shifting affinities for, affiliations with, as well as alienations from, those with whom he or she interacts at different sites constitutes a distinctly different sense of "doing research."

Ethnographer as Circumstantial Activist

It is appropriate in conclusion to come full circle and to place the literal methodological concerns developed in this review in terms of a particular ethos of self-perception commonly evidenced in multi-sited research out of the just-mentioned experience of positioning. The conventional "how-to" methodological questions of social science seem to be thoroughly embedded in or merged with the political-ethical discourse of self-identification developed by the ethnographer in multi-sited research. The movement among sites (and levels of society) lends a character of activism to such an investigation. This is not (necessarily) the traditional self-defined activist role claimed by the left-liberal scholar for his or her work. That is, it is not the activism claimed in relation to affiliation with a particular social movement outside academia or the domain of research, nor is it the academic claim to an imagined vanguard role for a particular style of writing or scholarship with reference to a posited ongoing politics in a society or culture at a specific historic moment. Rather, it is activism quite specific and circumstantial to the conditions of doing multi-sited research itself. It is a playing out in practice of the feminist slogan of the political as personal, but in this case it is the political as synonymous with the professional persona and, within the latter, what used to be discussed in a clinical way as the methodological.

In conducting multi-sited research, one finds oneself with all sorts of cross-cutting and contradictory personal commitments. These conflicts are resolved, perhaps ambivalently, not by refuge in being a detached anthropological scholar, but in being a sort of ethnographer-activist, renegotiating identities in different sites as one learns more about a slice of the world system. For example, in Martin's *Flexible Bodies* (64), she is an AIDS volunteer at one site, a medical student at another, and a corporate trainee at a third. Politically committed though she is at the start of her research, ethnographer though she is throughout it, the identity or persona that gives a certain unity to her movement through such disjointed space is the circumstantial activism involved in working in such a variety of sites, where the politics and ethics of working in any one reflects on work in the others.

In certain sites, one seems to be working with, and in others one seems to be working against, changing sets of subjects. This condition of shifting personal positions in relation to one's subjects and other active discourses in a field that overlap with one's own generates a definite sense of doing more than just ethnography, and it is this quality that provides a sense of being an activist for and against positioning in even the most self-perceived apolitical fieldworker.

Finally, the circumstantial commitments that arise in the mobility of multi-sited fieldwork provide a kind of psychological substitute for the reassuring sense of "being there," of participant observation in traditional single-site fieldwork. One often affiliates with literal activists in the space of multi-sited research, and given anthropology's past preference for focusing on subaltern or marginal subjects, such activists are often surrogates for one's "people" of traditional research. The emerging and circumstantial sense of activism that develops among ethnographers in a multi-sited space and their close personal affiliations with cultural producers (e.g., artists, filmmakers, organizers), who themselves move across various sites of activity, thus preserve for ethnographers engaged in multi-sited research an essential link with the traditional practice of participant observation, single-site ethnography in the peripatetic, translative mapping of brave new worlds.

References

1. Abu-Lughod, L., ed. 1993. Screening politics in a world of nations. *Public Cult.* 11: 465–606 (Special Segment).
2. Amherst Seminar. 1988. Law and ideology. *Law Soc. Rev.* 22(4) (Special Issue).
3. Appadurai, A., ed. 1986. *The Social Life of Things: Commodities in Cultural Perspective.* New York: Cambridge University Press.
4. Appadurai, A. 1990. Disjuncture and difference in the global cultural economy. *Public Cult.* 2:1–24.
4a. Balshem M. 1993. *Cancer in the Community: Class and Medical Authority.* Washington, DC: Smithsonian Inst. Press.
5. Boyarin, J. 1994. Space, time, and the politics of memory. In *Remapping Memory: The Politics of TimeSpace,* ed. J. Boyarin, pp. 1–24. Minneapolis: Univ. Minn. Press.
5a. Bright, Brenda J. Forthcoming. *Low Rider: Chicano Culture in the Time of the Automobile.* Berkeley: University of California Press.
5b. Bright, Brenda J. 1998. "'Heart Like a Car': Low Rider Cars and Hispano/Chicano Culture in Northern New Mexico." *The American Ethnologist* 25(4).
6. Brooks, P. 1984. *Reading for the Plot: Design and Intention in Narrative.* New York: Knopf.
7. Campbell, C. 1987. *The Romantic Ethic and the Spirit of Modern Consumerism.* Oxford: Blackwell.

8. Chicago Cultural Studies Group. 1992. Critical multiculturalism. *Crit. Inq.* 18(3): 530–55.

9. Clifford, J. 1994. Diasporas. See Ref. 47, pp. 302–38.

10. Comaroff, J., Comaroff, J.L. 1991. *Of Revelation and Revolution: Christianity, Colonialism, and Consciousness in South Africa.* Chicago: Univ. Chicago Press.

11. Comaroff, J., Comaroff, J.L. 1992. *Ethnography and the Historical Imagination.* Boulder, CO: Westview.

12. Coombe, R.J. 1995. The cultural life of things: globalization and anthropological approaches to commodification. *Am. J. Int. Law Polit.* 10(1): In press.

13. Deleuze, G., Guattari, F. 1988. *A Thousand Plateaus: Capitalism and Schizophrenia.* London: Athlone.

14. DeLillo, D. 1984. *White Noise.* New York: Penguin.

15. Derrida, J. 1981. [1972]. *Dissemination.* Chicago: Univ. Chicago Press.

16. Donham, D.L. 1990. *History, Power, Ideology: Central Issues in Marxism and History.* New York: Cambridge Univ. Press.

17. Downey, G.L., Dumit, J., Traweek, S. 1995. *Cyborgs and Citadels: Anthropological Interventions in Emerging Sciences and Technologies.* Santa Fe, NM: School Am. Res. Press. In press.

18. Dreyfus, H.L., Rabinow, P. 1983. *Michel Foucault: Beyond Structuralism and Hermeneutics.* Chicago: Univ. Chicago Press.

19. Escobar, A. 1993. Welcome to Cyberia: notes on the anthropology of cyberculture. *Curr. Anthropol.* 35:211–31.

20. Escobar, A. 1994. *Encountering Development: The Making and Unmaking of the Third World.* Princeton, NJ: Princeton Univ. Press.

21. Escobar, A. 1994. *Cultural politics and biological diversity: state, capital, and social movements in the Pacific coast of Columbia.* Presented at Guggenheim Found. Conf. "Dissent and Direct Action in the Late Twentieth Century," Otavalo, Ecuador, June 15–19.

22. Farmer, P. 1992. *AIDS and Accusation: Haiti and the Geography of Blame.* Berkeley: Univ. Calif. Press.

23. Featherstone M., ed. 1990. *Global Culture, Nationalism, Globalism, and Modernity.* London: Sage.

24. Feld, S. 1994. From schizophonia to schismogenesis: on the discourses and commodification practices of "world music" and "world beat." In *Music Grooves,* by C. Keil, S. Feld, pp. 257–89. Chicago: Univ. Chicago Press.

25. Ferguson, J. 1990. *The Anti-Politics Machine: "Development," Depolitization, and Bureaucratic Power in Lesotho.* New York: Cambridge Univ. Press.

26. Fischer, M.J. 1991. The uses of life histories. *Anthropol. Hum. Q.* 16(1) 24–27.

27. Fischer, A.M. 1995. (Eye) (I)ing the sciences and their signifiers (language, tropes, autobiographers): InterViewing for a cultural studies of science & technology. See Ref. 60. In press.

28. Fischer, M.J., Abedi, M. 1990. *Debating Muslims: Cultural Dialogues in Postmodernity and Tradition.* Madison: Univ. Wisc. Press.

29. Foley, D.E. 1990. *Learning Capitalist Culture: Deep in the Heart of Tejas.* Philadelphia: Univ. Penn. Press.

30. Friedland, R., Boden, D. 1994. *NowHere: Space, Time, and Modernity.* Berkeley: Univ. Calif. Press.
31. Friedman, J. 1994. *Cultural Identity and Global Process.* London: Sage.
32. Gaines, J. 1991. *Contested Culture: The Image, the Voice, and the Law.* Chapel Hill: Univ. NC Press.
33. Gilroy, P. 1993. *The Black Atlantic: Modernity and Double Consciousness.* Cambridge. MA: Harvard Univ. Press.
34. Ginsburg, F. 1989. *Contested Lives: The Abortion Debate in an American Community.* Berkeley: Univ. Calif. Press.
35. Ginsburg, F. 1993. Aboriginal media and the Australian imaginary. *Public Cult.* 5:557–78.
36. Ginsburg, F. 1994. Embedded aesthetics: creating a discursive space for indigenous media. *Cult. Anthropol.* 9(3):365–82.
37. Ginsburg, F. 1996. Mediating culture: indigenous media, ethnographic film, and the production of identity. In *Fields of Vision,* ed. L. Deveraux, R. Hillman. Berkeley: Univ. Calif. Press. In press.
38. Ginsburg, F., Rapp, R., eds. 1996. *Conceiving the New World Order: The Global Stratification of Reproduction.* Berkeley: Univ. Calif. Press. In press.
38a. Ginzburg, C. 1993. Microhistory: two or three things that I know about it. *Crit. Inq.* 20(1):10–35.
39. Gleick, J. 1987. *Chaos: Making a New Science.* New York: Penguin.
39a. Glick Schiller, N., Basch, L., Blanc Szanton, C. 1992. *The Transnationalization of Migration: Perspectives on Ethnicity and Race.* New York: Gordon & Breach.
39b. Glick Schiller, N., Fouron, N. 1990. "Everywhere we go we are in danger": Ti Manno and the emergence of a Haitian transnational identity. *Am. Ethnol.* 17(2):329–47.
40. Grasmuck, S., Pessar, P. 1991. *Between Two Islands: Dominican International Migration.* Berkeley: Univ. Calif. Press.
41. Grossberg, L., Nelson, C., Treichler, P. 1992. *Cultural Studies.* New York: Routledge.
42. Gupta, A., Ferguson, J. 1992. Beyond 'culture': space. identity, and the politics of difference. *Cult. Anthropol.* 7:6–23.
43. Gupta, A., Ferguson, J., eds. 1992. Space, Identity, and the Politics of Difference. *Cult. Anthropol.* 7(1) (Theme issue).
44. Hannerz, U. 1992. *Cultural Complexity: Studies in the Social Organization of Meaning.* New York: Columbia Univ. Press.
45. Haraway, D. 1991. A cyborg manifesto: science, technology, and socialist-feminism in the late twentieth century. In *Simians, Cyborgs, and Women: The Reinvention of Nature,* pp. 149–82. New York: Routledge.
46. Haraway, D. 1991. Situated knowledges: The science question in feminism and the privilege of partial perspective. In *Simians, Cyborgs, and Women: The Reinvention of Nature,* pp. 183–202. New York: Routledge.
47. Harding, S., Myers, F., eds. 1994. "Further Inflections: Toward Ethnographies of the Future." *Cult. Anthropol.* 9(3) (Special Issue).
48. Harvey, D. 1989. *The Condition of Post-modernity: An Inquiry into the Origins of Cultural Change.* Oxford: Blackwell.

49. Holub, R.C. 1991. *Jurgen Habermas: Critic in the Public Sphere.* New York: Routledge.
50. Lash, S., Friedman, J., eds. 1992. *Modernity and Identity.* Oxford: Blackwell.
51. Lash, S., Urry, J. 1987. *The End of Organized Capitalism.* Madison: Univ. Wisc. Press.
52. Latour, B. 1987. *Science In Action.* Cambridge, MA: Harvard Univ. Press.
53. Latour, B. 1988. *The Pasteurization of France.* Cambridge, MA: Harvard Univ. Press.
54. Laughlin, K. 1995. Rehabilitating science, imagining Bhopal. See Ref. 60. In press.
54a. Lindenbaum, S., Lock, M., eds. 1993. *Knowledge, Power and Practice.* Berkeley: Univ. Calif. Press.
55. Malinowski, B. 1922. *Argonauts of the Western Pacific.* New York: Dutton.
56. Marcus, G.E. 1986. Contemporary problems of ethnography in the modern world system. In *Writing Culture: The Poetics and Politics of Ethnography,* ed. J. Clifford, G. Marcus, pp. 165–93. Berkeley: Univ. Calif. Press.
57. Marcus, G.E. 1989. Imagining the whole: ethnography's contemporary efforts to situate itself. *Crit. Anthropol.* 9:7–30.
58. Marcus, G.E. 1992. The finding and fashioning of cultural criticism in ethnography. In *Dialectical Anthropology: Essays in Honor of Stanley Diamond,* ed. C.W. Gailey, S. Gregory, pp. 77–101. Gainseville: Fla. State Univ. Press.
59. Marcus, G.E., ed. 1993. *Perilous States: Conversations on Culture, Politics and Nation.* Late Eds. 1: *Cultural Studies for the End of the Century.* Chicago: Univ. Chicago Press.
60. Marcus, G.E., ed. 1995. *Techno-Scientific Imaginaries.* Late Eds. 2: *Cultural Studies for the End of the Century.* Chicago: Univ. Chicago Press.
61. Marcus, G.E., ed. 1996. *Connected: Engagements With Media at the Century's End.* Late Eds. 3: *Cultural Studies for the End of the Century.* Chicago: Univ. Chicago Press. In press.
62. Marcus, G.E. with Hall, P.D. 1992. *Lives in Trust: The Fortunes of Dynastic Families in Late Twentieth Century America.* Boulder, CO: Westview.
63. Marcus, G.E., Myers, F., eds. 1996. *The Traffic in Art and Culture: New Approaches to a Critical Anthropology of Art.* Berkeley: Univ. Calif. Press.
64. Martin, E. 1994. *Flexible Bodies: Tracing Immunity in American Culture From the Days of Polio to the Age of AIDS.* Boston: Beacon.
65. Miller, D. 1994. *Modernity: An Ethnographic Approach.* Oxford: Berg.
66. Mintz, S. 1985. *Sweetness and Power: The Place of Sugar in Modern History.* New York: Viking.
67. Myers, F. 1992. Representing culture: The production of discourse(s) for Aboriginal acrylic paintings. In *Rereading Cultural Anthropology,* ed. G.E. Marcus, pp. 319–55. Durham, NC: Duke Univ. Press.
68. Nader, L. 1969. Up the anthropologist—perspectives gained from studying up. In *Reinventing Anthropology,* ed. D. Hymes, pp. 284–311. New York: Pantheon.
69. Naficy, H. 1993. *The Making of Exile Cultures: Iranian Television in Los Angeles.* Minneapolis: Univ. Minn. Press.

70. Ong, A. 1987. *Spirit of Resistance and Capitalist Discipline: Factory Women in Malaysia.* Albany: State Univ. NY Press.
71. Ong, A. 1993. On the edge of empires: flexible citizenship among Chinese in diaspora. *Positions* 1:745–78.
72. Petric, V. 1987. *Constructivism-in-Film: "The Man With the Movie Camera," a Cinematic Analysis.* New York: Cambridge Univ. Press.
73. Pietz, W. 1993. Fetishism and materialism: The limits of theory in Marx. In *Fetishism as Cultural Discourse,* ed. E. Apter, W. Pietz, pp. 119–51. Ithaca, NY: Cornell Univ. Press.
74. Pred, A., Watts, M. 1992. *Reworking Modernity: Capitalism and Symbolic Discontent.* New Brunswick, NJ: Rutgers Univ. Press.
75. Rabinow, P. 1989. *French Modern: Norms and Forms of Social Environment.* Cambridge, MA: MIT Press.
76. Rabinow, P. 1995. *The polymerase chain reaction.* Unpublished manuscript.
77. Radway, J. 1988. Reception study: ethnography and the problems of dispersed audiences and nomadic subjects. *Cult. Stud.* 2(3):359–76.
78. Readings, B. 1991. *Introducing Lyotard: Art and Politics.* New York: Routledge.
79. Roseberry, W. 1989. *Anthropologies and Histories: Essays in Culture, History, and Political Economy.* New Brunswick, NJ: Rutgers Univ. Press.
80. Rouse, R. 1991. Mexican migration and the social space of postmodernity. *Diaspora* 1:8–23.
81. Sarat, A., Kearns, T.R., eds. 1993. *Law in Everyday Life.* Ann Arbor: Univ. Mich. Press.
81a. Savigliano, M.E. 1995. *Tango and the Political Economy of Passion.* Boulder, CO: Westview.
82. Scott, J.C. 1985. *Weapons of the Weak. Everyday Forms of Peasant Resistance.* New Haven, CT: Yale Univ. Press.
83. Silverman, D. 1986. *Selling Culture: Bloomingdale's, Diana Vreeland, and the New Aristocracy of Taste in Reagan's America.* New York: Pantheon.
84. Sklair, L. 1991. *The Sociology of the Global System.* Baltimore, MD: Johns Hopkins Univ. Press.
85. Smith, C. 1976. *Regional Analysis,* Vols. 1–2. New York: Academic.
86. Soja, E.W. 1989. *Postmodern Geographies: The Reassertion of Space in Critical Social Theory.* London: Verso.
86a. Solow, R. 1991. *New York Times,* Sept. 29, Sect. 4. p. 1.
87. Steiner, C.B. 1994. *African Art in Transit.* New York: Cambridge Univ. Press.
88. Stewart, K. 1995. Bitter faiths. See Ref 60. In press.
89. Strathern, M. 1991. *Partial Connections.* Savage, M.D.: Rowman & Littlefield.
90. Taussig, M. 1990. *The Nervous System.* New York: Routledge.
91. Taussig, M. 1992. *Mimesis and Alterity.* New York: Routledge.
92. Taylor, I., Barbash, I. 1993. *In and Out of Africa.* Berkeley: Univ. Calif. Extens. Cent. Media Indep. Learn. (Video).
93. Teitelman, R. 1989. *Gene Dreams, Wall Street, Academia and the Rise of Biotechnology.* New York: Basic Books.
94. Tsing, A. 1993. *In the Realm of the Diamond Queen: Marginality in an Out-of-the-Way Place.* Princeton, NJ: Princeton Univ. Press.

95. Turkle, S. 1984. *The Second Self: Computers and the Human Spirit.* London: Grenada.

96. Turner, T. 1991. Representing, resisting, rethinking: historical transformations of Kayapó culture and anthropological consciousness. In *Colonial Situations: Essays on the Contextualization of Ethnographic Knowledge*, ed. G.W. Stocking Jr., pp. 285–313. Madison: Univ. Wisc. Press.

97. Wallerstein, I. 1991. *Report on an Intellectual Project: The Fernand Braudel Center, 1970–1991.* Binghamton, NY: Fernand Braudel Cent.

98. Weiner, A.W., Schneider, J., eds. 1989. *Cloth and Human Experience.* Washington, DC: Smithsonian Inst. Press.

99. Willis, P. 1981. *Learning to Labour: How Working Class Kids Get Working Class Jobs.* New York: Columbia Univ. Press.

100. Wilmsen, E.N. 1989. *Land Filled With Flies: A Political Economy of the Kalahari.* Chicago: Univ. Chicago Press.

101. Wolf, E. 1982. *Europe and the People Without History.* Berkeley: Univ. Calif. Press.

102. Zonabend, F. 1993. *The Nuclear Peninsula.* New York: Cambridge Univ. Press.

Four

The Uses of Complicity in
the Changing Mise-en-Scène
of Anthropological Fieldwork (1997)

Rapport: *Report, talk. Reference, relationship; connexion,
correspondence, conformity. A state in which mesmeric action can be
exercised by one person on another.*

Collaboration: *United labour, co-operation; especially in literary,
artistic, or scientific work.*

Collaborate: *To work in conjunction with another.*

Complicity: *The being an accomplice; partnership in an evil action.
State of being complex or involved.*

Complice: *One associated in any affair with another, the latter being
regarded as the principal.*[1]

IN WHAT IS PERHAPS his most broadly influential essay, "Deep Play:
Notes on the Balinese Cockfight," Clifford Geertz opens with a tale of
fieldwork in which the rapport that is so much sought after by anthropologists among the peoples they study is achieved through a circumstance of complicity.[2] In 1958, Geertz and his wife moved to a remote
Balinese village to take up, in the tradition of Bronislaw Malinowski,
the sort of participant observation that has given distinction to the ethnographic method. Unfortunately, their initial efforts to fit in were met
with marked inattention and studied indifference: "people seemed to
look right through us with a gaze focused several yards behind us on
some more actual stone or tree."[3] However, their status changed dramatically about ten days after their arrival, when they attended a cockfight that was raided by the police. Geertz and his wife ran from the
invading police along with the rest of the village, and when they were
finally discovered by a policeman and questioned about their presence,
they were passionately defended by the village chief, who said they be-
longed in the village and did not know anything about any cockfight.
From the next morning on, their situation in the village was completely
different: they were no longer invisible, and they had indeed achieved

the kind of relationship that would allow them to do their work and
eventually produce the account of a cultural artifact that follows this
opening tale of fieldwork—an account that became a widely assimilated exemplar of a style of interpretive analysis in which deep meanings are derived from the close observation of a society's most quotidian events. Geertz concludes his anecdote by saying:

> Getting caught, or almost caught, in a vice raid is perhaps not a very gener-
> alizable recipe for achieving that mysterious necessity of anthropological
> field work, rapport, but for me it worked very well. It led to a sudden and
> unusually complete acceptance into a society extremely difficult for outsiders
> to penetrate. It gave me the kind of immediate, insideview grasp of an aspect
> of "peasant mentality" that anthropologists not fortunate enough to flee
> headlong with their subjects from armed authorities normally do not get![4]

In Geertz's anecdote I am primarily interested in the ironic entangle-
ment of complicity with rapport that he draws. Indeed, for anthropologists trained from the 1950s through the 1980s, rapport has been the
powerful shorthand concept used to stand for the threshold level of
relations with fieldwork subjects that is necessary for those subjects to
act effectively as informants for anthropologists—who, once that rapport is established, are then able to pursue their scientific, "outsider"
inquiries on the "inside."

The range of definitions given in the *OED* for the word *rapport*—
from "talk" to "relationship" to "conformity" to the unusual meaning of
"a state in which mesmeric action can be exercised by one person on
another"—aptly conveys the mix of senses of this key figure within the
ideology of anthropological practice. Of course, behind this figure are
the immensely complex stories, debates, views, and critiques that surround the relationships that anthropological fieldwork imposes. Since
the 1960s, this probing of fieldwork relationships has moved from informal, ethos-building professional talk—a regulative ideal—to a more
formal articulation found in both reflections on fieldwork and essays
on anthropology's distinctive method, discussions in which Geertz himself has been a seminal, though ambivalent, voice.[5]

Until recently, much of this discussion has assumed the essential desirability and achievability of rapport—it remains the favored con-
densed view and disciplinary emblem of the ideal condition of fieldwork—even while the path to rapport seems always to have been
fraught with difficulties, uncertainties, happenstance, ethical ambiguity,
fear, and self-doubt. However, there are now signs of the displacement
of this foundational commonplace of fieldwork, given the changing
mise-en-scène in which anthropological research is now frequently being constituted. It is probably a healthy sign that no replacement fig-

ure, as such, is emerging to take rapport's place. Rather, a deep reassessment of the nature of fieldwork is beginning to occur as a result of defining the different conditions in which it must be designed and conceptualized.

Purely as a means of lending perspective to and representing the set of changes that are affecting anthropological practice and the way that it is thought about, I have chosen in this essay to emphasize the concept of complicity. Indeed, many fieldwork stories of achieving rapport are in some way entangled with acts of complicity, as in Geertz's epochal anecdote. But while complicity has a certain kinship of meaning with rapport, it is also its "evil twin," so to speak. (In this regard, I appreciate the *OED*'s definitions of complicity as including both the "state of being complex or involved" and "partnership in an evil action.") In no way am I promoting complicity as a candidate for a new shorthand or commonplace of disciplinary practice in our changed circumstances—its "dark" connotations certainly don't lend it to that use. Rather, a focus on the term will serve as a device for tracing a certain critique, or at least complexation, of the valorized understanding of fieldwork relationships from within the reigning figure of rapport to an alternative conception of fieldwork relationships in which the figure of rapport has lost much of its power as a regulative ideal.

In the following section, then, I want to explore the ways in which Geertz dealt with the issue of complicity within rapport, since his representations of fieldwork represent for me the most subtle understandings of the traditional ideology of fieldwork practice at its apogee. Following that, I want to address two directions that critiques of ethnographic authority and rhetoric took in the 1980s, producing an unprecedentedly reflexive and critical perspective on fieldwork relations (a perspective that Geertz unquestionably helped to inspire and from which he interestingly has distanced himself).[6]

One of these directions displaces rapport with an ideal of collaboration that both preserves the traditional, enclosed mise-en-scène of fieldwork and avoids paying explicit attention to the issue of complicity that Geertz himself saw as so entangled with the very achievement of rapport. The other direction, aptly expressed in Renato Rosaldo's notion of "imperialist nostalgia,"[7] directly confronts complicity in fieldwork relationships within the broader historical context of colonialism in which the traditional mise-en-scène of ethnography has always been situated; but it fails to go beyond the ethical implications of that context to consider the cognitive ones.

Finally, I want to offer a conception of complicity that is largely free of the primary connotations of rapport. In so doing, I want to move beyond the predominant and troublesome ethical implications associated with complicity in past views of anthropological practice to an understanding of the fieldwork relationship that entails a substantially different vision of the contemporary mise-en-scène of anthropological research. Complicity here retains its ethical issues, but it does so in a way that forces a rethinking of the space and positioning of the anthropologist-informant relationship that is at the heart of fieldwork as it has been commonly conceived.

The larger stake of the discussion that I want to develop is indeed the current level of self-conscious awareness and response of anthropologists to the changing circumstances in which they now work—what I have referred to earlier as the mise-en-scène of fieldwork. Of course there have recently been many theoretical and direct conceptual discussions of these changing circumstances—the talk of transcultural processes, global-local relations, and deterritorialized cultures[8]—but it is not clear what, if anything, these discussions have meant for the deeply ingrained and reassuring ideologies of fieldwork practice. Until these macro-changes are understood at the heart of anthropology's distinctive method, in terms of the commonplaces and powerful figures by which anthropologists have conceived fieldwork as an ideology of professional culture, it is quite likely that the traditional conception in use of the mise-en-scène and the central relationship of anthropologist to informant will remain immune from the more radical implications of the new theoretical visions and discussions of anthropology's changing objects of study. A consideration of these changes within anthropology's sacred domain, so to speak, is precisely what I intend to initiate by tracing complicity as at first an integral but underplayed dimension of rapport that has eventually become an independent means of understanding how certain deep assumptions and commonplaces about fieldwork might finally be modified in line with otherwise clear perceptions among anthropologists about how their objects and contexts of study are changing.

Geertz and Complicity

But what is, to me anyway, most interesting about . . . these attempts to produce highly "author-saturated," supersaturated even, anthropological texts in which the self the text creates and the self that creates the text are represented as being very near to identical, is the strong note of disquiet that suffuses them. There is very little confidence here and a fair amount of outright malaise. The imagery is not of scientific hope, compensating inner weakness, à la Malinowski, or of bear-hug intimacy dispelling self-rejection, à la Read, neither of which is very much believed in. It is of estrangement,

hypocrisy, helplessness, domination, disillusion. Being There is not just practically difficult. There is something disruptive about it altogether.[9]

As we have seen in the cockfight anecdote, for Geertz a certain *kind* of
complicity generates rapport. In a manner characteristic of his signature style as a writer and thinker, in this passage Geertz seems to make
light of a figure or commonplace of his discipline—rapport—while
remaining passionately committed to *his* version of it—a version that
actually strengthens the figure in the shadow of his playful, trenchant
critique of it. He may disdain his discipline's too-easily assimilated
shoptalk—about, for example, the figure of rapport—but finally he
improves upon that talk and, in a committed way, preserves the traditional sense of the craft that the figure of rapport stands for. In "Deep
Play," the ethnographer's powerful and exemplary analytic magic that
follows the tale of complicity breaking into rapport is a testament to
this.

In the cockfight anecdote, complicity makes the outsider the desired
anthropological insider. It is a circumstantial, fortuitous complicity
that, by precipitating a momentary bond of solidarity, gains Geertz ad-
mission to the inside of Balinese relations (the means to ethnographic
authority) and converts the Balinese village into a proper mise-en-
scène of fieldwork—a physically and symbolically enclosed world, a culture for the ethnographer to live within and figure out. Very pragmatically, Geertz realizes that he can benefit from this complicity only by
presenting himself as a naïf, a person subject to events and looked out
for by others (and this vulnerability of finding himself on the side of
the village against the state and its agents, rather than representing
himself as someone officially there through the auspices of the state,
suggests both a shrewd and an ambiguous innocence about the historic
era in which anthropological fieldwork was then being done).[10]

So complicity in this particular famous tale of fieldwork is rather
neat and simple; it is an uncomplicated complicity that "breaks the ice"
and provides the anthropologist the coveted fictional acceptance that
will allow him to create the counter-"mesmerism" of rapport whereby
he is no longer invisible, as before, but will be indulged as a person.
But in a lesser-known paper on fieldwork, Geertz tells another more
complex, yet complementary, story from the field in which he considers how complicity, internal to the development of relations with
informants once he has gotten "inside," is deeply entangled with the
motivated fiction of sustaining rapport itself.[11] This paper tells how a
kind of complicity is necessary for sustaining the working relationships
of fieldwork, without which its very mise-en-scène—let alone rapport—
would not be possible in the anthropologist's imaginary. This paper,

"Thinking as a Moral Act: Ethical Dimensions of Anthropological Fieldwork in the New States," reveals Geertz's astute foresight of the possible
development of a hyperreflexivity upon the conditions of anthropological knowledge—a subject that, after a complicated treatment in this
paper, he turns away from in favor of accepting the fictions of fieldwork relations so that ethnographic interpretation and the historic anthropological project to which he is committed can continue (that is,
the project of U.S. cultural anthropology in the line of, for example,
Johann Herder, Franz Boas, Margaret Mead, and Ruth Benedict, among
many others).

In "Thinking as a Moral Act," Geertz describes a complicity of mutual interest between anthropologist and informant, subtly but clearly
understood by each, that makes rapport possible—indeed that constitutes, even constructs, it. Geertz calls this key rapport-defining act of
complicity an "anthropological irony" of fictions that each side accepts:

> One is placed, in this sort of work, among necessitous men hoping for radi-
> cal improvements in their conditions of life that do not seem exactly immi-
> nent; moreover, one is a type benefactor of just the sort of improvements
> they are looking for, also obliged to ask them for charity—and what is almost
> worse, having them give it. This ought to be a humbling, thus elevating,
> experience; but most often it is simply a disorienting one. All the familiar
> rationalizations having to do with science, progress, philanthropy, enlighten-
> ment, and selfless purity of dedication ring false, and one is left, ethically
> disarmed, to grapple with a human relationship which must be justified over
> and over again in the most immediate of terms.[12]
>
> What I am pointing to . . . is an enormous pressure on both the investiga-
> tor and his subjects to regard these goals as near when they are in fact far,
> assured when they are merely wished for, and achieved when they are at best
> approximated. This pressure springs from the inherent moral asymmetry of
> the fieldwork situation.[13]
>
> To recognize the moral tension, the ethical ambiguity, implicit in the en-
> counter of anthropologist and informant, and to still be able to dissipate it
> through one's actions and one's attitudes, is what encounter demands of
> both parties if it is to be authentic, if it is to actually happen. And to discover
> that is to discover also something very complicated and not altogether clear
> about the nature of sincerity and insincerity, genuineness and hypocrisy, hon-
> esty and self-deception.[14]

Here again, as in the cockfight anecdote, the broader context of
implication—that of colonialism and neocolonialism—that has so exercised the subsequent critics of ethnography is submerged in Geertz's
account, implied but not explicitly noted. The anthropology of the
1950s and 1960s was part of the great mission of development in the

new states—in the midst of which Geertz was a very American as well as an anthropological writer, accepting this mission with a certain resignation that did not particularly define a politics of fieldwork. That politics instead emerged in terms of the always slightly absurd but very human predicaments of a well-meaning outsider thrust among people with very different life chances. According to the presumptions of the development mission, themselves based on Western notions of liberal decency, the outsider was in some sense the model of a desired future.[15]

In Geertz's writings on his fieldwork of the 1960s and 1970s, we see first a virtual outline and summary of the major moves of later critique—built on the reflexive study of the conditions of anthropological knowledge not only in terms of its traditional mise-en-scène of fieldwork but also in terms of the broader historic contexts that Geertz tended to elide—and then a hesitation and a pulling back for the sake of sustaining a distanced practice of interpretation. Finally, as Geertz argues in his paper, "Thinking as a Moral Act,"

> I don't know much about what goes on in laboratories; but in anthropological fieldwork, detachment is neither a natural gift nor a manufactured talent. It is a partial achievement laboriously earned and precariously maintained. What little disinterestedness one manages to attain comes not from failing to have emotions or neglecting to perceive them in others, nor yet from sealing oneself into a moral vacuum. It comes from a personal subjection to a vocational ethic . . . to combine two fundamental orientations toward reality— the engaged and the analytic—into a single attitude. It is this attitude, not moral blankness, which we call detachment or disinterestedness. And whatever small degree of it one manages to attain comes not by adopting an I-am-a-camera ideology or by enfolding oneself in layers of methodological armor, but simply by trying to do, in such an equivocal situation, the scientific work one has come to do.[16]

Indeed, the Balinese cockfight essay itself enacts Geertz's position on critical self-knowledge in anthropological practice. Once the incident described in the opening reflexive fieldwork anecdote has authoritatively secured the standard and idealized condition of rapport, or "mesmeric" possibility, the work of interpretation proceeds by the participant who is still a detached observer, famously able to read Balinese culture "like a text." Geertz's shrewd perception of the complicit heart of the otherwise soporific, too-easy professional invocation of rapport, followed by his pulling back from further reflexive examination and its implications, probably has disturbed his critics more than if he had not bothered to make this move into reflexivity at all.

The fact that he *did* and that he then pulled back from looking too closely at the conditions of the production of anthropological knowledge—a topic that he brilliantly introduced at a time of maximum positivist hopes and confidence in the social sciences—is not a sign of the ambivalence or hesitation that are otherwise so much a part of Geertz's expository style of delivering insight. Rather, it is a sign of his commitment to the frame of reference in which anthropology could be done: the frame that the figure of rapport guaranteed and that Geertz played with, could see the critique of, but would not go beyond for the sake of a historic anthropological project that he had done so much to renew in the 1960s and 1970s and that defined for him a "vocational ethic." His concern—expressed in the passage with which this section opens and which first appeared in his 1988 book *Works and Lives* as a sideways commentary on that decade's seminal critique of anthropological knowledge—was over the malaise that an unfettered reflexivity, following his own opening, might lead to. And has it?

The Collaborative Ideal

> This possibility suggests an alternate textual strategy, a utopia of plural authorship that accords to collaborators not merely the status of independent enunciators but that of writers. As a form of authority it must still be considered utopian for two reasons. First, the few recent experiments with multiple-author works appear to require, as an instigating force, the research interest of the ethnographer who in the end assumes an executive, editorial position. The authoritative stance of "giving voice" to the other is not fully transcended. Second, the very idea of plural authorship challenges a deep Western identification of any text's order with the intention of a single author. . . . Nonetheless, there are signs of movement in this domain. Anthropologists will increasingly have to share their texts, and sometimes their title pages, with those indigenous collaborators, for the term informants is no longer adequate, if it ever was.[17]

One strong direction of the critique of anthropological rhetoric, representation, and authority that occurred during the 1980s reconceived the figure of rapport in terms of collaboration. Associated with the writing of James Clifford and loosely derived from Mikhail Bakhtin's notions of polyphony and dialogism as an alternative to the monologic authority of modes of voicing in the novel, the vision of a collaborative relationship between anthropologist and informant as authors of ethnography in the field has provided a strong reimagining of the regulative ideal of rapport in the ideology of anthropological practice. As presented by Clifford in a scholarly style of historical literary criticism, the collaborative ideal is less a methodological prescription or figure or fieldwork in a changing mise-en-scène than a rereading, an excavation, of certain overlooked dimensions of past ethnography. Its power, then, is in its suggestiveness of a more pleasing, post-1960s practice of thoroughly participatory fieldwork—and it is developed in a way that suggests that anthropologists need only consciously activate what was always there, an obscured dimension of classic fieldwork that was previously concealed by the monologic authority of the conventions of ethnographic writing.

Collaboration ("co-operation" in dialogue) thus replaces rapport ("relationship" or "connexion," with its connotation of a means or instrumentality for fulfilling the ends primarily of one of the partners—the initiating one—of the relationship). Theoretically, collaboration creates a figure for a much more complex understanding of fieldwork, but in Clifford's writing, which looks back at the ethnographic tradition through its classics and classics-in-the-making, this replacement figure is also very much forged in the traditional mise-en-scène of fieldwork—and in fact reinforces that traditional setting, giving it a needed new face, so to speak. The scene of fieldwork and the object of study are still essentially coterminous, together establishing a culture situated in place and to be learned about by one's presence *inside* it in sustained interaction. The collaborative ideal entails the notions that knowledge creation in fieldwork always involves negotiating a boundary between cultures and that the result is never reducible to a form of knowledge that can be packaged in the monologic voice of the ethnographer alone. But still, the polyphony implied in the idea of collaboration preserves the idea of the representation of a bounded culture, however nonreductive, as the object of study and reinforces the same habits of work that rapport valorized. The independent voices in collaboration still emerge within a distinctively other form of life. Perhaps because of the way this ideal was developed in the critique of anthropology—by excavating from *within* the tradition of ethnography—it inherited the limits of the mise-en-scène that had preceded it.

Of course, neither collaboration nor the idea of dialogism on which it is based necessarily implies the harmony of "united labour" in a scientific, literary, or artistic endeavor, as the *OED* definition suggests, and Clifford does not develop the idea with this connotation. The positive *OED* sense remains a potentiality, but more often than not, collaboration is conflicted, based on misrecognitions, coercions, and precisely the sort of ironies/complicities that Geertz cataloged so well in his writing on fieldwork. Clifford differs from Geertz only in finally not being personally tied to the scientific vocation of anthropology; thus, he can indulge a reflexivity that transforms the commonplace ideal of the fieldwork relation. Indeed, to recognize and legitimate as partners one's subjects of study and to generate only polyphonic texts would make something radically different of ethnography; but it wouldn't significantly change the traditional frame of study.

Collaboration does evoke the reflexive space and suggests new conventions for the normalized discussion of the complexities, ambiguities, and nuances of the anthropologist-subject relationship central to fieldwork. Yet Clifford's articulation of the ambiguities of this relationship still remains rather mute as to the different senses of complicity that surround, motivate, and make this relationship possible. In particular, the broader colonial context as it operates in collaboration, while a part of Clifford's discussion, is not strongly developed.[18]

In relation to the particular sense of complicity that I want to develop below, which corresponds to a break with the traditional mise-en-scène of fieldwork, Clifford's discussion of collaboration can even be seen as evasive. It goes somewhat further than Geertz's in recognizing how the broader context of the anthropological project is registered in fieldwork, but it recognizes this context *only* in terms of the long-standing question of anthropology's relationship to colonialism. What is missing in the evocation of the ideal of collaboration is the much more complicated and contemporary sense of the broader context of anthropology operating in a so-called postmodern world of discontinuous cultural formations and multiple sites of cultural production. This context is certainly shaped in part by a history of colonialism, but it cannot be fully represented by that venerable bête noire, which has long served as the broader context in commonplace professional ideology, ambivalently cradling the traditional mise-en-scène of fieldwork.[19]

In the imagining of collaboration as fieldwork, then, complicity has not been a very important component, either in its ethical sense or in its cognitive potential for reconfiguring the fieldwork scene itself. But by fully opening a reflexive space that went beyond Geertz's own self-limited explorations of the regulative idea of rapport, the figure of collaboration created the necessary ground for going further. The explicit dimension of complicity remained to be powerfully articulated—and again, with regard to colonialism as the broader context—as part of the 1980s critique of anthropology by Renato Rosaldo, perhaps the spoiler of all of fieldwork's other fictions.

Imperialist Nostalgia and Complicity

Processes of drastic change often are the enabling condition of ethnographic field research, and herein resides the complicity of missionary, constabulary, officer, and ethnographer. Just as Jones received visits from American constabulary officers during his field research, Michelle Rosaldo and I often used the missionary airplane for transportation in the Ilongot region. Jones did not police and we did not evangelize, but we all bore witness, and we participated, as relatively minor players, in the transformation taking place before our eyes.[20]

Moving in another direction from the possibilities foreseen by Geertz, Renato Rosaldo takes the critique of the traditional mise-en-scène to its limit and finally makes explicit the broader context of anthropology in the scene of fieldwork. This is where complicity potentially has its greatest power as a figure. Rosaldo's work has developed very much within the specific compass of interpretive anthropology that Geertz established in the 1960s and 1970s. As such, his essay "Imperialist Nostalgia" constitutes an appropriate expression of the evolution of Geertz's thinking on fieldwork, now in its most politicized form. Among the critiques of the 1980s, this essay is the most recognizable successor to Geertz's own writing.

The trenchant insight of this essay—indeed, another exemplar of anthropological irony, as Geertz called complicity in fieldwork—is that the key ideological sentiment that has allowed anthropologists to distance themselves from other foreign agents in the field is precisely the sentiment that both denies and constructs their own agency in that very same transformative process. As Rosaldo says, "My concern resides with a particular kind of nostalgia, often found under imperialism, where people mourn the passing of what they themselves have transformed. . . . When the so-called civilizing process destabilizes forms of life, the agents of change experience transformations of other cultures as if they were personal losses."[21] Here, Rosaldo captures and indicts the characteristic rhetoric of ethics that pervades ethnography, at the same time pinpointing the primary relation of complicity in fieldwork—not with the informant or the people, but with the agents of change. This is the politicizing complicity from which Geertz backed off, and about which the alternative view of collaboration was not blunt enough.

This politicization at the limits of the figure of rapport is achieved by placing a primary emphasis on what was the play of complicity in Geertz. Rather than simply being the ironic means to a rapport that cements the working bond between fieldworker and informant, complicity becomes the defining element of the relationship between the anthropologist and the broader colonial context. In so doing, the problem of the broader outside context—again, thought of as colonialism—is finally brought squarely to the inside of the fieldwork relation, something that the collaborative ideal achieved only intermittently or indirectly.

So where has Rosaldo's argument about "imperialist nostalgia" brought us in our tracing of the entanglements of complicity with the powerful regulative ideal of rapport? To the verge of talking primarily about complicity rather than rapport as constructing the primary fieldwork relation, and as such, to the brink of reconceiving the stubbornly held mise-en-scène of fieldwork to better accommodate a different kind of ethnographic project that is now emerging and being professionally normalized in anthropology.

In Geertz's writing, rapport requires that the anthropologist be complicit with the inside of a community or group of subjects. While not effacing the "insideness" essential to the fieldwork mise-en-scène, Rosaldo understands every apparent inside move the fieldworker makes as primarily complicit with the broader external context of colonialism. But, like Geertz's earlier politically muted critique of fieldwork and Clifford's contemporaneous critique of monologic authority in anthropological practice, Rosaldo's essay is still located within rapport and its mise-en-scène, though at its outer limit. As such, the recognition of the sort of complicity that brings the outside into the scene of fieldwork with the very arrival of the anthropologist—who can no longer protect herself with the nostalgia that preserves her difference from other agents of change—remains for Rosaldo a *moral* lesson, one for which there is little further response from within the traditional ideology of rapport. For Rosaldo, anthropology of the old sort either is over, is paralyzed by moralizing insight, or continues to be practiced as a tragic occupation, done in the full awareness of the pitfalls of its powerful rhetorics of self-justification.

With Rosaldo, then, we come to an impasse. The kind of sustained reflexivity that Geertz feared, turned away from, and has more lately confirmed for himself as leading to malaise has now been taken to its limit within the traditional project of anthropology, revealing the implication of complicity that has always shadowed the positive figure of rapport. But is this really the end?

Complicity and the Multi-Sited Spaces of Contemporary Ethnography

There exists a very strong, but one-sided and thus untrustworthy idea that in order to better understand a foreign culture, one must enter into it, forgetting one's own, and view the world through the eyes of this foreign culture. . . . of course, the possibility of seeing the world through its eyes is a necessary part of the process of understanding it; but if this were the only aspect it would merely be duplication and would not entail anything enriching. Creative understanding does not renounce itself, its own place and time, its own culture; and it forgets nothing. In order to understand, it is immensely important for the person who understands to be located outside the object of his or her creative understanding—in time, in space, in culture. In the realm of culture, outsidedness is a most powerful factor in understanding. We raise new questions for a foreign culture, ones that it did not raise for itself; we seek answers to our own questions in it; and the foreign culture responds to us by revealing to us its new aspects and new semantic depths.[22]

The transformation of complicity that I want to trace, from its place in the shadows of the more positive and less ethically ambiguous notion of rapport to its emergence as a primary figure in the ideology of fieldwork, is occasioned by the changing conditions of fieldwork itself and of its objects of study. These changing conditions are effectively stimulating the traditional mise-en-scène of fieldwork to be turned inside out within the professional ideology, and it is the figure of complicity that focuses this change.

Discontinuity in cultural formations—their multiple and heterogeneous sites of production—has begun to force changes in the assumptions and notions that have constructed the traditional mise-en-scène of fieldwork. Anthropologists, of course, continue to work intensively and locally with particular subjects—the substance of ethnographic analysis requires this—but they no longer do so with the sense that the cultural object of study is fully accessible within a particular site, or without the sense that a site of fieldwork anywhere is integrally and intimately tied to sites of possible fieldwork elsewhere. The intellectual environment surrounding contemporary ethnographic study makes it seem incomplete and even trivial if it does not encompass within its own research design a full mapping of a cultural formation, the contours of which cannot be presumed but are themselves a key discovery of ethnographic inquiry. The sense of the object of study being "here and there" has begun to wreak productive havoc on the "being there" of classic ethnographic authority.[23]

However complicity was implicated in the achievement of rapport in the critical versions of Geertz, Clifford, and Rosaldo, all three sustain the sense that the symbolic and literal domain of fieldwork exists inside another form of life—entailing crossing a boundary into it and exploring a cultural logic of enclosed difference (however fraught with difficulty the translation process is).

Once released from this mise-en-scène, complicity looks quite different. The focus on a particular site of fieldwork remains, but now one is after a distinctly different sort of knowledge, one for which metaphors of insideness or the crossing of cultural boundaries are no longer appropriate.

In any particular location certain practices, anxieties, and ambivalences are present as specific responses to the intimate functioning of nonlocal agencies and causes—and for which there are no convincing common-sense understandings.[24] The basic condition that defines the altered mise-en-scène for which complicity rather than rapport is a more appropriate figure is an awareness of existential doubleness on the part of *both* anthropologist and subject; this derives from having a sense of being *here* where major transformations are under way that are tied to things happening simultaneously *elsewhere*, but not having a certainty or authoritative representation of what those connections are. Indeed, there are so many plausible explanations for the changes, no single one of which inspires more authority than another, that the individual subject is left to account for the connections—the behind-the-scenes structure—and to read into his or her own narrative the locally felt agency and effects of great and little events happening elsewhere.

Social actors are confronted with the same kind of impasses that academics uncomfortably experience these days, and this affinity suggests the particular salience of the figure of complicity. But for the subjects of ethnography, these impasses are pragmatic problems that, for everyday life to proceed at all, require responses ranging from evasions and displacements to halfhearted investments in old theories or exotic constructions and idiosyncratic visions of the way the world works. In terms of the traditional mise-en-scène of fieldwork, most anthropologists have always understood themselves as being both inside and outside the sites in which they have been participant observers. That is, they have never naively thought that they could simply "go native" and in fact are critical of those among them who are so naive. Rather, they understand well that they always remain marginal, fictive natives at best. Still, they have always operated on the faith, necessary for the kind of knowledge that they produce, that they could be relatively more insiders than outsiders if only by mastering the skills of translation, sensitivity, and learned cultural competencies—in short, that they could achieve rapport.

In contrast, while it begins from the same inside-outside boundary positioning, investment in the figure of complicity does not posit the same faith in being able to probe the "inside" of a culture (nor does it presuppose that the subject herself is even on the "inside" of a culture, given that contemporary local knowledge is never only about being local). The idea of complicity forces the recognition of ethnographers as ever-present markers of "outsideness." Never stirring from the boundary, their presence makes possible certain kinds of access that the idea of rapport and the faith in being able to get inside (by fiction à la Geertz, by utopian collaboration à la Clifford, or by self-deception à la Rosaldo) does not. It is only in an anthropologist-informant situation in which the outsideness is never elided and is indeed the basis of an affinity between ethnographer and subject that the reigning traditional ideology of fieldwork can shift to reflect the changing conditions of research.

What ethnographers in this changed mise-en-scène want from subjects is not so much local knowledge as an articulation of the forms of anxiety that are generated by the awareness of being affected by what is elsewhere without knowing what the particular connections to that elsewhere might be. The ethnographer on the scene in this sense makes that elsewhere *present.*[25] It is not that this effect of fieldwork is currently unrecognized in anthropology, but it is always referenced in terms of an ethical discourse, and this frame does not get at what the more generative sense of the idea of complicity seeks to document.

This version of complicity tries to get at a form of local knowledge that is about the kind of difference that is not accessible by working out internal cultural logics. It is about difference that arises from the anxieties of knowing that one is somehow tied into what is happening elsewhere, but, as noted, without those connections being clear or precisely articulated through available internal cultural models. In effect, subjects are participating in discourses that are thoroughly localized but that are not their own. Douglas Holmes, whose research is discussed later, uses the term "illicit discourse" to describe this phenomenon, in which fragments of local discourses have their origins elsewhere without the relationship to that elsewhere being clear. This uncertainty creates anxiety, wonder, and insecurity, in different registers, both in the ethnographer and in her subjects.

This recognition of a common predicament is the primary motivation for thinking about the changed conception of fieldwork relationships in terms of complicity. It would be possible to understand our emphasis on the figure of complicity as the achievement of a different kind of rapport, but it would be a mistake to identify it with the precise construction of that figure in the traditional mode. The investment in the figure of complicity rests on highlighting this contemporary external determination of local discourses, marked and set off by the fieldworker's presence but free of the figures of rapport and collaboration that have traditionally characterized fieldwork. Free of these, complicity between an ethnographer whose outsideness is always prominent and a subject who is sensitive to the outside helps to materialize other dimensions that the dialogue of traditional fieldwork, conceived as taking place inside rapport, cannot get at as well. Only thus do we escape the tendency to see change as a disruption of what was there before—a disruption of a world in which the anthropologist might have been more comfortable and on the "prior-ness" of which he or she can still rely in exercising the assumptions of the traditional mise-en-scène of fieldwork, even in a site undergoing massive and long-term changes. In such cases, the formative expressions of anxiety that construct cultures in change and boundaries between cultures are likely to be either missed or rationalized in terms of prior cultural logics. Only when an outsider begins to relate to a subject also concerned with outsideness in everyday life can these expressions be given focal importance in a localized fieldwork that, in turn, inevitably pushes the entire research program of the single ethnographic project into the challenges and promises of a multisited space and trajectory—a trajectory that encourages the ethnographer literally to move to other sites that are powerfully registered in the local knowledge of an originating locus of fieldwork. This is what the notion of complicity as an aid in the rethinking of fieldwork potentially offers.

According to its *OED* definitions, *complicity*, compared to *rapport* and *collaboration*, carries a heavier load of ethical meaning and implication. However, this ethical sense is very different when complicity is evoked as a critical probe of the traditional figure of rapport in the writing of Geertz, Clifford, and Rosaldo—among others—than when it becomes the central figure used to explore the mise-en-scène of fieldwork in new circumstances. The usual ethical questioning of the fieldwork relationship relies heavily on exploring the dynamics of the assumed unequal power relations between ethnographer and subject, always weighted *structurally* on the side of the ethnographer, who is implicated in Western colonialism (which, as I noted earlier, has stereotypically defined the broader context of classic anthropological fieldwork). When the politicized nature of fieldwork has been highlighted in the past, it has been developed by calling anthropology to account for its colonial, and now postcolonial, complicities.[26]

This predictable construction of the ethical issues involved in fieldwork has become far too limited a means of addressing current changing views of the mise-en-scène of fieldwork in the broader context of multi-sited research. With theoretical metanarratives and frames of world-systems processes now under prominent debate and reformulation, a broader contextual framing for any location of fieldwork is less available to ethnographers. The shifting boundaries of the ethnographic project, as described above, are moving speculatively into this broader frame itself, treating it ethnographically through the multisited trajectory of research. This is partly because of the noted inadequacy and

loss of authority of both older and new formulations of metanarratives—like colonialism (or postcolonialism), Marxist political economy,
and globalization (an as-yet poorly theorized, but apparently necessary,
concept in wide currency)—and partly because of the changing nature
of the kind of material sought from and offered by fieldwork subjects
who think in terms of their connections beyond the local. This need to
deal more directly with the broader context of focused research without the aid of adequate frames created by other kinds of scholarship
leads to a much less determined and available context than does the
history of colonialism, for example, in considering the politics and ethical implications of contemporary fieldwork. Likewise, as the figure frequently evoked in past critiques of fieldwork to probe the ethical problems of a too-innocent figure of rapport, complicity specifically plays to
and constructs a different and more complex sense of the substance of
the ethnographer-subject relationship.

The changing contextualization for assessing the ethical implication
of complicity as the normal characterization of contemporary fieldwork
relationships is reflected in the shifting power valences of these relationships, as the fieldworker moves from site to site, and the often ethically ambiguous management by the fieldworker of the accumulation
of these developing relationships in specific situations. Of course, ethnographers have often been faced with such ethical issues within the
villages and communities in which they have worked, but in multi-sited
research, the broader context is in a sense entirely of the ethnographer's and his informants' own making, rather than attributable to
more abstract and already morally loaded forces such as capitalism and
colonialism. So, within the boundaries of a single project, the ethnographer may be dealing intimately and equivalently with subjects of
very different class circumstances—with elites and subalterns, for instance—who may not even be known directly to one another or have a
sense of the often indirect effects that they have on each other's lives.

The ethical issues in multi-sited research are raised by the ethnographer's movement among different kinds of affiliations within a configuration of sites evolving in a particular research project. The inequality
of power relations, weighted in favor of the anthropologist, can no
longer be presumed in this world of multi-sited ethnography. The fieldworker often deals with subjects who share his own broadly middle-class
identity and fears, in which case unspoken power issues in the relationship become far more ambiguous than they would have been in past
anthropological research; alternatively, he may deal with persons in
much stronger power and class positions than his own, in which case
both the terms and limits of the ethnographic engagement are managed principally by them. Here, where the ethnographer occupies a

marked subordinate relationship to informants, the issues of use and being used, of ingratiation, and of trading information about others elsewhere become matters of normal ethical concern, where they were largely unconsidered in previous discussions.

As I have remarked elsewhere the anthropologist, by virtue of these changing circumstances of research, is always on the verge of activism, of negotiating some kind of involvement beyond the distanced role of ethnographer, according to personal commitments that may or may not predate the project.[27] To what extent and on what terms can such activism be indulged within the activity of ethnography, and what are the consequences of avoiding it or denying it altogether for the continued achievement of the "disinterestedness" that Geertz argued for in the traditional mise-en-scène of research? These are the questions that define the much more complicated ethical compass of contemporary fieldwork for which the past understanding of ethnography (in the throes of more abstract world historical forces) can no longer serve as an adequate frame of assessment.[28]

What complicity stands for as a central figure of fieldwork within this multi-sited context of research, and particularly as characterizing those relationships that work effectively to generate the kind of knowledge engaged with the outside that I evoked earlier, is an affinity, marking equivalence, between fieldworker and informant. This affinity arises from their mutual curiosity and anxiety about their relationship to a "third"—not so much the abstract contextualizing world system but the specific sites elsewhere that affect their interactions and make them complicit (in relation to the influence of that "third") in creating the bond that makes their fieldwork relationship effective. This special sense of complicity does not entail the sort of evading fictions that Geertz described as anthropological irony, in which anthropologist and informant pretend to forget who and where they otherwise are in the world in order to create the special relationship of fieldwork rapport. Nor is this the covered-up complicity of fieldwork between the anthropologist and imperialism, as is described in Rosaldo's essay. Rather, complicity here rests in the acknowledged fascination between anthropologist and informant regarding the outside "world" that the anthropologist is specifically materializing through the travels and trajectory of her multi-sited agenda. This is the *OED* sense of complicity that goes beyond the sense of "partnership in an evil action" to the sense of being "complex or involved," primarily through the complex relationships to a third.

The shared imagination between anthropologist and informant that creates a space beyond the immediate confines of the local is also what projects the traditional site-specific mise-en-scène of fieldwork outward toward other sides. The loaded and more commonly acknowledged ethical implication of complicity glides here into its cognitive implication for the design and purview of fieldwork, turning the traditional mise-en-scène inside out. It will be recalled that for Rosaldo, the recognition of fieldwork as complicity was a stopping point for ethnography, a possibly paralyzing insight revealing how anthropology in its most self-justifying rhetoric participates in the broader context of an "evil partnership" with colonialism. In contrast, complicity as a defining element of multi-sited research is both more generative and more ambiguous morally; it demands a mapping onto and entry of the ethnographic project into a broader context that is neither so morally nor so cognitively determined as it appeared in previous critiques of rapport.

In conclusion, I want to offer a brief consideration of the developing research project of Douglas Holmes, in discussion with whom I worked out a number of the ideas presented in this paper concerning the value of recasting the mise-en-scène of fieldwork in terms of the figure of complicity. Holmes's project traces and examines in situ the discourses of the contemporary European right, frequently placing him in disturbing relation to his subjects. It is thus a dramatic example of the politics of fieldwork in multi-sited space, where the risk of complicity in its full negatively moral sense of "evil partnership" is alive at several levels. Certainly not many of the several other arenas of research in which multi-sited agendas are emerging are as charged.[29] Here there is the challenge of the fieldworker treating with a modicum of sympathy subjects whom, as a citizen, he would certainly otherwise oppose and revile. The doctrine of relativism, long considered a partial inoculation of the anthropologist against ethically questionable positions in far-off places, does not work as well in fieldwork among fascists and Nazis— the complicities of fieldwork relationships establishing strong affinities between ethnographer and subject in relation to a shared world or arena of discourse will not allow for a distancing relativism in the field. For Holmes, this problem is captured in his attempt to understand ethnographically the circulation of illicit discourse in contemporary Europe.

Illicit Discourse

Holmes's project examines how cultural struggles are shaping European politics in the post-cold-war era. In explaining the background of his research, he writes: "The project has a prehistory that stretches back to the mid-1980s and the Friuli region of northeast Italy—the terrain of Carlo Ginzburg's studies of sixteenth-century agrarian cults

and inquisitorial persecutions."³⁰ Elsewhere he writes, "While pursuing
an ethnographic portrayal of this domain, I encountered for the first
time what appeared to be a rough antipolitics that seemed to subvert
the formation of an independent political outlook and identity. In subsequent years these marginal sensibilities and aspirations insinuated
themselves into the heart of European political discourse."³¹ More recently, Holmes has made fieldwork sites of the European Parliament in
Strasbourg and the offices of the openly racist and neofascist British
National Party in the East End of London. From his work in Strasbourg, he has published a 1991 interview with Bruno Gollnisch, professor of Japanese law and literature at the University of Lyons, who was
elected to the European Parliament as a member of the Technical
Group of the European Right, the chairman of which is Jean-Marie Le
Pen; and from his London fieldwork he has produced an interview
with Richard Edmonds, who is the national organizer of the British
National Party.³²

Holmes's project is to piece together the manifestations, resemblances, and appeals of certain related discourses that have made
themselves present in settings like Friuli, Strasbourg, and East London,
among others. For the most part, he is not guided by a map of transnational and transcultural "flows" or "scapes"—the cartographic or di-
agrammatic imagery is inapt for the discontinuous spaces in which he
works. The lines of relationship between the discourses in these different sites are not at all charted, and this uncertainty or even mystery as
to the genealogies in the spread of right-wing discourses is in part what
makes them formidable to both analysts and those who wish to oppose
them. What Holmes brings to the enterprise is an ethnographic ear for
the perversions of discourse in different settings that mark and define
the changing social character of the right. What is challenging about
these discourses for the ethnographer is that they are not alien or
marked off from respectable ranges of opinion but in fact have deep
connections with them. They deserve to be listened to closely before
being exoticized as a figment of the politically extreme or being ethically condemned too precipitously. This calculated and imposed na-
ïveté, necessary for fieldwork to be conducted at all, is potentially the
source of greatest strength and special insight of ethnographics analysis, leading to both the "complex or involved" sense of complicity as
well as exposure to complicity's other sense, of "being an accomplice,
partnership in an evil action."

The working conceptual frame for Holmes's multi-sited fieldwork—
what conceptually defines the affinities among sites whose connections
are not otherwise preestablished—lies in his notion of "illicit discourse," which he describes as follows:

An illicit discourse aims at reestablishing the boundaries, terms, and idioms of political struggle. The resulting political practice is deconstructive. Its authority is often parasitic, drawing strength from the corruption, ineptitude, obsolescence, and lost relevance of the established political dogmas and agendas. *Its practitioners negotiate and map the points of contradiction and fatigue of particular positions.* They scavenge the detritus of decaying politics, probing areas of deceit and deception. By doing so they invoke displaced histories and reveal deformed moralities. They strive to introduce the unvoiced and unspeakable into public debate. Established political forces resist these "illicitudes," defining those who articulate them as racists, terrorists, bigots or as some form of essentialized pariah (italics mine).[33]

Different senses of the notion of complicity abound in Holmes's fieldwork. But the particular sense that is relevant to my argument here, and to other multi-sited research projects, concerns not the heightened ethical question of dealing with the odious from the necessarily open and cordial demeanor of the fieldworker wanting access, but the more subtle issue of the *cognitive/intellectual* affinity between the ethnographer and the purveyor of illicit discourse in different locations (as keyed by the statement that I have italicized in the quotation in the previous paragraph). Despite their very different values and commitments, the ethnographer and his subjects in this project are nevertheless broadly engaged in a pursuit of knowledge with resemblances in form and context that they can recognize. This constitutes the most provocative and potentially troubling sense of complicity in the fieldwork relationship.

What particularly struck Holmes in his fieldwork was the agile appropriation by people marked as objectionable of all sorts of registers of familiar discourse. He was being neither beguiled nor fooled by his informants—he was not complicit with them in this very direct normative sense. Rather, he was simply surprised by what was available in their discourse—its range of overlap and continuities with familiar and otherwise unobjectionable positions. When a researcher is dealing with extremes on either end of the political spectrum, the anthropological assumption is often that one is dealing with the cultlike, the exotic, and the enclosed (and, to some degree, anthropologists might be attracted to subjects in new terrains where they can analogically reproduce their traditional gaze). Extremists are supposed to be like exotic others, living within their own cosmologies and self-enclosed senses of the real. In such a construction, fieldwork complicity with them is highly artificial and not as troubling—it becomes, again, simply complicity to facilitate professional rapport. But when Holmes actually deals with as sophisticated and subtle a speaker as Gollnisch or as cunning a one as Edmonds, what is disrupted in the classic anthropological view is the notion that these speakers are "other"—that they have an "inside" that is distinctly *not* the fieldworker's.

While Holmes does not share his subjects' beliefs—nor does he fear being seduced in this way—he is complicit in many respects with their discourse and critical imaginary of what shapes political cultures in contemporary Europe. They share a taste for deconstructive logics and for, in short, understanding changes in terms of the infectious dynamics of illicit discourse. However differently they normatively view its operation, they share the same speculative wonder about it. By the fluid, appropriative capacity of right-wing discourse, Holmes finds himself being brought closer to his informants, who are accomplished ideologues/theorists/storytellers. His informants are as responsible for this connection (if not more so) as is Holmes—who, as fieldworker, would otherwise be thought of as the frame setter—and in this way, illicit discourse as experienced in fieldwork is particularly infectious.

Complicity not only raises difficult ethical questions here, but, in so doing, it also provides an opening to more general questions posed in "honest" intellectual partnership with fascists. What marks distinctive difference in the mise-en-scène of multi-sited fieldwork more generally is this unexpected affinity/complicity—more cognitive than ethical— between the fieldworker and the (in Holmes's case) vile informant. Because they are not the usual subjects, the anthropologist looks for other connections that triangulate him and them, and this is what pushes the ethnography elsewhere—in search of other connections, other sites. Finally, Holmes does not fear moral complicity in his fieldwork relationships in any obvious way; rather, he is constantly in danger of becoming an accomplice in the mutual making of illicit discourse because of the commonalities of reference, analytic imaginary, and curiosity that fieldworker and subjects so productively share—each for their very different purposes.[34]

A Concluding Note

After a strong critical reflection in the 1980s upon the historical project of cultural anthropology as a discipline, articulated through an assessment of its rhetorical traditions, we are now in the midst of a rethinking of the ideology of its distinctive method of fieldwork. Much is at stake in this, since it touches upon the core activity that continues to define the discipline's collective self-identity through every anthropologist's defining experience. The figure of rapport has always been acknowledged as being too simplistic to stand for the actual complexities of fieldwork, but it has had—and continues to have—great influence as a regulative ideal in professional culture. As were many other issues concerning anthropology's contemporary practice, the more troubling figure of complicity shadowing that of rapport was explored in Clifford Geertz's landmark essays of the 1960s and 1970s, written with his signature turn-of-phrase style of deep insight combined with considerable ambivalence. He significantly furthered the anthropological tradition with renewed intellectual power while pragmatically managing the doubt that comes with any exertion of an acute critical capacity. The exercise undertaken in this paper, of amplifying the implication of this shadow figure of complicity for the changing circumstances of anthropological fieldwork without proposing it as a new regulative ideal, is offered in the continuing spirit of Geertz's own seminal balancing of ethnography's possibilities and problems at another, very different moment in the history of anthropology.

Notes

1. *Oxford English Dictionary*, 1971 compact ed., s. v. "rapport," "collaboration," "collaborate," "complicity," "complice."

2. The most common source of this essay ("Deep Play: Notes on the Balinese Cockfight") is Clifford Geertz, *The Interpretation of Cultures* (New York, 1973), 412–53, but it was first published in *Daedalus* 101 (Winter 1972): 1–37, and as an undergraduate at Yale, I first heard Geertz deliver a version of it at a colloquium in the mid-1960s. This essay was remarkable for its elegant condensation of virtually all of the major styles and moves that were to make interpretation within the context of ethnography such an attractive research program throughout the 1970s and 1980s, not only in anthropology but also especially in social history and in the new historicist trend in literary criticism, among other methods and disciplines. Segments of "Deep Play" could be easily appropriated as models for different tasks of cultural analysis as these were becoming prominent in a variety of fields. For example, the opening anecdote on which I focus served as a model of the kind of fieldwork story that gets the writer into the material. The rhetorical technique of opening with such a story was to become a major (and now perhaps, dully repetitive) strategy of both writing and analysis in ethnographic, historical, and literary scholarship.

3. Geertz, "Deep Play," 412.

4. Ibid., 416.

5. By now, the literature of fieldwork accounts as well as the critical literature on fieldwork itself are both vast and diverse. For recent assessments in line with the argument here, see Akhil Gupta and James Ferguson, eds., *Culture, Power, Place: Explorations in Critical Anthropology* (Durham, N.C., 1997); Akhil Gupta and James Ferguson, eds., *The Concept of Fieldwork in Anthropology* (Berkeley, 1997); George E. Marcus, ed., *Critical Anthropology Now: Unexpected Contexts, Shift-*

ing Constituencies, New Agendas (Santa Fe, 1997); and George E. Marcus, "Ethnography in/of the World System: The Emergence of Multi-Sited Ethnography," *Annual Review of Anthropology* 24 (1995): 95–117.

6. Standard references for these critiques include James Clifford and George E. Marcus, eds., *Writing Culture: The Poetics and Politics of Ethnography* (Berkeley, 1986); George E. Marcus and Michael Fischer, *Anthropology as Cultural Critique: An Experimental Moment in the Human Sciences* (Chicago, 1986); James Clifford, *The Predicament of Culture* (Cambridge, Mass., 1988); and Renato Rosaldo, *Culture and Truth: The Remaking of Social Analysis* (Boston, 1989).

7. Renato Rosaldo, "Imperialist Nostalgia," in *Culture and Truth*, 68–87.

8. See, for example, Arjun Appadurai, *Modernity at Large: Cultural Dimensions of Globalization* (Minneapolis, 1996), and Susan Harding and Fred Myers, eds., *Further Inflections: Toward Ethnographies of the Future*, theme issue of *Cultural Anthropology* 9, no. 3 (1994).

9. Clifford Geertz, *Works and Lives: The Anthropologist as Author* (Stanford, 1988), 97.

10. We can compare the relative inattention of Geertz to broader complicities of presence (characteristic of the scholarly zeitgeist of the development era of the 1950s and 1960s) to Renato Rosaldo's explicit reflection on his own circumstantial complicity with the historic forces of colonialism (characteristic of a post-1970s zeitgeist in which tales like that of the cockfight incident can no longer be told innocently).

11. Clifford Geertz, "Thinking as a Moral Act: Ethical Dimensions of Anthropological Fieldwork in the New States," *Antioch Review* 28, no. 2 (1968): 139–58. Again, compare the ironies of fieldwork fictions in this essay of the development era, in which scholarly distance not only remains possible but is considered the most desirable outcome, to James Clifford's reassessment of Marcel Griaule in the field: James Clifford, "Power and Dialogue in Ethnography: Marcel Griaule's Initiation," in *Observers Observed: Essays on Ethnographic Fieldwork*, ed. George Stocking (Madison, 1983), 121–56, one of the key works that placed anthropological fieldwork intimately in colonial context. The way to knowledge for Griaule is through a certain humbling, which puts the desirability of the return to the anthropological "vocation" in doubt.

12. Geertz, "Thinking as a Moral Act," 150–51.

13. Ibid., 151.

14. Ibid., 154–55.

15. In Clifford Geertz's recently published, memoirlike *After the Fact* (Cambridge, Mass., 1995), written with the hindsight knowledge of the murderous turbulence that was to sweep through Indonesia following his years of fieldwork, there is this same matter-of-fact noting of the broader historic dramas and contexts of moments of anthropological fieldwork. These are conveyed with a weary resignation, in which striking insights are encompassed in turns of phrase full of the kind of detachment and wryness that has angered his younger critics.

16. Geertz, "Thinking as a Moral Act," 156.

17. James Clifford, "On Ethnographic Authority," *Predicament of Culture*, 51.

18. Again, Clifford's essay on Marcel Griaule is probably his most explicit and strongest piece on the colonial context and shaping of fieldwork relations. Interestingly, neither Clifford nor the *OED* points to the very common and darker connotation of the term *collaboration* that arose with its special use during World War II (as in *collaborating* with Nazis in occupied countries). In this sense, the connection of the term with *complicity* is of course most prominent.

19. This more complicated and contemporary broader context has begun to be constructed as a rhetorical, theoretical, and ethnographic exercise—for example, in the "Public Culture" project as reflected in the journal of that name and in the recent volume, cited above, by Appadurai, *Modernity at Large*. Also important for thinking about the scene of fieldwork in the different broader context of global political economy is the formulation of and debate about the notion of "reflexive modernization"; see Ulrich Beck, Anthony Giddens, and Scott Lash, *Reflexive Modernization: Politics, Tradition, and Aesthetics in the Modern Social Order* (Stanford 1994). It should be noted that Clifford's more recent work is a strong move beyond his earlier concentration on the historical context and conventions of the ethnographic mise-en-scène; see his *Routes: Travel and Translation in the Late Twentieth Century* (Cambridge, Mass., 1997).

20. Rosaldo, "Imperialist Nostalgia," 87.

21. Ibid., 69–70.

22. From Mikhail Bakhtin, *Speech Genres and Other Essays*, quoted in Paul Willeman, *Looks and Frictions: Essays in Cultural Studies and Film Theory* (Bloomington, Ind., 1994), 199.

23. In addition to the general discussions on the emergence of multi-sited ethnography, referenced in note 5, see, for a very specific example, the excellent description by Sherry Ortner of the materialization of this multi-sited space in her fieldwork among the now dispersed members of her high school class, Sherry B. Ortner, "Ethnography Among the Newark: The Class of '58 of Weequahic High School," *Michigan Quarterly Review* 32, no. 3 (1993).

24. Discussions about reflexive modernization (see note 19) are for me the most searching theoretical discussions available of this mode of being.

25. Geertz saw this clearly, but he argued that the anthropologist and the informant, joined in the complicity of "anthropological irony," blunted these insights in a calculated way through the achievement of rapport by mutual, self-interested, and pragmatic fictions. The sense of complicity that I evoke here is quite different; it is based precisely on the anthropologist and his subject *not* engaging in the fictions that achieve rapport.

26. Under the powerful stimulus of postcolonial studies that have emerged through the writings of scholars such as Edward Said, Gayatri Spivak, Homi Bhabha, and those of the Subaltern Studies group, an important body of work in anthropology has developed reassessing both colonialism and its legacies. In reflecting new exchanges between anthropology and history as well (especially those that have come out of the University of Michigan and the University of Chicago), it has made ethnography's traditional broader context of colonialism itself a complex object of study. While this work overlaps somewhat with the as-yet halting attempts to provide large, systematic perspectives on what is meant

by the term *globalization*, its program still remains within a frame that I believe takes a more conservative position on challenging the regulative ideology of ethnographic practice. As such, the ethical critique of fieldwork in this body of scholarship, although immensely enriched, is still expressed restrictively in terms of anthropology's complicity with colonialism and its legacies—categories that do not encompass the diversity of fieldwork relationships that have been created in anthropology's contemporary forays into, for example, science studies, media studies, and political economy.

27. Marcus,"Ethnography in/of the World System," 113–14.

28. The more complex ethical compass of multi-sited research can be read into Emily Martin's pioneering *Flexibile Bodies: The Role of Immunity in American Culture from the Days of Polio to the Age of AIDS* (Boston, 1994). While the explicit discussions of complicities operating in this research are not that developed or rich in Martin's book, she does map very well the special kind of moral economy that emerges from doing multi-sited fieldwork.

29. Multi-sited projects are beginning to emerge prominently in the forays of anthropological research into media studies, the study of science and technology (an outgrowth of the diverse interests of the prominent subfield of medical anthropology), the study of environmental and indigenous social movements, the study of development through the activity of NGOs (nongovernmental organizations), the study of art worlds, and the study of diasporas. I myself learned the methodological issues of multi-sited research through my long-term study of dynastic families and fortunes, and the worlds that they make for others: George E. Marcus, *Lives in Trust: The Fortunes of Dynastic Families in Late-Twentieth-Century America* (Boulder, 1992). While none of these arenas have generated projects with ethical issues of complicity quite as stark as the ones Douglas Holmes has encountered in his fieldwork among the European right, each does place anthropologist and local subject in uncomfortable, but interesting, relationships of mutual complicity in relation to an imagined world of outside sites of activity in which they have very different interests.

30. Douglas R. Holmes, *Cultural Disenchantments: Worker Peasantries in Northeast Italy* (Princeton, 1989).

31. Douglas R. Holmes, "Illicit Discourse," in George E. Marcus, ed., *Perilous States: Conversations on Culture, Politics, and Nation*, Late Editions 1 (Chicago, 1993), 255.

32. The Bruno Gollnisch interview forms the body of Holmes's "Illicit Discourse," and the Richard Edmonds interview appears in "Tactical Thuggery: National Socialism in the East End of London," in George E. Marcus, ed., *The Paranoid Style at Century's End*, Late Editions 6 (forthcoming).

33. Holmes, "Illicit Discourse," 258.

34. As a citizen, experiencing events largely from a distance and through the available media of journalism, one is inoculated against the heterogeneous seductions of the odious—but not as an ethnographer. For example, an Italian reader of Holmes's Gollnisch interview was not at all impressed with Gollnisch's discourse, which he found easy to see through and situate. This reader responded from an activist political position on the left, whose own discourse has a long history of being shaped by an embedded dialectic of distanced rela-

tionship to the changing guises of the European right. But close-up, from the necessary openness of ethnography, Gollnisch is seductive, at least for a moment. This persuasiveness of the moment makes illicit discourse effective in its own political project just as it pulls the ethnographer in as well, making him an accomplice even as it does so in the name of the latter's own distinctive scholarly project, conceived in a tradition of disinterested fieldwork.

Part Two

TRACES IN PARALLEL ETHNOGRAPHIC PROJECTS

Five

Power on the Extreme Periphery

THE PERSPECTIVE OF TONGAN ELITES IN THE MODERN
WORLD SYSTEM (1980)[1]

THIS ESSAY develops implications of Immanuel Wallerstein's world-system perspective for contemporary elite formation in the Kingdom of Tonga, which although unique in its development as a monarchy, reflects similar conditions in Polynesian and other island nation-states generally. In world-system terms, Polynesia is literally on the extreme periphery, composed of island societies with limited land resources, overpopulation, a cash crop economy tied to world markets, overseas labor migration, and dependence on external sources—other states, private business, and church organizations—for investment capital. The special problems of mini to small states have been well noted in the literature on development and international relations (e.g., see Vital 1967, 1971; Benedict 1976; UNITAR 1971). Yet the fact that these states are conventionally analyzed in conceptual terms appropriate to any nation-state unit, regardless of size and relative position in a world system of states, is itself a bias of viewing the periphery from the perspective of a Western core, which exported its forms of political and economic organization to the rest of the world.

In the theoretical conclusion of Wallerstein's study (1974) of the origins of the European world-economy during the sixteenth century, he made two fundamental points which can be elaborated to constitute a general research orientation for studying elite perspectives on the periphery: (1) "World-economies then are divided into core-states and peripheral areas. I do not say peripheral *states* because one characteristic of a peripheral area is that the indigenous state is weak, ranging from its non-existence (that is, a colonial situation) to one with a low degree of autonomy (that is, a neo-colonial situation)" (p. 349); (2) ". . . one of the key elements in analysing a class or a status-group is not only the state of its self-consciousness but the geographical scope of its self-definition" (p. 351).

Wallerstein discounts the significance of states as analytical units in considering peripheral areas and emphasizes the direct apprehension of the perspectives of local status groups and social classes within them.

The nation-state model and identity is the way that core states view the periphery, but it may be only one way, among others, that peripheral elites—broadly, those with political power and who control the distribution of resources in their locales—view their own conditions or their position in the world. Taking on the apparatus of state organization was an imposed or self-selected adaptation in peripheral areas, which was the necessary mode of integration into a world of nation-states. However, this mode did not always overlap exactly with possible alternative self-definitions of a population as, for example, a people, a culture, or a chiefdom/kingship. The artificiality of nation-state status thus has added a measure of flexibility to the activities of elites in backwater areas of the world system; it is one public face or context which they could present at home and internationally as a means of both justifying and explaining their actions.

The geographical self-definition of established and emergent elites on the extreme periphery is likely to be international, if not global, in scope. In certain areas of the world—particularly island areas such as the Pacific—European penetration merely added a larger dimension to an existing tendency for local populations to view their social worlds in broad geographical terms. Post-contact elites among these populations became or stayed elites by attending to this new horizon of social definition. Old elites had an initial advantage in assimilating and interpreting changes for their populations, but eventually their own character as elites also changed as their functions became defined by foreign-derived political and economic institutions, which brought them into closer emulative and subordinate relations with colonial powers than the rest of their populations.

Middle classes of Western core states historically became conscious of themselves in the framework of their nation-state boundaries. In contrast, contemporary elites of the extreme periphery, who adhere to models of Western middle classes, are conscious of their participation in cultures where social relations span nation-state boundaries. In the presence of long-term migration and overseas communities, the relative scale of the home mini-state as a "place"-focused cultural identity changes against the background of an emerging "diaspora"-focused alternative cultural identity. The existence of instrumental family networks spanning locales—especially those created and nurtured by elites—sustains the range of options through which individuals view their life possibilities and fields of activity. The resource and opportunity base even for those elites who reside permanently within their home societies may still be conceived by them materially and ideologically as a set of international possibilities, embodied in dispersed family networks, with anchors in different places abroad.

Historically, Tonga has experienced two distinct periods of peripheral integration into a changing capitalist world system, associated with two distinct processes of elite formation. The first period of integration was as a self-imposed monarchical state under English protection, lasting from the last nineteenth century to the late 1960s. The second period since the late 1960s has been as an independent state with multilateral ties to other states, and most importantly, with flows of permanent migration to various locales abroad as well as variable flows of temporary labor migration between Tonga and those places abroad where permanent Tongan populations are growing. Elite formation was localized and closely controlled by the kingship during the first period, but during the second period, when a Tongan diaspora has developed, both old and new elites must be seen in their formation and orientations to social activity on a scale commensurate with the international dispersion of the contemporary Tongan population.

In Tonga, as elsewhere in the Third World, socioeconomic development, like westernization before it, has foremost been the ideology of state-craft in the management by periphery elites of relations with core and patron states. It has been one salient way by which peripheral states take on the identity which core states recognize and expect of them. However, aside from rhetoric and ideology, the present Tongan monarch is distinguished by his very aggressive and committed plans for Tonga's development as a prosperous nation-state, which have been crafted with Tongan mini-state limitations in mind. These plans seek an economic role for Tonga independent of its status as an overpopulated agrarian society tied to world market fluctuations for certain commodities.

The King's development ambitions for Tonga must be understood not merely in the context of a conventional nation-state model of Tongan society as a state among states, but more critically in the context of the international dimension of contemporary Tongan social organization. This dimension is itself a consequence of a historically subordinate and peripheral integration into a world system where Tongan elite formation has depended on the development of international family networks, yielding a kind of parasitic access to resources and opportunities in richer locales. These networks represent diversified economic activity which increases the degree of autonomy and flexibility of groups of individuals in relation to both local and overseas political and economic institutions. This is a "boot-straps" kind of development of family groups in the interstices of states, which some Tongans (by definition, the elites) are able to convert into position and personal power within the nation-state framework at home. Such overseas development of family networks is a phenomenon which occurs throughout the contemporary world, but it is Tonga's relative smallness of scale as a nation-state entity which

makes the effects of diffuse international development of families so
much greater on local nation-state development. The remainder of this
essay is a descriptive elaboration of these points about Tongan elites,
during the two historic periods noted.

1875–1965: The Reigns of the First Three Tupou Monarchs— A Period of "Hothouse" Development

Tupou I's declaration of a constitutional monarchy for Tonga in 1875
was a conscious adaptation to increasing European colonization of
Polynesia. The declaration was preceded by Tupou's treaty making with
foreign powers to secure formal recognition of Tonga's political independence as well as by his growing suspicions concerning the ambitions of the Australian controlled Wesleyan mission. The Wesleyans im-
planted a strong church organization in Tonga, through which much
of the early westernization occurred, and their support was significant
in Tupou's ability to consolidate his own power among the major
chiefly factions. During the scandal-ridden reign of Tupou II (1893–
1917), Tonga reluctantly became a British Protectorate. Under the
long and stabilizing rule of Queen Sālote (1917–1965), British protection came to be appreciated and nurtured by the monarch as an asset
to her culturally conservative reign. The British shielded Tonga from
the turbulence in world politics and economics and also provided the
funnel through which the introduction of external influences could be
closely controlled by the kingship (except for the massive Allied presence during World War II). The social reforms of Tupou I took shape
in the everyday lives of Tongans during the reigns of his successors,
and Tonga experienced a "hothouse" development typical of monarchies, preserved and protected by the British (Marcus 1978).

During the past century, Tonga has remained principally an agrarian
economy with the increasing use of money dependent on cash-crop
production and external injections from patron states, remittances,
and most importantly, from direct investment by overseas church organizations to develop their Tongan missions (see Bollard 1974). At the
base of society has been a small-holding peasantry, with secure tenure
in hereditary plots of land, who have fluctuated in their participation
in commercial agriculture. At the top of society, a highly centralized
kingship has overseen the operations of a weak state bureaucracy and
largely autonomous church hierarchies which reach to all villages and
towns of the kingdom. A nobility with hereditary privileges and estates
was retained, composed of some of the most powerful chiefly lines of
the old order, but the nobles have been considerably constrained in
their formal powers and in what they have been able in fact to exploit

from the land and people of their estates. A commoner elite gradually developed in the new order, composed of those who have been prominent as family groups in the church hierarchies (often the children or siblings of leading clergymen), who have distinguished themselves in the local system of education, and who have been eventually rewarded with bureaucratic positions. Gradually, distant or forgotten chiefly connections among these commoners have been renewed and elaborated only after they had validated their status through achievements in the new institutions. They were thus truly an elite created from a process of westernization rather than covertly old-style elites in a new form.

Local commerce has been in the hands of a segment of the Tongan elite who are the descendants of European traders who had settled in Tonga. These so-called half-caste families, of German, English, and Scandanavian heritage, have occupied an ambiguous position in the kingdom—on the surface integrated into a homogeneous culture, but having specialized functions as merchants. These Tonganized Europeans have also acted at various times as close advisors and representatives of the King, especially in managing relations with overseas Europeans. Large portions of their wealth acquired in Tonga have been spent and invested abroad, thus making them among the first Tongans, along with the Royal Family itself and their close aristocratic kin, to create family networks and resource bases abroad. The first overseas university degree was earned by the present monarch in the early 1940s, although a number of prominent noble and commoner families had already been educating their children in overseas church affiliated schools. Permanent residence, purchase of land overseas, and the exploitation of other opportunities have often followed the sending of children overseas (principally to New Zealand) to be educated, just as education is the oft-stated impetus for current internal migration within the Kingdom from the outer islands to the capital.

During the first three reigns of Tupou monarchs, then, Tongan elite formation was largely an internal process. In a highly centralized kingdom, the economic infrastructure of the society has been most heavily developed on the main island of Tongatapu, and particularly in and around the port capital of Nuku'alofa (Sevele 1973). In recent decades, the drift of population has been from outer regions to Tongatapu, thus artificially accentuating already overcrowded conditions in the kingdom. While never losing their regional and village associations, elite families had already clustered as residents of the capital during the reigns of Tupou II and Queen Sālote. At present, the old commoner and noble elite (including the part-European families) compose 30–40 families based in Nuku'alofa, with continuing linkages both to their outer island regions of origin (mainly through their holding of hereditary plots of land) and to the newer overseas concentrations of Tongans.

These families, conceived in their dispersed form, constitute the contemporary focus of an elite subculture in Tonga. As noted, they have become elites, not through entrepreneurship (with the exception of the part-Europeans), but by making niches for themselves in new institutions, controlled by the kingship and church organizations. Economically, the Tongan elite should be seen collectively as accumulators and redistributors of the local resources of Tongan society both through family networks and through positions which they control within government and church hierarchies. Here, resources should be understood broadly as land, jobs, privileged statuses, and the establishing of preferences among clients and kin for distributing controlled values and goods of all kinds.[2] Carol Smith (1976) emphasized the importance of elites as controllers of modes of exchange and distribution in agrarian societies, and noted that when dendritic market systems organize peripheral economies, local political and economic elite subcultures, clustered in market centers such as port towns, assume wide-ranging control of the distribution of "goods" of all kinds to their respective populations. Their elite status lay not so much in the direct ownership control of productive resources such as land, as in the control of a population's consumption habits.

Even during the long period of Tonga's "hothouse" development as a monarchy, there was a collective level of awareness and sensitivity among Tongans to their regional and international position in relation to other states. This kind of awareness is by now a cultural ideology, supported by Tonga's central historic achievement of preserving both its independence and its kingship. In relative terms, this "world" view has been most sophisticatedly and consciously developed among Tongan elite families, and of course most notably among the Royal Family and its aristocratic kinsmen, who for so long under Sālote, monopolized the management of Tonga's position in relation to its British protector and others. However, consistent with the general cultural pattern of emulating those of the highest status, the old commoner elite under Sālote also achieved a sophistication about Tonga's leverage in a world of more powerful states, especially about how they might use their position at home to build part of their futures abroad, at first in New Zealand, but then under Tupou IV, in the United States as well.

1965–Present: The Reign of Tupou IV—The Internalization of Tongan Culture

The contemporary period of Tongan history, particularly since its attainment of full independence in 1970, can be seen in terms of two related trends. These have opened the Tongan state and people to multiple linkages with particular core and semi-peripheral societies, most of which border the Pacific. First, since his succession in 1965, Tupou IV has aggressively sought a source of foreign capital to fund major projects which would set the development of Tonga on a course leading to a position as one of the world's rich and relatively autonomous mini-states. At the same time, continuing investments by overseas churches and the periodic injection of foreign capital, associated with the King's persistent cultivation of friendships and personal diplomacy with parties in a variety of countries, have stimulated a number of modest projects in tourism and small industry.

Second, shortage of land, increasing population, and Tongan fascination with the sources of influence which changed their society have led during the past three decades to large concentrations of Tongans who live in certain overseas locales. Their rootedness abroad is now apparent, and linkages of variable intensity and content with home kin have important effects on the Tongan economy and social structure. In the short term, and particularly since 1970, there have been great fluctuations in flows of temporary migration between Tonga and New Zealand, primarily, and these have been governed largely by conditions in the New Zealand economy. Unpredictable remittance flows back to Tonga, accompanied by a steadily increasing demand for imports, have had an overall destabilizing effect on the Tongan home economy. Temporary migration has also been a potentially new source of elite formation in Tonga, or at least, a source for the appearance of a broader-based Tongan middle class (a middle class in the sense of possessing the locally interpreted symbols and attributes of modernity, so long available only to a much more restricted noble and commoner elite).

Over the years, the King has conducted negotiations with private and government parties in the United States, Australia, New Zealand, Japan, India, Saudi Arabia (1973), Russia (1977), and most recently, Libya. Several of these negotiations have apparently ended without clear results; others have been mutually sustained as long-term personal friendships; others have resulted in suspect deals and losses for Tonga; while others have given the kingdom leverage in aid requests to regional patrons (for example, the recent courting of the Russians, which, intended or not, attracted New Zealand's concern). The negotiations seem aimed at finding one large investor to subsidize Tongan development, which has been conceived differently over the years in terms of specific schemes.

The King's moves to take a main chance for Tonga, improving dramatically its position as a mini-state in the overall community of nations, is a bold game with considerable risks. Finding a backer for

Tongan development could replace the diffuse dependency and economically stagnant conditions characteristic of most peripheral states with a very narrow kind of clientage.

This bold strategy of development for Tonga as a nation-state should be interpreted in the broader context of the simultaneous development of the Tongan people as a dispersed population, of which Tonga itself is only one, albeit still the most important, locus. It is difficult to know how many thousands of Tongans are living abroad, since there are no reliable census figures concerning them. Based on my own rough estimates,[3] there are over 30,000 Tongans permanently resident abroad compared to a current population in Tonga of approximately 100,000. The largest concentrations are in New Zealand (particularly, Auckland), Australia, Fiji, the United States (particularly, Hawaii, California, and Utah, although there is a sprinkling of Tongans throughout the United States), and much less so in Britain. The numbers as well as wealth of overseas Tongans are increasing relative to the home population. Intermarriage, church and private sponsorship, overstaying temporary visas, and primarily, education have been the footholds which have led to the permanence in migration.

Important issues for understanding this kind of Tongan development are the characteristics of the networks which are maintained between permanent overseas Tongans and Tongans at home—how long network configurations last and what kinds of relationships and transactions compose them. Consideration of these issues is still somewhat academic since overseas concentrations are relatively very recent and the long-term characteristics of family networks barely established. Even the old elite overseas networks have only been developed since World War II, and most have not yet been challenged by such expectable weakening factors as the decline in involvement of second generation overseas Tongans with their relatives in Tonga.

These permanent overseas concentrations of Tongans are to be distinguished conceptually from the flows of temporary migrant labor during the 1970s, since only rarely do the temporary migrants lay down roots abroad, at least not without the assistance of permanent Tongan residents. The control by family networks with permanent migrant branches of this flow of temporary migrants, as one of their resources or fields of enterprise, is a tantalizing question on which I have little systematic evidence.

In referring to Tongans overseas, I use the word concentration rather than community. On the basis of the elite networks which I have studied, it appears that although Tongans do associate with one another abroad and there are organizations which bring them together such as overseas branches of Tongan churches, they are far more dispersed and isolated from one another in host societies, than in comparison, for example, to Samoans. My impression is that Samoans have more of a community identity than Tongans abroad. Also, they identify each other and themselves, by village of origin in Samoa. As in Albert Wendt's novel, *Sons for the Return Home*, even Samoans who spend decades abroad retain aspirations that they or their children will eventually make a triumphal, permanent return home and will use what they have achieved abroad to enhance their positions in their villages of origin. In contrast, permanent Tongan migrants seem much more culturally self-sufficient abroad, while maintaining their strongest ties of support with specific kin, rather than villages, at home. If this is in fact a real difference, it might have something to do with the extension abroad of fundamentally different kinds of local organization at home between Tonga and Samoa—that is, the key importance of village and community organization in Samoa characterizes overseas Samoans; its relative unimportance in Tonga characterizes overseas Tongans.[4]

While international ties of cooperation permeate the entire Tongan home population, their strength, regularity, and durability are highly variable and of unknown patterning.[5] It is clear that such networks are most strongly developed and anchored among the old and new elite families, clustered in the capital. For these families, elite status had depended during the "hothouse" period on the accumulation and coordinated sharing of resources in dispersed networks within the kingdom, and this feature of elite formation has merely expanded in space with the internationalizing dimension of Tongan social organization. As noted, segments of the old elite were the first to establish their interests as families abroad, and more recently, they have been in the most favored position to travel and spend long periods overseas. The internationalizing of elite networks characterizes to a lesser degree even the most traditional segment of the old elite—the nobility—with their most important inherent advantages closely tied to the nation-state model of Tonga as a society (Marcus 1980). There is also a small, but growing new elite or middle class joining the slow circulation of elites at the center of Tongan society. These are families catapulted to prominence by the extraordinary achievements of one or more of their members usually in education overseas, who return to Tonga and are coopted into the local system of church and state offices. The advantage to the kingship of such co-option is that it has an increasingly large pool of previously unrecognized talent to draw back to Tonga, thus giving it an alternative to sole dependence on domestically established noble and commoner elite families.

These old and new elites represent the extreme end of a diverse continuum. They are distinguished by features which make their networks appear more consistently "structured"—a coordinated mix of resources and an internal authority structure, anchored by an unambiguous elite identity in Nuku'alofa society, even though their overseas branches may be anonymous as members of a diffuse Polynesian minority. In contrast, there are many other Tongans who have achieved wealth and distinctions abroad, but who have no anchorage in Tonga by which to convert these resources into elite status; they are merely the pride of their undistinguished kinsmen at home. Such successful overseas Tongans tend to cut most substantive ties with their networks. However, there are anomalous cases where they fund and support relatives at home, who thus become economically well off in Tonga, but ironically, who are unable to trade on this acquired relative wealth to improve their local personal status. These cases index the formation of a stunted middle class in Tonga as a product of receiving overseas advantages combined with limited possibilities for local social mobility. The increasing occurrence of such cases epitomizes a contradiction in the alternative diaspora and homeland models of Tongan social structure.

Possibilities in the context of an internationally dispersed population are thus the crucial framework for assessing the life chances even for people who will remain lifelong residents of Tonga. To be able to migrate is not essential for economically enhancing a family's position in Tonga. Rather, the capacity to call on international resources, continually or on important occasions, has become a crucial factor in influencing its local economic conditions. The lowest stratum in contemporary Tonga are those totally dependent on the nation-state framework and the limited resources it embodies without any overseas options at all. Elites and an emergent middle class, in contrast, are those not only with the greatest potential options abroad, realized through family connections, but also those who successfully organize to play them.

The heuristic intent of this essay precludes a discussion of the dynamics of relationships within elite family groups, but it might be useful merely to list resources, which I have recorded as having been shared through active exchange within geographically dispersed elite kin networks. Property, businesses, positions, jobs, reputation, and influence with local authorities are typical kinds of resources developed by old and new elite families with footholds abroad. Table 1 contains resource listings for one old commoner elite family and one new commoner elite family.

TABLE 1

OLD ELITE	NEW ELITE
In Tonga:	*In Tonga:*
1 high church office	strong influence in a minority
1 school principal	church
3 in executive bureaucratic positions	1 high bureaucratic position
1 airline clerk	3 middle-level civil servants
ownership of garage/gas station	1 executive at radio station
taxi-business	hereditary interest in 3 agricultural allotments (leasing of 5 others); considerable commercial agriculture
mild chiefly associations/long-time reputation as elite	2 Nuku'alofa town allotments
1 retail business/shop	2 retail businesses
hereditary interest in 6 agricultural allotments (4 around Nuku'alofa)	1 PhD employed in Tonga
hereditary interest in 5 town allotments (residential property in Nuku'alofa)	3 teachers
	In Hawaii:
In Hawaii:	handicraft business
handicraft business and importer	ownership of rental property
yard-cleaning business	3 persons at the university
5 wage-earners (3 skilled; 2 unskilled)	*In California:*
ownership of residential property	1 gas station operator and owner
3 individuals seeking university degrees	2 residential properties
	2 employed at San Francisco airport
In New Zealand:	*In Utah:*
residential property	3 employed at unskilled jobs (1 permanent; 2 temporary residents)
secondary school education of children	1 teacher
In Fiji:	*In New Zealand:*
university lecturer	1 person in transport work
	1 rental property
	1 residence
	2 in secondary school
	1 at university

Both families can be seen as anchored in Nuku'alofa with various kinds of options that are being exploited in different overseas locales. An interesting question is under what conditions might the center of gravity of these families change from a focus in Tonga to a focus abroad, while still not yielding, as a group, any options completely, including those in Tonga. It is the possibility of such shifts within dispersed family networks which might eventually change the central position of the Tongan nation-state relative to the international distribution of the Tongan population. At present, the focus of most such cooperating, but dispersed families is still in the homeland. There is a tendency for the particularly well-off overseas to grow apart from their home networks rather than to build their positions within them, or else for particular individuals resident abroad to contemplate an eventual return home. For example, young, highly educated Tongans, whose university degrees would bring deference in Tonga, could originate overseas branches of their families, but they would often prefer to trade on their educational qualifications at home, if the opportunity to be co-opted to a place in the Tongan institutional order arises.

The fact that commoner elite families must mediate high prestige roles at home and a relatively low or marginal status as minorities abroad does not generate the kind of cognitive dissonance which Westerners might anticipate. Social contexts in which options occur are kept quite separate in the activities of dispersed family networks, and thus there is no conceptual bar to developing any new options in separate contexts. Janitors in New Zealand are as much a part of the family network as are bureaucrats at home (and some bureaucrats even work as janitors when they reside temporarily abroad). This capacity to integrate all kinds of resources, geographically separated, is one of the key elements of economic strength and flexibility in elite family networks.

It is worth offering a speculative scenario to suggest where the present internationalizing trend of Tongan culture might lead. A fully internationalized Tongan culture would result from an international scale of family operations, still tied to kin at home, which would equal or exceed in economic value the Tongan national product. While the homeland might never lose its symbolic and emotional importance for permanent migrants in the retention of a Tongan cultural identity, it might become decentered as the political and economic focus of the Tongan people. Tonga might remain merely a struggling nation-state in the face of flourishing overseas concentrations in places such as Hawaii and California, residents of which would continue to affect the overall conditions of Tongans at home by their selective participation and contributions in persisting family networks. With this futurist scenario in mind, we can now return to view the King's ambitious development program from a particularly Tongan perspective.

The King's efforts to find a strong base for Tonga's development take-off, even at the risk of its becoming a narrowly defined client state, can be understood, on one hand, as the kingship's continuing assertive orientation to a world of more powerful states, on which the historic pride and popular image of the Tupou monarchs in Tongan society have been based. On the other hand, it can be understood as an effort to preserve Tonga's position as *both* the economic and symbolic center of an internationalizing culture. Migrant dispersion generates an alternative model of Tongan development as an international population which challenges the model of Tongan development as a nation-state. This former model of development against which the King's must be vigorously played involves the appearance of family networks, most prominently among the established elite subculture, but which is also a pervasive feature of the Tongan home population at large. Most Tongans have instrumental linkages of some sort with overseas concentrations. The development aims of the King are thus in part an effort to retain the Tongan state as the center of a society in centrifugal motion.

More practically and realistically at present, this clash of development contexts should be seen narrowly as an affair of elites. All of the Tongan national elite families now have an international dimension, and thus see their fields of activity as a strategic mix of options in the framework of dispersed family networks which span different places, each with different kinds of opportunities, and one such place is Tonga itself. Those who play the nation-state/homeland option most strongly and see it as a markedly more important option than others include the Royal Family, certain of the noble families, and old commoner elite families with a greater vested interest in the running of Tongan bureaucratic institutions. In one sense, the monarch represents those who see Tongan resources as more important than others, and he has perhaps expectedly been most involved in the aggressive and innovative development plans for Tonga as a place.

For the rest of the elite, the nation-state option remains important, but in comparison to the high bureaucratic and aristocratic elite, it now takes a more modest place among other possibilities which can be pursued opportunistically. They see themselves flexibly as participants in both contexts of development, but are not overly committed to either one. Their development as families still anchored in Tonga, aids Tonga's development as a nation-state, an option controlled by and heavily invested in by the kingship-focused subset of families. Yet, this conventional nation-state model of development is simultaneously challenged by the possibility of such families decisively switching abroad their tentative and relative commitments among options in the present general trend of migration. The development moves of those playing heavily the nation-state option can be seen as an attempt to improve Tonga's position, not so much as an extreme peripheral state involved in a world system of states, but as the core of its own migrant periphery.

Conclusion

Despite its special monarchical development, Tonga is not unique in the Pacific or elsewhere in its dual faces as a small nation-state and an internationalizing population, which are mediated as resource options in elite formation. Particularly in Polynesia, the relativizing of the political and economic significance of the homeland in the appearance of a diaspora characterizes a number of other societies such as Samoa, Niue, and the Cook Islands. The extent and nature of international dispersions in relation to island states need further investigation to see if they accord with the considerable impact such internationalization has had on the elite segments of local Tongan society.

Perhaps the most interesting previous formulation which fits with the perspective offered here is Silverman's model (1969) of option maximization, suggested as the pervasive value orientation among Banaban (Ocean) islanders. This model is certainly relevant for many other Micronesian and Polynesian peoples. Silverman was concerned with a people who had been resettled from Ocean Island, rich in phosphate, to Rabi Island, Fiji. Of the several contexts in which the Banaban people acted to "touch" all their options without foreclosing any, one of the most striking has been the deft handling by the Banaban leadership of their international relations. To their considerable advantage, they have maintained their identities both as a people under colonial rule in Fiji and as owners of their economically rich homeland. Forced into internationalization, they defined and played their place-focused options in the shadow of more powerful states to whom they were formally a dependent and territorially anomalous people of the extreme periphery.

The Tongans have experienced very different historical conditions than have the Banabans in that they are internationalizing from the most advantageous kind of outcome of the colonial process in the Pacific—the preservation of their kingship and relative independence as a state—while the Banabans internationalized from the much more negative outcome of the same process—resettlement. Still, in contemporary times, both peoples find themselves in much the same situation as cultures exploiting whatever resources they can define in global perspective. Particularly for the Tongan elite, the mixing and playing of options internationally has been as important for them as it has been for the Banaban leadership, even if Tongan elites, in contrast to the Banaban, do not represent a unified, situated population, but rather reflect in distinctions among themselves the contradictions of competing social structural models.

The notion that the Tongans may be demonstrably following culturally distinctive strategies, which also characterize other historically related cultures in their area of the world, raises an interesting point about the particular relevance of cultural anthropology to the study of world events in peripheral areas. There may be a positive relationship between the visibility of cultural differences in the world system and peripherality. That is, the relations among large states of the core and semi-periphery are so thoroughly mediated by a rationalized nation-state model that cultural differences in the conduct of political economy with and between these states may be extremely subtle and their precise significance in doubt among Western scholars who have concerned themselves with world-system topics. In contrast, because the pressure is off backwater nation-states, so to speak, manifest distinctive cultural orientations, associated with a peripheral area such as the Pacific, might permeate state-craft among its component societies and nation-states. Peripheral states can perhaps afford the kind of cultural variability and creatively in their operations which larger states cannot. These tend instead to homogenize their relations under the discipline of the political models of the dominant core in the process by which Wallerstein (1974) has distinguished world systems from world empires.

Finally, the leverage of periphery elites lay in the range of options by which they operate in backwater societies. The advantage relative to the center is that these elites can deal flexibly in alternative frameworks whereas the core is tied to one dominant model of the nation-state which it has proliferated. Perhaps only on the periphery is elite formation importantly affected by a pervasive "worldview." In more substantial states, interacting with the core, the nation-state framework is a more formidable constraint on how self-definition develops among elites.

Those that remain behind in societies of the extreme periphery may never become better off without connecting with migrant dispersion, but internationalization itself eventually offers possibilities for at least a more broad-based economic mobility than would be otherwise possible in island states such as Tonga. Actual outcomes depend on how well migrants do and how strongly they maintain ties with kin at home. The quality of network relationships, outside the old elite and emerging middle class in Tonga, deserves more investigation as does the possible mediation and control by established elite networks of opportunities for those outside them to tap international options.

Notes

1. A longer version of this paper was presented at a symposium on dependency and development in the Pacific, during the annual meeting of the Association for Social Anthropology in Oceania, Galveston, Texas, February 1980. This paper is based on my fieldwork in Tonga during the summer months of 1972, a full year in 1973–74, and a brief visit in 1975. In addition, between 1974 and 1978, I attempted to track specific family networks, during brief visits to Auckland, Suva, Honolulu, Salt Lake City, and San Francisco.

2. These are the well-recorded traditional functions of chiefship in Polynesia, and there is some justification for claiming that new elites function in a manner similar to traditional chiefs. This is particularly so in the institutionalized patterns of collection and distribution of money, goods, and services to and from the population at large, as they are mediated by the clergy in the hierarchical organization of church congregations. However, historically and culturally, the functions of the Tupou era elites have their own specific manifestation which accords more realistically with the integration of periphery elites and markets into an international economic system, controlled by core and semi-peripheral states.

3. During my research, I could find no official or other statistics on numbers of temporary and permanent Tongan residents in the various overseas locales I visited. I did have the opportunity to discuss the size of concentrations of Tongans with permanently resident Tongans in each locale I visited, and in some places, I had access to church lists. From these discussions and lists, I derived the 30,000 estimate, which is regrettably, rough, but I think on the conservative side.

4. The long-standing adaptive mimicry by Tongans of Europeans as well as the traditional Tongan use of kinship/genealogical categories to locate themselves culturally in space and time, in preference to village/place orientations, might in part account for the salience among Tongan migrants of family networks across international spaces with the absence of strong insulating overseas communities.

5. Since the tracing of ties for the entire internationalized Tongan population would be difficult, given the diffuseness of the phenomenon, my claims here are based specifically on readings of my data for elite families, which show very clearly the importance of international networks in their formation as elites, and of my earlier, sketchy, but suggestive data for one island community (Marcus 1974).

References

Benedict, Burton, 1967, *Problems of Small Territories,* London, Athlone Press.
Bollard, Alan E., 1974, *The Impact of Monetisation in Tonga,* Unpublished MA thesis, University of Auckland.

Marcus, George E., 1974, "A Hidden Dimension of Family Development in the Modern Kingdom of Tonga," *Journal of Comparative Family Studies*, 5, 1, 87–102.

——— 1978, "Land Tenure and Elite Formation in the Neotraditional Monarchies of Tonga and Buganda," *American Ethnologist*, 5, 3, 509–534.

——— 1980, *The Nobility and the Chiefly Tradition in the Modern Kingdom of Tonga*. The Polynesian Society, Memoir No. 42, Wellington.

Sevele, F. V., 1973, *Regional Inequalities in Socio-Economic Development in Tonga: A Preliminary Study*. Unpublished PhD dissertation, University of Canterbury, Christchurch, N.Z.

Silverman, M. G., 1969, "Maximize Your Options: A Study in Values, Symbols, and Social Structure," in *Forms of Symbolic Action*. Robert F. Spencer (ed.). Proceedings of the American Ethnological Society, University of Washington Press, Seattle.

Smith, Carol A., 1976, "Exchange Systems and the Spatial Distribution of Elites: The Organization of Stratification in Agrarian Societies," in *Regional Analysis: Social Systems*, Carol A. Smith (ed.). Academic Press, New York.

UNITAR (United Nations Institute for Training and Research), 1971, *Small States and Territories: Status and Problems*. Arno Press, New York.

Vital, David, 1967, *The Inequality of States: A Study of the Small Power in International Relations*, Oxford University Press.

——— 1971, *The Survival of Small States*. Oxford University Press.

Wallerstein, Immanuel, 1974, *The Modern World-System*, Academic Press, New York.

Six

The Problem of the Unseen World of Wealth for the Rich

TOWARD AN ETHNOGRAPHY OF COMPLEX CONNECTIONS

(1989)

THIS ESSAY is an effort to outline a major challenge (as well as opportunity) for a developing ethnography of modernity within anthropology through ironic reference to a traditional anthropological problem in the traditional arena of traditional society. The focus is on how the construction of order in everyday (modern or traditional) life depends on the postulation of at least dual, parallel worlds, one of which is unseen. In a broader sense, this essay reflects an effort to recast, but sustain, the comparative framework so central to anthropology's identity as ethnography and equally central to the discipline, to expand its capacity for representation in posing new questions and new objects for study.

The foundation of cultural order among the Kaluli, the people of the Great Papuan Plateau of New Guinea so vividly represented by the Schieffelins and Steve Feld, rests on the positing of an unseen world that intimately parallels the happenings of everyday life. As Edward Schieffelin has written:

> In talking about the people of the other world, the Kaluli use the term *mama*, which means shadow or reflection. When asked what the people of the unseen look like, Kaluli will point to a reflection in a pool or a mirror and say, "They are not like you or me. They are like that." In the same way, our human appearance stands as a reflection to them. This is not a "supernatural" world, for to the Kaluli, it is perfectly natural. Neither is it a "sacred world," for it is virtually coextensive with and exactly like the world the Kaluli inhabit, subject to the same forces of mortality. . . . In the unseen world, every man has a reflection in the form of a wild pig . . . that roams invisibly on the slopes of Mt. Bosavi. The man and his wild pig reflection live separate existences, but if something should happen to the wild pig, the man is also affected. If it is caught in a trap, he is disabled; if it is killed by hunters of the unseen, he dies. [1976:96–97]

Phenomenologically, this unseen world is experienced through an aesthetic of sounds and sounding, as Steve Feld (1982) has recounted. In the richly diverse sounds of the forest, the unseen world is always present for the Kaluli. What happens is always here and there, never being fully present. In this sense, the Kaluli would be Derrida's own model of Rousseau's primitive who defies logocentrism: they live largely without the Western metaphysics of presence, and thus represent the antithesis of the desire for self-sufficiency, for the unqualified and the unmediated. Yet, while known by the Kaluli in everyday life in an episodic, commonsensical, and fragmented way, the unseen world is systematically imagined in ritual (the Gisaro) and discourse through mediums who, roughly like an ethnographer, have been to this other world and have *seen* what ordinary persons can only *hear* traces of. Communication with the unseen world and authoritative interpretations of events in the here and now world of the Kaluli thus depend on the coherent vision of mediums, who at certain moments give presence and order to Kaluli culture by creating primarily visualized representations (rather than sounded evocations) of the unseen world within the fully sensed world of the here and now.

Unlike the case of the medium who is known to have actually been to the unseen world, this doppelganger world, paralleling the Kaluli here and now, poses for their alien ethnographer a problem that potentially subverts his/her own use of the framing concept of culture, itself, that effectively bounds and conventionalizes the Kaluli as an entity to be studied and written about. After all, the alien ethnographer has only the Kalulis' here and now account of the other part of themselves to go on: that is, the activities of the varied inhabitants of the unseen world. This would not be so significant for an orderly representation of Kaluli culture (since one always receives as ethnographic data self-representations based on comparative representations of significant cultural others, such as the Nuer giving an account of the Dinka, or the Tongans of the Samoans, or the Americans of the Russians) if it were not for the fact that life in the unseen world is so intimately and inherently a part of what it is to be Kaluli in the here and now. The unseen world and the Kaluli here and now are so completely separate, yet so completely determine one another, that an ethnography of one without the other might be felt to be keenly unsatisfying. As Edward Schieffelin expresses it for the Kaluli:

> There was no feeling of enmity between the Kaluli and the *mamul* over this, for how was one to know when he killed a wild pig that it was the reflection of someone else and not just an animal? Kaluli seemed to look on this as one of those tragic facts of life that must simply be accepted. . . . There is a more

or less cheerful acceptance of the fact that everything is paid for by some-
body somewhere and that from time to time one must receive the lumps
himself. [1976:101]

Like contemporary visions in the West of the modern world system, or
like Gregory Bateson's cybernetic ecology of mind, so for the Kaluli,
the seen—the illusion of full presence—and all that is unseen are
complexly linked and mutually constituted. The difference is that the
Kaluli person is acutely aware of this all the time, while we are only
becoming so, it appears.

What is the ethnographer then to do in his/her empirical quest for a
full or at least satisfying account of Kaluli cultural order? Literally
search out the denizens of the unseen world on Mt. Bosavi so as to do
fieldwork among them and, thus, represent this other parallel, yet independent side of Kaluli life? The ethnographer often travels and
hunts with the here and now Kaluli on Mt. Bosavi, the place of the
unseen world, but it is never literally found—seen and therefore
grasped by means of representation—either by the ethnographer or by
the Kaluli, yet its traces abound in the rich Kaluli aesthetic of sound.

Finally, what prevents the cultural entity conventionally posited by
the ethnographer in the field and then constructed in the ethnography
from breaking up in the face of two parallel worlds, one fully accessible
to Western common sense, the other intractably not so, is precisely the
assignment of the unseen world to matters of belief. While the ethnographer treats the unseen world respectively "as if" it were real, parallel, independent, yet implicated in constituting plainly observed Kaluli life, he or she has no apparent choice but finally to represent the
unseen world as fully encapsulated by the here and now Kaluli cultural
order, as fully present in the conventional category of ethnographic
description, their "beliefs."[1]

So far, this discussion may seem merely a naïve replaying of the very
sophisticated classic discourse in British anthropology and philosophy
about the rationality of beliefs, especially supernatural beliefs, among
so-called primitive peoples (for the latest in this tradition see the Hollis
and Lukes volume, *Rationality and Relativism* [1982], especially the paper by Sperber). However, I want to take my fanciful conjuring of the
potential reality of the unseen world as an object of study for the ethnographer in an entirely different direction, one that leads from the
worlds of the Kaluli to those of the dynastic wealthy in the contemporary United States, and to the problem of rendering an account of the
latter. *Their* "unseen worlds," roughly like that of the Kaluli in relation
to their here and now, are much less problematic ontologically—the
unseen worlds of money and wealth tracking the here and now world

of the rich have a very demonstrable, independent, and separate existence.[2]

What I like so much about Edward Schieffelin's ethnography of the Kaluli is that he resolutely dissociates any connotation of the mystified or the sacred from his account of the unseen world; in so doing, he does not let it slip easily into the conventional category of the religious. Although he must still assign it to the category of belief, or worldview, of the Kaluli, he succeeds in expressing the continuously human quality of the unseen world with the Kaluli here and now—in one regard, it is merely another world for the Kaluli (like another people in the next valley), but one that is resolutely and reciprocally tied seamlessly to their self-understandings of who they are and what they do. Accounts of Amazonian worldviews come close to the sort of account that Schieffelin offers (for example, Reichel-Dolmatoff's [1971] representation of the Tukano cosmos) but they usually rest within the category of religion and never push toward the seeming reality and naturalness of these unseen worlds for Western readers. It is the phenomenological work on sound and emotion by Steve Feld and on socialization by Bambi Schieffelin as a complement to Edward Schieffelin's ethnography that so persuasively locates the unseen world in the fragmented, commonsensical realm of everyday life experience, rather than in the vision-oriented frameworks of ritual and narrative discourse that are the habitual foci of so much ethnography—and that distance such a world as a matter cosmological and supernatural. The unseen world of the Kaluli, as represented by the Schieffelins and Feld, much more than the Tukano cosmos, as represented by Reichel-Dolmatoff, for example, is a phenomenon that suggests being studied like any other ethnographic subject even though it finally cannot be, at least without a leap into imaginative fiction (see note 1) that would fashion a here and now account of this world, as if the ethnographer were there, from the diverse Kaluli reports of it.

The ethnographic treatment of the Kaluli thus brings me to the very edge of a methodological and theoretical problem in the practice of ethnography in societies of self-styled modernity and progress, to which I now want to turn. Unseen doppelganger worlds, the equivalents of that of the Kaluli, are equally as consequential for groups of ethnographic subjects in modern societies, yet they really are unproblematically capable of conventional definition and empirical investigation. What becomes of the focused, local order of culture in ethnographic research when it is understood in terms, like the Kalulis', of at least dual, spatially distanced, complexly connected, and mutually determined simultaneous worlds? Does the ethnographer remain, as he is obliged to do among the Kaluli, with here and now accounts of these worlds, or does he move to grasp them empirically and, in so doing, to reconfigure the fundamental ground upon which ethnographic narratives and representations of cultural order have traditionally been made? How does the ethnographer in his/her own academic culture, rather than the Kaluli in their here and now world, handle a subject that is never definitively or self-sufficiently present anywhere, but is continually and *partially* constructed in parallel, simultaneous, but separate contexts?[3] Such is a subject like the contemporary dynastic rich, among other late twentieth-century Americans.

The dynastic fortunes that I have studied in Texas over the past few years are complex creations of various kinds of experts and of lineages of descendants two to four generations away from founding entrepreneurial ancestors. A dynasty is commonsensically a family, but after much experience with this form of social organization, I find that it is primarily a fortune instead. Concentrations of old wealth, however, have no one particular locus or materialization; in short, they have no presence. Rather, a fortune has multiple, simultaneous manifestations within a variety of interconnected but isolated social contexts that encompass the long-term fates and daily lives of literally hundreds of people. In initiating my research, I followed common sense and took the family—literal flesh-and-blood descendants, and particularly those who seemed to be leaders or in positions of authority—for the dynasty. I soon discovered in their here and now lives the profound influence of the equivalent of the unseen world among the Kaluli—the complex world of highly specialized expertise that through an elaborate division of labor, not only structured the wealth but, also, created doppelganger facsimiles of the descendants—roughly similar to the Mt. Bosavi wild pig reflections of Kaluli persons—variously constituted as clients, beneficiaries of trusts, wealth shares in computerized strategies of investment, and accountants' files. While the unseen world is richly registered through sound and imagery in the here and now of the Kaluli, it distinctly is not among the descendants within dynastic families. Being true to the metaphysics of presence that shapes their individualism, they always presume that they are self-sufficiently in control of their lives, while being vaguely aware, more so than other Americans probably, that they are constantly being moved about and determined as bearers of wealth and credit in worlds of money and finance.

Now there is a great deal of variation from fortune to fortune in how elaborately this unseen world that constitutes the organization of wealth has evolved. When the fortune is still in the form of original assets like land or businesses, closely held and managed by family members, the unseen world is relatively undeveloped (but this situation is rare for large fortunes beyond the second generation). Large fortunes generally have family offices that attempt to centralize and keep control of the fortune's diverse manifestations in the larger worlds of law, finance, and corporate business, as well as look back toward the family and do various welfare services for descendants—the gray denizens of such offices are the analogues of the Kaluli mediums. These days, such offices either turn into ramifying bureaucracies themselves, represented coherently only by the mythic order of the organizational flow chart or, given their conservative and conserving nature, cannot really manage effectively the fortune's interests in the risk environments of investment markets, and farm out functions, sharing the power to manage and reinvent the descendants with external expert agencies.

In my eventual direct ethnographic probing of the unseen world of the dynastic rich—something the Schieffelins and Feld could not do for that of the Katuli—my aim was to juxtapose a representation of the independent, simultaneous, and parallel copies of descendants, as diffused and animated through the complex practices of experts, to that which I was composing from my initial commonsensical work on the phenomenological, here and now existences of dynastic families. Eventually, I began tentatively to work the other way, from the other, reciprocal perspective—that is, to know a family first as the business of trust departments, accountants' calculations, investment managers' decisions, and the work of law offices and, then, to become acquainted with it as flesh-and-blood descendants. What was keenly apparent to me from this exercise (not as successful ethnographically, as one might imagine, as moving from the family to the doppelgangers in the world of money and capital, rather than vice versa) was that the real locus of order in a dynastic formation was one that had no presence or place at all, although it was full of traces in the practices and discourses of the separate, parallel, blindly cooperating worlds of experts and descendants, mutually constructing and representing one another all the time—I refer, of course to wealth itself. While there are channels, connections, between the worlds of experts and descendants, the construction of wealth on an everyday basis depends on a largely autonomous parallel processing—an elaborate division of work, sentiments, and interests that construct, in separate spheres, persons as money and money as persons.

Crises of value and valuation bring a shock of mutual recognition to descendants and their doppelganger, monied counterparts of the unseen world and, thus, give the ethnographer a sort of conventional, situated here and now access to a phenomenon that must be otherwise monitored and represented in the dual phenomenological dimensions I have been discussing. The death of the patriarch or matriarch, insurgency by disgruntled descendants, or a crash—or if one prefers, a correction—in the stock market, all these are occasions when wealth, usually in its totality, must be given a precise value through an inventory and valuation of assets. But it is impossible to precisely value great wealth, and the effort, or need, to do so threatens the illusion of solidity on which the order of both the identities of descendants and the work of experts are routinely based. The process of mutually representing each other as unseen, vaguely imagined, but foundational worlds for activities in their own spheres is profoundly shaken by having to declare value, according to the discipline and requirements of economic operations, when either a person/owner dies, as in the death of a patriarch, or wealth dramatically declines, as in a stock market crash. The dynasty with which I am most familiar had suffered, in the period of one month in 1987, the death of its patriarch and a decline of cumulative worth in the recent stock market crash. While this has meant severe disorder for the family, fortune, and experts in the sudden merging of connected worlds kept apart and partial, it ironically has meant order for me as their ethnographer, who, long trying to cope with a disseminated subject diffused across many contexts, now finds a conventional, illusory presence to grasp in the focusing and locusing crystallizations produced by crisis. Presumably when their order of parallel unseen worlds eventually returns, so will the challenge of disorder to the tradition of ethnographic method and representation in which I practice.

In conclusion, I want to make it clear that dynasties are not a special case or an exotic phenomenon in the problems that their study poses for the ethnography of modernity. Scientists, professionals, as well as the credit-card carrying middle-class are potential ethnographic subjects who must be studied as disseminations, as always and partially here and there. Nor has the inclusion of another connected world, in the conventional ethnographic focus on the here and now of a single group of subjects, preserved the assumptions of presence merely by broadening the purview or bounding of the ethnographic project. Rather, the actual move to investigate an unseen world has put into question, within the ethnographic framework and eventual text itself, the fixing of meaning or the spatio-temporal pinpointing of phenomena. After all, the doppelganger world of descendants, out of their control, if not infinite, at least seems so. The constraints of the academic community and discipline, of the production of books, and the cognitive capacities of the individual ethnographer finally bound and strategically define subjects and worlds for them. Thus, the illusion of order in a disseminating world of meanings, particularly at the nexus where persons and money mutually represent one another, is produced as a common interest in and across the very different contexts of the banker, the lawyer, the patriarch or matriarch, and finally, the ethnographer.

Notes

1. Outside the bounds of acceptable ethnographic narrative, even in the so-called experimental moment, there is a choice: one could compose a (science?) fictional account of the unseen world, derived from Kaluli reports, but written as standard ethnography comparable to the mode in which one writes about the Kaluli here and now world. The effect would be to bring to life textually the world that the Kaluli believe to exist and be an intimate part of their everyday life anyhow, to be placed alongside the ethnographically observed Kaluli here and now. The unseen world would be represented according to both the anthropologist's conventions of realism and to the essential reality that the Kaluli claim for it. The result would perhaps disturbingly jumble the categories of fiction and non-fiction in ethnographic writing, but it would look quite familiar and legitimate to science fiction afficionados—perhaps Ursula LeGuin comes closest to home for anthropologists here.

2. Of course I am on the well-trod path here of Marx's central notion of commodity fetishism (or more generally, just fetishism) as metaphorically evoking the complexly connected mimetic relationships between persons and their materialized reifications in capitalist societies. And in this regard, all I am suggesting in this paper is a literal ethnographic tracing and development of this key Marxist insight about the cultural order of capitalist societies. My only complaint about Marx's formulation (although I certainly understand it, given the kind of critical uses that Victorian writers effectively made of representations of the "primitive"—that is, to point to certain irrationalities in civilized, modern thought and practices) is that the metaphor of fetishism emphasizes the self-delusionary aspect of mystification at the heart of capitalist relations—something like the positing of the Kaluli unseen world that exists, not anywhere else, but in the fetishization of sounds of the forest. This mystification can only be demolished for Marx by a true (scientific) understanding of how capitalist production treats human labor. By relegating it to the realm of the irrational (which fetishism in the world of the primitive connotes), mystification (and culture) is overlooked as an object of study, as an observable set of social practices that simultaneously constitute persons and impersonal processes in capitalist societies. By assigning the fetishized relationships of a capitalist culture to "superstructure" as a figment of irrational mentality, Marx does not encourage the grounded study of mystification in capitalist culture, as I do here. The contemporary ethnographers of the Kaluli resolutely reject a fetishized connotation for the unseen, but quite natural and commonsensical "other," world of their "primitives," thus reflecting the very different contemporary intellectual context in which the primitive is written about from Victorian times. The point is to resist the Victorian habit (followed by Marx in his positivism) of assigning primitive unseen worlds to fetishism or supernaturalism, in short, to argue in-

stead for their naturalness and commonsensical reality. Thus free of the metaphor of fetishism, Marx's postulation of the mutual representation of men and
commodities (or money) opens up for direct inquiry complex parallel processes that construct social identities in capitalist cultures.

3. Aside from the "simultaneous unseen world" challenge that I am developing in this essay to the metaphysics of presence inherent in the way cultural
order is typically represented in ethnography, there is another mode for reconfiguring the self-contained ethnographic subject that is emergent in innovative
strategies for writing history into ethnographies conventionally focused on here
and now subjects. For example, the most significant aspect for me of Michael
Taussig's long and complicated *Shamanism, Colonialism, and the Wild Man*
(1987) is his expression of shaman-client relations and the experience of healing in contemporary Colombia as a profound version of cultural criticism and
accommodation that can only be understood as such by seeing these anthropological staples as the response to the turbulent historical conditions of geno-
cide and terror, the methodically redundant account of which occupies well
over the first half of the book. Diffused in this temporal dimension, the conventional ethnographic interest in shamanism becomes the locus of indigenous
experience for coming to terms at once with both the present and past of this
region of Colombia, and with the wild man who is both there in the healing
and in the always present "unseen world" of the past.

References

Feld, Steven. 1982. *Sound and Sentiment: Birds, Weeping, Poetics, and Song in Kaluli
Expression.* Philadelphia: University of Pennsylvania Press.

Hollis, Martin, and Steven Lukes, eds. 1982. *Rationality and Relativism.* Cambridge MA: M.I.T. Press.

Reichel-Dolmatoff, Gerardo. 1971 [1968]. *Amazonian Cosmos: The Sexual and Religious Symbolism of the Tukano Indians.* Chicago: University of Chicago Press.

Schieffelin, Edward L. 1976. *The Sorrow of the Lonely and the Burning of the
Dancers.* New York: St Martin's Press.

Taussig, Michael. 1987. *Shamanism, Colonialism, and the Wild Man: A Study in
Terror and Healing.* Chicago: University of Chicago Press.

Seven

On Eccentricity (1995)

Eccentricity has always abounded when and
where strength of character has abounded.
(John Stuart Mill)

WRITING THIS ESSAY has provided me with an opportunity to pull together two major strands of argument in a recently completed study of mature American dynastic families and fortunes, *Lives in Trust* (1992), so as to think more about a lingering puzzle that I frequently encountered in this milieu: that of eccentric behavior and identity. Eccentricity has indeed been a particularly difficult social psychological category to address systematically and analytically in social science writing, except to simply describe the behaviors and biographies of famous eccentrics. Here, I want to develop some theoretical ideas about eccentricity relevant to the particular locus of my work: contemporary dynasties in which persons are formed by being both subjects and objects of great power, wealth, and sometimes, celebrity.

One main line of argument in my research had to do with the extreme salience among heirs to inherited wealth of the mediated nature of their lives. To a greater extent and awareness than most persons in modern (postmodern?) society, the identities of the extremely wealthy are multiply authored by agents and agencies over which they have variant and often limited control. Perhaps the key example is the management of individual shares of ancestral wealth through a complex division of labor among experts such as lawyers, bankers, investment consultants, and so on—fiduciaries, in short—which in turn amounts to the construction over time of a doubled, parallel self of an heir that might be experienced by him or her as something akin to a doppelganger, or familiar, produced by a mostly hidden world of expertise. Other kinds of doubled selves are authored by journalists, philanthropic clients, corporate executives, public relations and media consultants, and even scholars like me. An heir's relation or response to his or her keen awareness of these multiply authored, doubled, parallel selves in different vaguely understood spheres of production will constitute one important frame for the understanding of eccentricity in contexts of great power, wealth, and celebrity.

The second line of argument, deriving from a special case of the first, concerns the question of the efficacy of ancestral (often patriarchal) authority within the family of heirs/descendants itself despite modern conditions of widespread skepticism about and resistance to anything like the personal exercise of patriarchal upper-class authority by a dynastic leader. This kind of authoritative leadership has often devolved by the third generation upon the hidden world, to which I referred, constituted by the division of expert labor. Still, in many dynasties, ancestral figures continue to exert considerable, and particularly intimate, power in the lives of even the most resistant and skeptical descendants. This is the kind of invisible ancestral world of authority among traditional peoples that anthropologists are accustomed to studying, but here, instead, is a world of authority among capitalist dynasts without the aid of sacred rituals, shamans, or supporting cultural articulations of belief in such authority. How, then, does the ancestor otherwise have efficacy among wealth-bound moderns?

The answer I posed was framed in terms of postulating a deeply embedded, recurrent, and pervasive discourse of distinction and socialization within descendant families that was concerned *primarily* with both shaping and evaluating the personhood of family members, especially in relations across generations. Of course, this might be seen as the hyperdevelopment of the way that a collective ideology of its own special peculiarity or distinction is inculcated in the individuals of any family. In dynastic families, however, ancestral figures constitute a standard of "character" that is especially salient in the assessment of persons, by parents of children, by siblings of each other, and ultimately by children of parents. Besides distinctive notions of family character on which the distinction or honor of a family rests, descendants also often harbor distinctive ideas or family theories of how ancestral personhood is transmitted and distributed. These are often a mix of something like Frazerian mimetic theories of magic and eugenic notions.

In any case, my interest in the efficacy of ancestral authority under adverse modern conditions came to rest on ideologies of distinction, and particularly on how dynasts are constituted as distinctive persons. The cohort of mature dynasties with which I was concerned are now in their third to fifth generations and originated in the later nineteenth century through the founding fortunes accumulated by entrepreneurial capitalists who accomplished the economic integration of American society. In their contemporary period of maturity, distinctive personhood seems to rest now as much upon an ambivalently constructed valorization of eccentricity as upon models of obviously virtuous and positive character that particular families produced generation after generation among their members. This fetishization, so to

speak, of eccentricity within certain families I studied is what stimulated me to think more analytically about the phenomenon of eccentricity itself in dynastic contexts, which is the main concern of this
essay.

A digression is useful here to give a specific historical context to the
theoretical speculations of this chapter. It concerns heightened, self-
conscious fascination with eccentricity as a marked collective cultural
formation among upper classes in American society at certain junc-
tures. Unfortunately, such a history has yet to be written (but see Hall
1982), so in presenting this brief portrait, I have relied largely on discussion with Peter Dobkin Hall, my collaborator on *Lives in Trust* and
incomparable historian of New England upper classes and their role in
shaping national institutions.

Character discourse, as diffusely permeating relations within the upper-class families of Boston, was not only a key means of socializing
children to the already strong structures of class authority in the family
and supporting institutions (colleges, charities, professions) but also
the exemplary model of virtuous personhood toward which aspiring
entrants to elite life should strive. Such aspirants included the post–
Civil War cohort of entrepreneurial capitalists, based in growing urban
centers across the United States, who eventually succeeded in cultural
status and economic power the colonial gentry elites of New England.
This is the cohort with whose fourth- to fifth-generation descendants I
was mainly concerned in my research. But just as these later metro-
politan elites were beginning to form up in the early nineteenth century, Hall suggests, the virtuous notion of character began to shift from
meaning those attributes which make an individual or trait distinctive
to meaning the bundle of behavioral attributes that make an individual
dependable or reliable. Thus, while character, as an exclusive quality,
"the right stuff," so to speak, retained this mystique for a time in the
context of socialization to authority within upper-class families, it lost
its precise prestigious hold over society at large and rising classes within
it. Character discourse in the original sense, then, involuted upon the
internal dynamics of upper-class families themselves. Character as de-
pendability now fit within the work discipline of capitalist expansion,
and lost its particular, exclusive aristocratic edge.

There is no doubt that the New England gentry explicitly felt themselves in decline at a number of points during the long process of their
replacement by new elites—particularly during the 1840s and 1850s,
and again at the turn of the nineteenth century. It was during these
times that there was a marked collective preoccupation with eccentricities among themselves—when eccentricity became a theme of literature, social commentary, autobiography, and family memoir produced

by this class. At such times, I would argue, eccentricity served as both a preoccupation with decline and the rather perverse expression of a final essence of class exclusivity and honor.

The national upper class that finally succeeded the cultural dominance of the old New England gentry classes into the twentieth century was to a certain extent a product of the educational institutions and cultural models of class institutions of this originary (and only) American aristocracy. Within the dynastic families of this class, based on the amassing of great business fortunes, there was an attempt to reinstantiate a character discourse of the exclusive type for the purposes of inculcating authority among descendants by controlling their persons, so to speak, by evaluations according to models of distinctive, virtuous family character. However, the social tide was against this as an efficient technique of class solidarity, since elite formation in the increasingly diverse United States had long since escaped the narrow channels of prestige defined by Boston Brahmins, Philadelphia gentlemen, and New York gentry. With the decline of these aristocrats, there was no longer the class institutional support for patriarchal authority within dynastic families. Socialization to dynastic authority (but not necessarily class authority) of children by the subtle evaluation and shaping of their persons according to distinctive standards of very specific family character has indeed remained efficacious. However, the preoccupation with eccentricity—making a collective family fetish of it from the labeling and marking of particular family members across generations as eccentrics—has remained a means, alternative to character, of creating a strong family ideology among descendants in a mature dynasty that seems to be breaking up, except for the arrangements of sharing wealth that continue to tie individuals together. While I have not noted among "old wealth" upper classes of the twentieth century a repeat of the moments of collective class preoccupation with eccentricity that marked periods of self-perceived decline among the old gentry elite during the nineteenth century, categorically eccentric behavior within individual family histories has remained a variable but widespread component of a mature dynasty's collective self-awareness, a salient counterpoint to the usual effort to establish intimate family identification in persons by distinctive evaluation of character. While ambivalently discussed and focused upon, eccentricity also serves to mark distinction and honor, when there are few other resources with which to do so.

In the history of American upper classes and dynastic families, then, eccentricity is far from being obviously deviant, nonconformist behavior. Rather, it is the untamed or undomesticated side of positively valorized "character." It is what replaces this character discourse of a particular class or individual dynasty in decline as a sort of last bulwark of resentful privilege, an indulgence imposed upon the masses (or simply, others) as a last resort in the desire for distinction. Eccentricity here is inflected with exclusivity and excess—the unself-conscious characteristics of personhood among some of its members that a whole class or a single dynasty self-consciously draws upon to define its final excruciating, but exclusive, predicament. Finally, such a class or dynasty, by becoming preoccupied with distinctive eccentricity among its members and elevating this eccentricity to an emblem of collective condition, where a highly influential standard of character once held, makes society, which no longer recognizes it in any mystified way, now suffer its excesses.

The Strangeness of Eccentricity, or the Limiting Conditions of an Intractable Category

Now I attempt to define the distinctive features of the concept of eccentricity as a set of behaviors and an identity. This must needs be an exercise of specifying as much what eccentricity is *not* as what it is, since it is clearly a category that hovers between very positive and negative associations. For example, the defining nonconformism of eccentricity might be associated with the worthless "drunkard and fool" epithet that is a judgment always awaiting failures in dynastic families, or it might be associated with various kinds of clinically assessed mental illness, or it might, alternatively, be associated with the gift of originality and genius. As I noted, most studies of eccentrics have simply occupied themselves with marveling at the occult spectacle of eccentricity through providing biographical descriptions of famous eccentrics. In the following discussions of the distinctive features of eccentrics, I steer between aspects that seem to capture a defining essence for eccentricity—but any one of which singly fails to do so—and I will primarily be concerned with the ambiguities in how the category itself gets constructed.

Eccentricity by definition and situation is *not* clinical, or within the realm of neurosis and pathology, even though it is often discussed and understood as if it were mental illness. The one monographic study that I found on eccentricity (Weeks and Ward 1988) indeed approached eccentric behavior in terms of formal protocols of personality disorder. While descriptively useful, it violates a boundary that sustains eccentric behavior in embedded social life distinct from mental illness. In fact, well-known eccentrics may move into medical or therapeutic treatment, but from an ethnographic perspective, it is useful to try to understand eccentricity this side of clinical observation, so to speak, existing as a fully viable form of life in society, a feature that indeed distinguishes it as eccentricity, as *not* mental illness.

In an interesting recent book (1992), Louis Sass attempts to link historic theories of madness to the aesthetics of high modernism. His linking argument is that both modernism and madness are produced through and in selves that "suffer" from hyper-self-awareness, even to the sensation or effect of a loss of self. Eccentrics, I would argue, in contrast, exhibit very little self-awareness or self-consciousness in the sense of introspection. Rather, they are hyperaware that their selves are being constructed elsewhere by other agencies, that they are keenly aware of their selves being multiply authored. Thus, eccentricity arises not so much from an extreme awareness of self, but from an extreme awareness of how one's self is being constructed by other agencies. This key feature of eccentricity recalls the distinctive condition of doubling or mediation in self-construction that characterizes heirs to great wealth, which I mentioned in the introduction to this essay, and which will be elaborated in terms of the notion of mimesis in a following section. The point, here, is that eccentrics do not produce interesting introspective discourses about the self, or their own behavior and identity. They are more likely to engage with and comment upon the production of their selves by other agencies, and this engagement is less likely to be in the form of literal discourse than in the form of the behaviors, performances, and habits that constitute eccentricity itself.

A corollary to this last feature is that "eccentric" is rarely if ever a term of self-reference but is a label of social judgment of a particular person's behavior. One could thus easily and conveniently focus on eccentricity as a matter of social construction, more in the eye of the beholder than in the mind of the eccentric person, who, as I have noted, is distinctively not self-aware enough to provide an interesting account of his or her own eccentricity as a personal matter. From the perspective of the social judgment and attribution of eccentricity to particular persons, especially of great wealth, power, or celebrity, eccentricity is often associated with the distortion effect or excess associated with the bearing of great wealth or the exercise of great power. That is, merely bearing great wealth or exercising great power is quite exotic in the imaginations of most people; unless the powerful or wealthy person works at seeming common, he or she is vulnerable to seeming eccentric merely by the condition of excess in which he or she is embedded.

Eccentricity is thus constitutive of received myths of power and wealth. It is simply the "distortion effect" of the wielding of great power, the possessing of great wealth, or even of the experiencing of fame upon the person, rather than an intrinsic, psychological characteristic of the person (which indeed is the emphasis of the therapeutic/pathological version and context of eccentricity). This means that there is a fundamental ambiguity in the attribution of eccentricity in a person's wielding of great power: a person might be eccentric in relation to the doubling/mimetic situation that I will discuss further (what might be termed the "doppelganger effect," in distinction to the "distortion effect"), or more often, eccentricity is constructed from a social judgment or perception whereby the wielding of great power or bearing of great wealth as an activity of excess by a person lends itself to the labeling of that person as eccentric.

The judgment by society of rich, powerful, or famous eccentrics is bound to be tinged with class resentments. When a standard of positively valued character—the so-called role model of aspiration for socially mobile others—declines and eccentric excess takes its place, such eccentricity, while being the last bulwark of distinctive nonconformity for the family that comes to revel in it as their own predicament, becomes associated by a larger public with a certain aggressive superiority that the rich and powerful as eccentrics are able to impose and that stands for a presumed entitlement to bend the environments over which they have control toward indulging their nonconformist excesses. The eccentric rich, thus, have the capacity to normalize the institutions and personnel they control in line with what others judge as their peculiarities. Therefore the public associates a certain meanness and injustice with wealthy eccentricity.

There is thus always an aspect of class resentment or desire associated with eccentricity, even when it is identified and labeled among persons of middle- or lower-class (working-class) standing, as it is on a widespread basis in English society. In such an explicitly class-bound society as England, the bemused nonconformities of working-class and middle-class eccentrics have something of the privilege and pretension of aristocracy—sort of an existential claim, when material conditions do not permit it, of the sort of distinction of excess that is normally indulged by the powerful and the wealthy. The same is perhaps true of American society, but being less explicitly class-bound in its social thought, eccentricity is predominantly associated with the lavishly powerful, wealthy, and famous, and when it is not, and it also escapes clinical assessment as mental illness, its class associations are much more muted and masked.

Perhaps the relevant analogy here is: as the (class-privileged) dilettante is to the hard-working serious professional, so eccentricity is to character. The defining feature of eccentricity in this regard is the willingness of people, the public, to indulge it, and even respect it. This willingness affords to the one labeled an eccentric—even of modest middle-class or working-class standing—a certain deference that is usually reserved for those who are clearly able to impose their eccentricity, which in upper-class history is a peculiar deformation of character of a class in decline.

Finally, referring back to the earlier key point about the lack of personal self-awareness in eccentrics, individuals who have been labeled and focused upon as eccentric seem to be distinguished by obsessions and construction of fetishes. While there are elaborate psychological theories about both obsession and fetishism that ground these in notions of how personality is formed, I prefer to focus on the specifically microsocial conditions that might give a context to eccentric obsession. This of course does not exclude the equal importance of purely psychological dynamics. Indeed, eccentric obsessions and fetishes are the medium by which a person deals with the extreme awareness of the doublings and the multiple authorship of his or her self by other agencies elsewhere. In this speculation, the older meanings of obsession and fetishism (investment by evil spirits and ritualistic orientation toward objects of enchantment) will be more relevant than their domesticated uses in clinical judgments and theories about personality disorder. They may indeed mark personality disorders in contexts of eccentricity, but because eccentricity in its own bounding as a concept is distinct from pathology, I prefer to consider the obsessions and fetishes that characterize eccentric behavior socially and relationally, and this is what brings us back to the older, "primitivist" associations of the terms.

The following, then, are some of the specific kinds of behaviors that constitute lives that have been characterized as eccentric, again with the dynastic context of great wealth in mind.

1. In the context of great wealth, extreme hoarding behavior, or miserliness, and/or extreme extravagance in expenditure. An example is the apocryphal story of the Rockefeller who would not spare a dime for a phone call. Another is the Hearst castle. A third is the revelation of the impoverished conditions in which Howard Hughes lived.

2. Extreme privacy or withdrawal from most social contacts, as in the case, again, of Howard Hughes, or J. D. Salinger, or Greta Garbo.

3. Fear of infection, disease, or subversion (the form of eccentricity closest to the clinical definition of paranoia), resulting in rituals of either extreme cleanliness, or the opposite, or in a variety of body and food obsessions.

4. Inversions of commonsense habits, gender identifications, and dress. These deal with nonconformism in the presentation of self socially and are most likely to be judged as self-conscious strategies in which there is an intention to be eccentric.

Indeed, when eccentricity becomes the collective emblem of distinctive identity among a social class or a mature dynasty in decline, peculiarities of behavior can become hypostatized and self-conscious as a perverse form of privilege, but I would argue that the whole range of observed eccentric behaviors in their individual manifestations, as opposed to being seized upon as the emblem of class or family ideology, are obsessions and fetishes that have much more to do with the "mimetic faculty," as Walter Benjamin termed it and Michael Taussig has recently made much of (1992a, 1992b).

Mimesis, or the Occult, Exotic Sense of Eccentricity

In some way or another one can protect oneself
from evil spirits by portraying them.
   (Michael Taussig)

The story of my family! The story of my family
in my town: I didn't think about it; but it was in
me, this story, for the others; I was one, the last
of this family; and I had in me, in my body, its
imprint and in countless habits of action and
thought, that I had never considered, though
the others recognized them clearly in me, in
my way of walking, laughing, greeting. I
believed myself a man in life, an ordinary man,
who lived day by day a basically idle existence,
however full of curious errant thoughts; no, no,
no, I could be an ordinary man for myself, but
not for the others; for the others I had many
summary features, which I hadn't made or
given to myself and to which I have never paid
any attention; and my belief that I was an
ordinary man, I mean even my idleness, which I
believed truly mine, was not mine for the
others; it had been given me by my father, it
derived from my father's wealth; and it was a
fierce idleness, because of my father.
   (Luigi Pirandello)

The varieties of behavior defining eccentricities enumerated above are, in contexts of descent within family/fortune complexes of inherited wealth, manifestations of obsessions and fetishes that define the relationship of heirs to the agencies that produce their doubles. Recall the defining feature of the eccentric as the person whose own sense of self is most strongly developed as a keen awareness that his or her self is doubled and multiply authored.

In writing about this feature of the construction of dynastic authority, I drew upon an extended analogy with life in traditional society, particularly as described in the ethnography of the Kaluli people of New Guinea by Edward and Bambi Schieffelin and Steven Feld (see Marcus 1992, chap. 5). The foundation of cultural order among the Kaluli rests on the positing of an unseen world that intimately parallels the happenings of everyday life. Phenomenologically, this unseen world is experienced through an aesthetic of sounds and sounding, as Steve Feld has recounted. In the richly diverse sounds of the forest, the unseen world is always present for the Kaluli. While known by the Kaluli in everyday life in an episodic, commonsensical, and fragmented way, the unseen world is systematically imagined in ritual through mediums who, roughly like an ethnographer, have been to this other world and have seen what ordinary people can hear only traces of in the sounds of the forest.

Communication with the unseen world is primarily mimetic rather than discursive. That is, it depends on performance and the senses—a making contact through imitating, an embodying—rather than on discourse. Copying what is seen in vision or heard as sounds makes the other world present and gives humans some control over their doubles in an otherwise inaccessible sphere. I argued that the experience of sharing in a great concentration of inherited, abstract wealth is similar to the Kaluli's sensing of an unseen world that parallels theirs in which actions in either world have direct consequences for the other. Here I want to argue that, at least for eccentric heirs to great wealth, the mode of relationship or communication between themselves and the unseen world of wealth production and management is, as for the Kaluli, mimetic rather than discursive. In this sense, eccentric obsessions and fetishes are primarily mimetic concerns.

Mimesis itself has been the recent subject of interesting theoretical elaboration by Michael Taussig (1992a, 1992b), who in turn has been inspired by Walter Benjamin and his alternative to purely language-based approaches to the understanding of modern life. The critical notion in Benjamin on which Taussig meditates (1992a, 23) is the idea of "the radical displacement of self in sentience—taking one outside oneself. No proposition could be more fundamental to understanding the visceral bond connecting perceiver to perceived [and connecting eccentric heir to wealth, I would interject] in the operation of mimesis," says Taussig. The so-called mimetic faculty, operating through obsessive habit, takes the eccentric heir into the alterity of hidden worlds where wealth is produced in the operation of economics and accounting while his or her self is doubled as literally an "account" of economic value.

In place of a discourse of the self, then, or the social construction of the self, to which ethnographers have generally looked as the source of data on the basis of which to theorize the self as a cultural phenomenon, we have mimesis—a thoroughly performative, censorial, and un-self-conscious response to the social conditions that define one's self-hood—conditions that involve hidden or only partially understood parallel worlds of agency. The obsessions and fetishism that constitute mimesis might be seen as efforts to copy or embody, and thus control, powerful versions of one's self that are produced elsewhere. Such performative mimesis has no discourse itself and resists the social construction of it in terms of external social judgments of eccentricity.

Eccentricity, no longer operating under the illusion that family or class is in charge of its own identity, is an effort to recapture the power or aspects of the self that are constantly being produced elsewhere. The eccentric self is nothing other than this engagement with its dynamic peripheries and has no center itself (i.e., no self-consciousness of a centered self)—such a self is thus literally off-center or ec-centric.

Descriptively, the strength of this argument about the mimetic nature of eccentricity in contexts of great wealth, fame, and power depends on demonstrating in particular cases the relationship of obsessions and fetishes to the hidden worlds of agency in which one is keenly aware that one's self and identity are being authored elsewhere. And the frame for thinking about this is the two arguments about the alternative sources of contemporary dynastic authority with which I began this essay: eccentric mimesis oriented to the world of wealth and public image in the hands of a division of expert labor, and eccentric mimesis oriented to the ancestor, who, through the power of evaluative character discourse that permeates families of dynastic descendants, inhabits the body and mind of the heir.

Regarding eccentric mimesis oriented to agencies of self production in the worlds of wealth, expertise, and public relations that construct dynasty, it is useful to think of the situation as ironically the reverse of Marx's famous commodity fetishism, in which the hidden relations of persons are visibly manifested in the relations of things (through the autonomy of the economy): for dynastic descendants, hidden relations of things (the production of persons as wealth shares, traded, invested, and circulated as abstract economic value) are manifested directly through the visible relations of persons belonging to dynastic families among themselves and toward others. The doppelganger clink of money is the parallel world that constantly inhabits the immediate life world of the dynastic heir.

In his study of the socialization of children of privilege in American society, Robert Coles conjured this through the trope of "entitlement":

> I use the word "entitlement" to describe what, perhaps, all quite well-off American families transmit to their children—an important psychological common denominator, I believe: an emotional expression, really, of those familiar, class-bound prerogatives, money and power. The word was given to me, amid much soul-searching, by the rather rich parents of a child I began to talk with almost two decades ago, in 1959. I have watched those parents become grandparents, seen what they described as "the responsibilities of entitlement" get handed down to a new generation. When the father, a lawyer and stockbroker from a prominent and quite influential family, referred to the "entitlement" his children were growing up with, he had in mind a social rather than a psychological phenomenon: the various juries or committees that select the Mardi Gras participants in New Orleans' annual parade and celebration. He knew that his daughter was "entitled" to be invited here. . . . He wanted, however, to go beyond that social fact; he wanted his children to feel obligated by how fortunate they were, and would no doubt always be. . . . He talked about what he had received from his parents and what he would give to his children, "automatically, without any thought," and what they too would pass on. The father was careful to distinguish between the social entitlement and "something else," a "something else" he couldn't quite define but he knew he had to try to evoke if he were to be psychologically candid . . . . "My wife didn't know what I was talking about when I first used the word. She thought it had something to do with our ancestry! Maybe it does! I don't mean to be snide. I just think our children grow up taking a lot for granted, and it can be good that they do, and it can be bad. It's like anything else; it all depends. I mean, you can have spoiled brats for children, or you can have kids who want to share what they have. I don't mean give away all their money! I mean be responsible, and try to live up to their ideals" (1977, 363–364).

Coles's construct from his data here is just one of many rationales for the situation among the wealthy and heirs to wealth, which evokes the sense that the wealthy person is distinctive and not ordinary by the responsible connection she or he has to the lives of others, which in some unspecified way constitutes the heir's own. There are various sorts of uncritical, self-satisfying rationales and rationalizations for accepting this condition as a bearer of wealth and privilege, like the attitude of entitlement that Coles explores above. But eccentrics, in short, are those heirs who refuse (feel compelled not?) to accept such

rationales. Instead, they try to get beyond the fetishized (in the Marxist sense) immediate relations that hide the money and power relations that lay behind them, and deal directly with the constructions of
self that these impersonal spheres produce. The various categories of
eccentric behaviors mentioned in the previous section can be understood as different sorts of tactics for so doing. But, as suggested, such
behaviors as tactics are not self-conscious, but rather are mimetic—
behaviors seeking connection, embodiment, perhaps power, over
one's self produced by the manipulation of money or image. The
eccentric child of wealth, thus, might radically cut himself off from
the immediate everyday privileges of wealth through living the life of
an impoverished hermit while in seclusion trying to manipulate, acting extravagantly in, the very unseen spheres of wealth in which his
self has its strongest existence and effects. In the space of seclusion,
that other world is manipulated through indices, icons, and representatives from that unseen world of one's true existence. Such indeed is
the eccentricity of Howard Hughes, as we will explore further in the
next section.

Regarding eccentric mimesis oriented to the unseen world of ancestral authority embodied in oneself by the inculcation of character
discourse, the focus is upon bodily obsessions. Many persons as they
grow older find themselves uncannily repeating the habits, looks, and
peculiarities of particular forebears, but this sensation is generally
much more salient in families defined by ideologies of descent and
dynastic authority. Eccentricity is the extreme case of this—what I
have called the dynastic uncanny. The descendant's self becomes synonymous with the ancestor's through the bodily and behavioral imita-
tion of a dominant forebear. Luigi Pirandello's Moscarda (1990) is a
poignant case: a young man of prominent family who looking in the
mirror one day notices a feature of his nose that reminds him of his
father and transforms his existence. He ends by giving away the family
property, to the consternation of the local gentry. This may appear to
be extreme self-awareness, but really it is the extreme awareness of
the other—one's double—which mysteriously and irresistibly inhabits
one's self that one had thought to be integral, separate, and distinct.
In traditional societies the ancestral sphere is separate from and parallel to that of everyday life, but for eccentric descendants it invades
one's body and behavior, as a form of possession. Again, my suggestion is that certain behaviors characteristic of eccentrics might be understood in terms of mimetic ancestral doubling within a living descendant who has become the ancestor while still being him- or
herself. Eccentricity is the expression and management of this mimetic doubling.

The Case of Howard Hughes

Howard Hughes is one of those famous eccentrics—perhaps the most famous in the recent past—the mere telling of whose biography defines the nature of eccentricity. The latter became possible, following his death in 1976, when a spate of very detailed works on Hughes appeared. Perhaps the most detailed biography was by Donald Barlett and James Steele (1979). From the perspective of this chapter, the major limitation of this work is the authors' assumption that Hughes's eccentricities were intended or willed dimensions of his personality. For them, Hughes's eccentricities—his closely guarded privacy, his extravagant and reckless investment projects, the personal risks he took as a pilot—were motivated by the desire to preserve the integrity of self, even to make a monument of it. For example, as they conclude, "From the beginning, Howard Hughes had an overpowering urge to become a legend in his own lifetime. He wanted the world to notice and to marvel at what it saw. He wanted to show others that he was every bit the man his father had been" (1979, 622).

My alternative, which I believe is as consistent with the evidence, if not more so, is that Hughes had hardly any self-awareness at all. He certainly was not a person who desired to inflate something that was hardly existent as a self-conscious, centered construct. Instead, Hughes controlled vast resources and businesses from hermitlike, ascetic, even mortifying isolation, protected and exquisitely served by Mormon attendants in what amounted to the systematic annihilation of an integral, centered self in the effort to observe, manipulate, and control the representations of his self that were created in the disembodied management of the various projects of his immense inherited fortune.

Hughes was intimately present among all of these projects and wealth constructions through a massive flow of memoranda and directives. After a career as a shy, reticent Hollywood film magnate and aeronautics entrepreneur, Hughes retreated to a suite of rooms at his Desert Inn in Las Vegas from which he ran his empire by memos for most of the rest of his life. One has to picture an unkempt man living in filth, on a starvation diet, most of the time naked, who nonetheless made his presence felt through memos in a number of complex business deals that involved him in CIA operations, land deals, government military contracts, and organized crime interests. Although sometimes his executives, intermediaries, and assistants populating the complex structure of his interests were out of his control, it is remarkable given the primitive and withdrawn personal conditions in which he lived how much rational direction Hughes in fact exercised over his empire. To me, this is consistent with the basic condition of the wealthy dynastic eccentric oblivious to personal conditions but vibrantly operating in terms of his doubled selves, produced by the agents and agencies that manage his wealth.

Barlett and Steele note that even as Hughes's mental condition deteriorated over the years,

> he never forgot that the outside world would not look kindly on his bizarre behavior, and so he took great pains to keep it a secret and to perpetuate the image he had so carefully nurtured. How else can his remarkable performance in the 1972 telephone press conference be explained? The Hughes who spoke to newsmen that day had spent the previous fifteen years in complete seclusion, going nude daily; allowing his hair, fingernails, and toenails to grow for months; refusing to bathe; urinating in jars, sealing the jars, and storing them in his bedroom closet; and living in mortal fear of germs. Yet when newsmen discreetly asked him to comment on wild rumors about his personal habits and appearance, Hughes chuckled and put them at ease. Yes, he too had seen a sketch of himself in a magazine showing him with hair falling about his shoulders and nails curling over the ends of his fingers. "The first thing I said was how in the hell could I sign documents that I have been signing," he told the reporters. "I would have gotten tangled up in these fingernails . . . I have always kept my fingernails at a reasonable length . . . I take care of them the same way I always have—the same way I did when I went around the world and times when you have seen me and at the time of the flight of the flying boat, and *every other occasion I have come in contact with the press*." (1979, 626; italics mine)

One of the contexts in which Hughes's disembodied self had always lived was the creations of the image makers of the media, and he did not disappoint them on this occasion. It was Hughes's many eccentric obsessions of separation and withdrawal that kept him an empty center, so that his complete attention was directed to managing his multiple authored doubled selves, not particularly in the interest of making a legend of any essential self—of which he was not aware—but of participating in the many selves and different spheres that his parallel world of hidden wealth created. As Barlett and Steele note, Hughes had a keen sense of affairs and human nature far from himself, but not in direct relations:

> While Hughes's mind was adept at absorbing complicated technical material, there was no place in it for human beings. Yet despite his inability to relate individually either to men or to women, Hughes displayed a surprising grasp of human nature. He knew what motivated people—their hunger for wealth, their thirst for power, their fascination with sex . . . [yet] Hughes's estrange-

ment from other human beings went a long way toward explaining the de-
meaning way in which he treated so many people [around him], orchestrating their daily lives down to and including instructions on what food they
should eat and where they should park their cars. (1979, 623–624)

Thus, he lived fully at a distance in the abstract worlds of wealth and
power in which his doubled self was decisive and vital, and hardly at all
in his immediate day-to-day world of controlling obsessions.

Eccentricity on the Edges

In my own experience with dynasties, I met no Howard Hughes nor
any family in which the strain of eccentricity had become its collective
preoccupation, an ideology of distinction of the last resort, as among,
for example, Boston aristocrats of the nineteenth century. Still there
was what might be identified as eccentric behavior, as developed in this
chapter, and a family awareness of it in every family of dynastic descendants with which I became acquainted. For example, the man who
made a fetish of work discipline, going ceremoniously to and from his
cellar office each day, even though it was never clear what work he
actually did there; the woman, a noted collector of antique porcelain,
who dressed only in clothes of the 1950s (when she was a teenager),
acquired from secondhand shops; the couple who threw lavish parties,
in the middle of which they retired for bed; and so on. While each of
these instances would need to be studied within its dynastic context
(i.e., the context of the doubling of the self by "hidden world" agencies
elsewhere), for me, they recall in a parallel way (but of course, situated
very differently) the "lads," nonconformist English working-class
schoolboys, whom Paul Willis wrote about (1977), and who saw
through their immediate relations to the secret, abstract (hidden
world?) labor basis of capital.

    Likewise, dynastic eccentrics are evoking their abstract doppelganger
selves produced as wealth shares and images (rather than labor) in the
parallel worlds of wealth, fame, and power, which both serve and dominate dynastic persons. However, while the nonconformity of the working-class lads channels them to the factory floor, dynastic eccentrics are
destined for treatment in the world of mental health professionals, or
they are left to stagnate in the purgatory of their particular, indulged
obsessions. They are then, perhaps, to be finally claimed by their families in decline—losing ground to the dynastic authority of experts and
managers—as a replacement for character discourse in a last-ditch
grabbing at the residue of family distinction.

References

Barlett, Donald L., and James B. Steele. 1979. *The Life, Legend, and Madness of Howard Hughes.* New York: Norton.

Coles, Robert. 1977. *Children of Crisis.* Vol. 5. *Privileged Ones.* Boston: Atlantic Little, Brown.

Hall, Peter D. 1982. *The Organization of American Culture, 1700–1900: Private Institutions, Elites, and the Origins of American Nationality.* New York: New York University Press.

Marcus, George E., with Peter D. Hall. 1992. *Lives in Trust: The Fortunes of Dynastic Families in Late Twentieth Century America.* Boulder: Westview Press.

Pirandeilo, Luigi. 1990. *One, No One, and One Hundred Thousand.* Translated by William Weaver. Boston: Eridanos Press.

Sass, Louis A. 1992. *Madness and Modernism: Insanity in the Light of Modern Art, Literature, and Thought.* New York: Basic Books.

Taussig, Michael. 1992a. *Mimesis and Alterity.* New York: Routledge.

———. 1992b. "Physiognomic Aspects of Visual Worlds." *Visual Anthropology Review* 8:15–28.

Weeks, David Joseph, with Kate Ward. 1988. *Eccentrics: The Scientific Investigation.* London: Stirling University Press.

Willis, Paul. 1977. *Learning to Labour.* New York: Columbia University Press.

Part Three

THE CHANGING CONDITIONS OF PROFESSIONAL CULTURE IN THE PRODUCTION OF ETHNOGRAPHY

Eight

On Ideologies of Reflexivity in Contemporary Efforts to Remake the Human Sciences (1994)

FAR TOO LITTLE of the discussion of postmodernism over the past decade has occurred at the level of the terms, practices, and internal debates of particular disciplinary traditions. As a result, some of its most important and transformative influences on the way that research is done have been all too easy to dismiss as posturing. It is especially important to establish the terms in which postmodernism has been recognized and debated in relation to particular sets of disciplinary practices since the term "postmodernism" itself has such delegitimating associations. Ironically, most of those who have been profoundly influenced by it in their own thinking consider it an object or referent to be applied to others—definitely not to themselves—and view the term with ambivalence and suspicion, even as a fatal attraction. Thus, in effect, the specific disciplinary discussions of postmodernism have usually occurred in *other*, more discipline-specific terms.

In anthropology, the debate has centered on the critique of ethnography as mode of both inquiry and writing. The emergence of various styles of reflexivity in ethnographic writing has come to stand for, accurately or not, the influence of (or, for some, infection by) postmodernism. Much of this essay will consider the kinds of interests at stake in the various positions taken on reflexivity in the writing of ethnography.

In the United States, discussions of postmodernism have been elaborated over the past decade and a half from specific references to aesthetic styles in art, architecture, and literature to a more generalized radical critique of styles of discourse and research in all of the humanities and social sciences. Postmodernism has been given theoretical substance by the works of the French poststructuralists (who themselves, apart from Lyotard, temporarily, had little use for the term), works which only became available through frequent translation in the early 1980s. Existentially, postmodernism has been powered by the widespread feeling that the conditions of social life (especially in the West, and especially in the frame of American postwar hegemony) were undergoing a fundamental transformation, a breakup of the world order, systemically conceived, into fragments that have not yet assumed new, readily identifiable configurations. This world of established but unstable institutions rapidly generating emergent forms of diversity has defined the social conditions of a *postmodernity* for which the ethos, at least, of *postmodernism* as a style of knowledge production is particularly appropriate. Both in revealing the conditions of postmodernity and in enacting them, postmodernist writing has been a seductively attractive mode for defining radical, contemporary cultural criticism.

Yet it is important to understand that the critiques of disciplinary traditions (especially in their post–World War II penchant for privileging and desiring to reproduce the perceived achievements of the natural sciences) were already well under way before the early 1980s, when the specter of postmodernism took shape in general awareness. Postmodernism merely intersected with the developing internal critiques of such fields as literature, history, sociology, law, philosophy, and anthropology, both radicalizing and consolidating them. As suggested above, postmodernism has been sustained as an "alien other" by the internal critics of disciplinary traditions who assimilated its powerful and radical aspects for their own purposes, while holding postmodernism itself at arm's length as an object of suspicion and ambivalence. Everyone would speak vaguely of postmodernism; few would claim to be postmodernists. But all the while, its seductive example of extremity has been radicalizing, consolidating, and promoting alternatives for practice in the ongoing internal critiques of disciplinary traditions.

In anthropology, the ethos of postmodernism has intersected specifically with the strong critique of ethnographic rhetoric and writing that powerfully brought together and rearticulated three separate strands of critique. These strands, which had been developing in Anglo-American anthropology since the 1960s and even before then, included (1) the exposure of the "messiness" of fieldwork as a social science method through an outpouring of "trial-and-tribulation," "confessional" accounts; (2) the contextualization of anthropology in the history of colonialism, particularly during the periods of decolonization for the British and of the Vietnam War for the Americans; and (3) the not-yet-pointed critique from hermeneutics of anthropological styles of interpreting language, culture, and symbols. Influenced by literary theory (as influenced in turn by poststructuralism), by the kind of rhetorical critique of history developed by Hayden White, and by a renewed interest in the history of anthropology itself, a group of anthropologists, historians, and theorists of literature and language, with whom I and other members of my department have been associated, produced work from the mid-1980s on (including, most prominently, *Writing Culture* [Clifford and Marcus 1986], but also *Anthropology as Cultural Critique* [Marcus and Fischer 1986], *The Predicament of Culture* [Clifford

1988], and *The Unspeakable* [Tyler 1987], among others) that articulately brought to the surface our profound discontents with the state of anthropology. The power of this intervention was in critique rather than in defining a new paradigm or setting a new agenda. That critique has legitimated new objects and new styles of research and writing, as well as a shift from the historical purpose of anthropological research toward its long-standing but underdeveloped project of cultural critique. It has also tended to reorient the relevant interdisciplinary interests of anthropologists toward the humanities, as it became obvious that the most energetic thinking about culture, especially in cross-cultural and transcultural frameworks, had been coming from such literary scholars as Edward Said, Gayatri Spivak, and Homi Bhabha.

The frame of postmodernism, by this time an interdisciplinary focus or sign of radical critique, has merely enhanced the radical critical tendencies within anthropology, which were once again brought powerfully to the surface in the mid-1980s' attention to the language, conventions, and rhetoric by which anthropological knowledge has been produced through ethnography. The effect of postmodernism has thus been to hold anthropology accountable for its own potential radical critique, which it had submerged in its legitimation as an academic field. How, and to what degree, alternative possibilities for work within the ethnographic tradition might emerge from the specific practices and responses that the critique of the mid-1980s, now labeled (justly or not) postmodern, are questions that I want to take up. But before doing so, I want to make certain observations, in the form of a list of points, about how postmodernism has posed predicaments for the writing practices of anthropologists, what new tendencies it has encouraged, and what old ones it has radicalized.

1. Regardless of their stated commitments to interdisciplinary work through the devaluing of disciplinary traditions, or to postmodern nonconformity in the way that research is conceived, I have not seen any works by anthropologists which have not validated the practice of ethnography (this is *not* the same thing as validating ethnographic authority, but rather the validation of ethnography as central to the identity of the discipline in its new interdisciplinary, postmodern milieu). Thus, while old forms of ethnography may have been called into question, ethnography itself, in terms of its possibilities beyond its disciplinary uses so far, has not been. In fact, different conceptions of ethnography (and the fieldwork it entails) define the limits within which postmodern reimaginings in anthropology can occur. Outside anthropology, the practice of ethnography (especially among exotic others) con-

tinues to define anthropology's mystique, appeal, and identity for its interdisciplinary partners in history, feminism, film studies, comparative literature, and elsewhere.

2. What postmodernism has meant specifically for anthropology is a license to create an interesting traffic between the cognitive techniques of the now-classic aesthetic, avant-garde modernisms (e.g., early twentieth-century literary modernism, or Russian Formalism, or, especially, the later avant-gardes of the 1920s and 1930s, such as the surrealists). There have been no innovative moves in so-called experimental ethnography so far that have not had a modernist history. What *is* new (and perhaps shocking) is the open use of modernist sensibilities and techniques having to do with reflexivity, collage, montage, and dialogism in an empiricist genre with a strong scientific claim to constructing reliable knowledge about other ways of life. The struggle in contemporary works of so-called postmodern anthropology is between the currently liberating techniques and cognitions of a modernist sensibility and the continuing desire to report objectively on a reality other than the anthropologist's own. Maybe it is the conditions of postmodernity in the cultural situations encountered by anthropologists that make this belated migration from the sphere of art to the sphere of aspirant science at least feasible. In this heady enterprise, the responsibility of experimental ethnographers (or theorists of ethnography) is to understand the fate of certain techniques of radical critical aestheticism (such as montage, negative dialectics, and Brechtian theater) in their earlier appearances and to ensure that their current application does not represent a nostalgia for aesthetics against a villainous positivism.

3. Again, I want to raise here the question of the anthropologist's explicit relation to a postmodernist identity. As I noted earlier about the discussions of postmodernism that I have read, it is rare that anyone will claim for him or herself personally a postmodernist intellectual style—will indeed say, "I am a postmodernist." Rather, for those who have written most cogently about postmodernism (e.g., David Harvey [1989], in *The Condition of Postmodernity*, or John Rajchman [1987], in his excellent short essay "Postmodernism in a Nominalist Frame: The Emergence and Diffusion of a Cultural Category," where he conveys ironic amazement that such a "motley and elastic range of things" could become such an object of fascination), the term has a phantom referent, but it is certainly not oneself. While a critical attitude may be taken toward others' practice of it, rarely do the features attributed to this intellectual style fail to rub off on the critic (e.g., by the end of his book, Harvey has assimilated the sensible dimensions of postmodernism, while eschewing its extremism; through such critical engagement, he ends up infected by it, becoming a postmodernist

perhaps in spite of himself). So in anthropology, where the label "post-modern anthropologist" is usually applied hostilely to the critics of ethnography, it is rare to find anyone (save Stephen Tyler; see below) who will own up to it, but more common to note that those making the attribution end up claiming postmodernist innovations for themselves, save for its excesses. In effect, by the logic of academic fashions, everyone seems to want to be "with it," more than ever, but at the least cost to the orientations in which they have previously vested themselves. Postmodernism, being a *bricoleur's* art, can, of course, tolerate that.

4. The very few cases in which postmodernists identify themselves as such or enact postmodernism in their writing are instructive. Stephen Tyler is the only one among the group associated with articulating the critique of ethnography who explicitly champions postmodernism and enacts it in his writing (see, e.g., Tyler 1987). This entails a radical and endlessly parodic mode of writing. With brilliant consistency and resolution, Tyler creates a thoroughly parodic discourse about parody. While full of powerful insights about language, writing, orality, and especially ethnographic representation, his bold experiment seems, finally, limiting. He develops some nearly unbearable truths that would make it difficult to claim a special importance or justification for any practice of ethnography.

Yet, short of Tyler's bold attempt at endless self-parody, championing postmodernism while also claiming to be practicing it leads one into serious contradictions. This occurs, for instance, in a recent paper by Rosemary Coombe, who states, "As a postmodernist, I believe that form has implications for the issues that we address and that conventional forms of discourse limit and shape the realities we recognize" (Coombe 1991: 1857). Indeed, what follows looks and reads pretty much like a law journal paper, as Coombe submits to most of the conventions of legal discourse (careful citations, long footnotes, etc.), perhaps in spite of herself. Subverting such standard conventions of discourse does seem to be a sign of experimentation in ethnographic writing (as we will see in the discussion of "messy" texts, below), but this is more an indication of tensions in the "messiness" of a text in which a new kind of study is struggling to be born out of an older framework than a self-conscious claim or conceit of being postmodernist by doing "it" in one's writing. Although this conceit fails in the case of Coombe and succeeds in the case of Tyler, neither one models a likely replacement for the tactic of dealing with postmodernism as an infectious object to be held at arm's length.

5. The following are three of the most important effects that key features associated with postmodernism have had on current anthropological practice:

a. Cultural translation, which is what ethnography is, never fully as-
similates difference. In any attempt to interpret or explain another
cultural subject, a surplus of difference always remains, partly created by the process of ethnographic communication itself. Thus
radical, intractable difference, as in Lyotard's notion of the *differ-
end*, confronts the idea of difference in the liberal concept of culture which has dominated Anglo-American anthropology and
which historically triumphed (in parallel with the pervasiveness of
late capitalism's consumer culture) over the concept of culture
that developed within an earlier, evolutionary frame of social
thought. Culture as the object of ethnography is predicated on the
notion that the difference of others can be fully *consumed*, that is,
assimilated to theory and description by cracking codes of structure, through better translation, and so forth. The postmodern
idea of radical or surplus difference counters the liberal concept
with the premise that difference can never be fully consumed, con-
quered, experienced, and thus that any interpretive framework
must remain partly unresolved in a more serious sense than is usually stipulated as a matter of "good manners" in doing interpretive
work. Radical, surplus difference is a fundamental challenge and,
as such, a stimulus to remaking the language and forms of ethnographic writing.

b. Associated with the above, the postmodern premise that there is
no possibility of a fixed, final, or monologically authoritative
meaning has radicalized anthropology's internal critique of its own
forms of representation by challenging the authority on which
they have been based. It has also undermined the practice of a
kind of interpretation from which authoritative meanings could be
derived (the kind of interpretive practice that Geertz had earlier
promoted, which constituted cultures through the metaphor of
text, and the practice of interpretation through the metaphor of
reading).

c. The postmodern notions of heterotopia (Foucault), juxtapositions, and the blocking together of incommensurables (Lyotard)
have served to renew the long-neglected practice of comparison in
anthropology, but in altered ways. Juxtapositions do not have the
obvious meta-logic of older styles of comparison in anthropology
(e.g., controlled comparisons within a cultural area or "natural"
geographical region); rather, they emerge from putting questions
to an emergent object of study whose contours, sites, and relationships are not known beforehand, but are themselves a contribution of making an account which has different, complexly connected, real-world sites of investigation. The postmodern object of

study is ultimately mobile and multiply situated, so any ethnography of such an object will have a comparative dimension that is integral to it, in the form of juxtapositions of seeming incommensurables or phenomena that might conventionally have appeared to be "worlds apart." Comparison reenters the very act of ethnographic specificity by a postmodern vision of seemingly improbable juxtapositions, the global collapsed into and made an integral part of parallel, related local situations rather than something monolithic and external to them. This move toward comparison as heterotopia firmly deterritorializes culture in ethnographic writing and stimulates accounts of cultures composed in a landscape for which there is as yet no developed theoretical conception.

These three challenges to the conventional ways and premises by which ethnography has been conceived lead to the "messy text," manifestly the most complex and interesting form of experimentation with ethnographic writing now being produced.

Messy Texts, or Worlds-Apart Cultural Criticism

While many in anthropology have acknowledged at least the therapeutic value of the 1980s critique of ethnographic writing, there has also been a widespread nervousness, a fear that this has gone on for too long and, as a result, is leading anthropology in unproductive directions, a conviction that innovations in the form of ethnography cannot possibly carry the burden that abstract theoretical discourse and clear distinctions between arguments and supporting data once did. Contra those who want to move quickly beyond the notion of experimentalism, I remain convinced that the form ethnographies might take continues to be a key question for theoretical and research-design discussions, especially those that confront the issues of postmodernist styles of knowledge production and of real social conditions of postmodernity among our subjects.

To me, the most interesting experiments (sometimes in spite of themselves) confront the problem that ethnography, which is centrally interested in the creativity of social action through imagination, narrativity, and performance, has usually been produced through an analytic imagination that is both comparatively impoverished and far too restrictive, especially under contemporary conditions of postmodernity. For example, once we know (or analytically "fix" by naming) that we are writing about violence, migration, the body, memory, and so forth, we have already circumscribed the space and dimensions of our object of study—we know what we are talking about prematurely. But we can

also be sure that our object of study will always exceed its analytic circumscription, especially under conditions of postmodernity.

The mark of experimental, critical work is its resistance to this too-
easy assimilation of the phenomenon of interest by any given analytic,
ready-made concepts. Such resistance is manifested in a work's messy
many-"sited"-ness, its contingent openness to the boundaries of the object of study (which emerge in the heterotopic space of the work,
whose connections by juxtaposition are themselves *the* argument), its
concern with position, and its derivation/negotiation of its analytic
framework from indigenous discourse, from mappings within the sites
in which the object of study is defined and among which it circulates.
The contemporary works I have in mind, by no means all from within
the ethnographic tradition, but all of which have worked well for me in
teaching, are *Primate Visions: Gender, Race, and Nature in the World of
Modern Science* by Donna Haraway (1989); *Debating Muslims: Cultural Dialogues in Postmodernity and Tradition* by Michael M. J. Fischer and
Mehdi Abedi (1990); *Shamanism, Colonialism, and the Wild Man: A Study
of Terror and Healing* by Michael Taussig (1987); and *Lives in Trust: The
Fortunes of Dynastic Families in Late Twentieth-Century America* by myself,
with Peter Dobkin Hall (Marcus 1992).

Although the authors of these texts are often conscious of themselves as engaged in experimental work, there is much more to these
texts, which struggle with conventional forms in order to provide new
cognitive mappings, than special pleading, self-indulgence, avant-gard-
ism, or staging a genius act. These authors refuse to assimilate too
easily or by foreclosure the object of study, thus resisting the kind of
academic colonialism whereby the deep assumption permeating the
work is that the interests of the ethnographer and those of her subjects
are somehow aligned. There are at least three other motivations for
producing "messy texts":

1. These texts arise simply from confronting the remarkable space/time
compression that defines the conditions of peoples and cultures globally
(this is, of course, the defining empirical feature of the condition of postmodernity for such theorists as David Harvey and Anthony Giddens). This
raises the problem of giving an account of everyday life in which what was
formerly incommensurable becomes related or at least contiguous, with the
global, or aspects of the global process, now encompassed by the local, and
purely local meanings no longer a sufficient object of study.

2. These texts wrestle with the loss of a credible holism, so important in
previous ethnographic writing, especially functionalist accounts. In messy
texts, there is a sense of a whole, without an evocation of totality, that
emerges from the research process itself. The territory that defines the object

of study is mapped by an ethnographer who is within its landscape, moving and acting within it rather than being drawn in from a transcendent, detached point.

3. Messy texts are messy because they insist on their own open-endedness, incompleteness, and uncertainty about how to draw a text/analysis to a close. Such open-endedness often marks a concern with an ethics of dialogue and partial knowledge, a sense that a work is incomplete without critical, and differently positioned, responses to it by its (ideally) varied readers.

Thus, the important questions to pose about messy texts concern how they end (openly, with utopian hope, pragmatic resolution, etc.), what space they lay out, and how the conceptual apparatus (and the *naming* of its object) emerges as a function of the hesitation to assume conceptual or analytic authority by fiat. However, it should be clear that messy texts, aside from the features that I have listed, are by no means uniform in their sensibilities or theoretical influences, nor are they models for a new genre of critical work. I find them interesting as *symptoms* of a struggle to produce, within the given formats and practices of analytic writing, unexpected connections and thus new descriptions of old realities and, in so doing, to critically displace sets of representations that no longer seem to account for the worlds we thought we knew, or at least could name.

Indeed, most ethnographers are not writing messy texts, but the specter of postmodernism (and postmodernity) with which the appearance of such unusual writing is associated has been a subject of widespread discussion, and, at the level of what most anthropologists might or might not do differently than before, postmodernism comes down to the "sign" of reflexivity—how much (if any) and in what form should it appear in one's ethnographic work?

Ideological Strategies of Reflexivity

It is now time to back up and consider what sorts of discussions of postmodernism in contemporary anthropology and other fields that share a strong identification with and valorization of the practice of ethnography open up the possibility of "messy text" experimentation. The crucial turn, it seems to me, has been the new positions taken toward self-critical reflexivity in ethnographic writing. The sometimes heated debate over the desirability of reflexivity marks the opening up of the ethnographic tradition to new possibilities, to a departure from the ideology of objectivity, distance, and the transparency of reality to concepts, toward a recognition of the need to explore the ethical, political, and epistemological dimensions of ethnographic research as an integral part of producing knowledge about others. Rather than taking up the theory and philosophy of reflexive practice itself, my concern here is the complex politics of theory (the different positions taken, interests implied, and stakes defined) that the discussion of postmodernism, specifically in terms of reflexivity in ethnography, has engendered.

I do not arbitrarily choose reflexivity as the loaded sign of these politics, but from the point of view of an (amateur) ethnographer of these politics. I have noted that "reflexivity" is the label used in common currency to stand for possible but as-yet unrealized alternatives in the production of ethnography. For me, then, reflexivity is not so much a methodological matter as an ideological one that, in turn, masks anxiety about a broader, but less conceivable postmodernism. In this regard, Graham Watson's (1987) paper "Make Me Reflexive—But Not Yet: Strategies for Managing Essential Reflexivity in Ethnographic Discourse" draws an important distinction between essential reflexivity and derived, or as I call it, ideological reflexivity. Essential reflexivity is an integral feature of all discourse (as in the indexical function of speech acts); one cannot choose to be reflexive or not in an essential sense—it is always a part of language use. What remains is how to deal with the fact of reflexivity, how to handle it strategically for certain theoretical and intellectual purposes. And this is the ideological dimension of reflexivity that interests me here. In the current polemics about the use of reflexivity, one encounters, for example, a frequent bad-faith, flippant dismissal of reflexivity, or, among those who favor it, competitive, "more reflexive than thou" positions, as in *Writing Culture* (Clifford and Marcus 1986), where Paul Rabinow criticizes the arch-critic of ethnography, James Clifford, for not being sufficiently self-critical. (A charge of insufficient critical reflexivity has also been a main line of attack by feminists on the mostly male critics of ethnography, for being *mostly* male.)

To portray the quality of the polemics about reflexivity, I offer three personal samples. The first one illustrates bad-faith dismissal (with, behind it, the hope that it will go away, or at least go the way of all minor fashions); the other two examples are of the "more reflexive than thou" variety, signaling the agonism of those who validate reflexivity, but have very different agendas in so doing.

Example 1
"But as the Fijian said to the New Ethnographer, 'That's enough talking about you; let's talk about me'" (cited in Judy Stacey's [1990] book *Brave New Families* as taken from Marshall Sahlins's essay "The Return of the Event, Again," reprinted in *Clio in Oceania* [Sahlins 1991], but this is also a joke in wide circulation among anthropologists).

Example 2
Pierre Bourdieu, as heard in an address to the senior chieftains of American sociology while visiting the University of Chicago during my year (1988–89) at the Getty Trust and as reported in a letter to George Stocking, my neighbor at the Getty:

> Bourdieu made several notably caustic comments about George Marcus, from whose brand of "nihilistic" and "narcissistic self-criticism" he clearly wanted to distinguish himself. "Reflexivity is [meant to be] a means to understand and refurbish the tools you will use." In addition, he cited Marcus as an example of the trans-national distortion effect. They [Rice University anthropologists] take ideas "from people they don't know, things they don't understand, put them in an atmosphere of campus radicalism. . . . They think they are Parisians, but they are nothing." To think you can be an American Habermasian is necessarily to forget [and paradoxically so] that there are social modes of production affecting those ideas.

The note I did not send to Bourdieu:

> Dear Pete,
>
> Heard about your performance in Chicago. Thanks for making us a part of the canon, and sharing your cultural capital.
>
> Salut,
> Georges from Houston

Compare Bourdieu's comments, above, with the following observation, made by John Rajchman in "Postmodernism in a Nominalist Frame":

> It [postmodernism] is like the Toyota of thought: produced and assembled in several different places and then sold everywhere. . . . Postmodernism is a sign of the loss of the colonial model of a universal culture spread out to educate the world at large. It is rather theory for a post-colonial world of products made and sold in different places without a center. It is like the *lingua franca* of this world; it can be made and consumed everywhere and nowhere. (Rajchman 1987: 51)

Example 3
In "Suspending Anthropology's Inscription: Observing Trinh Minhha Observed," Sarah Williams, a graduate of the History of Consciousness Program at the University of California, Santa Cruz, defends by way of clarification reviews of Trinh's work published in the *Visual Anthropology Review*. In so doing, she takes the opportunity to offer the following observations about me, in commenting on an article of mine on a different subject that had been published in the same journal:

> Despite Marcus' critical observations regarding the situatedness of anthropology as an academic discipline within the primary ideological industry of

modernist society—the university—he does not maintain a critical language
within his own text regarding the institutionalized culture of his profession.
Despite his championing of subversive ethnographics in recent texts such as
Michael Taussig's *Colonialism, Shamanism, and the Wild Man* [*sic*], Marcus' own
comments do not incorporate any of the sensibilities, any of the alternative
practices of knowing and representing about which he comments. (Williams
1991: 8)

In the "more reflexive than thou" frame of polemic, Williams's comment refers to the point I made earlier about the likely contradiction
encountered by those who embrace a postmodernist identity and who
insist that you must practice what you preach, that your writing practices cannot simply be positioned differently or apart from their objects
of critique (e.g., academic discourse), but must exemplify (perform)
the critique of other discourses. While this may not be the same thing
as the idea that you have to be boring in order to write on boredom,
Williams does require the radical "piggy-backing" of subject and object—you must exemplify what you write about. This is, indeed, a major thrust of the innovative writing coming from and occurring within
feminist scholarship. But save for the relentless self-parody practiced by
Tyler, such an injunction, if rigorously observed in the frame of producing ethnography or any other kind of academic work, is likely to be
undone either by the constraining conventions of publishers or by a
failure to communicate to any but the most narrow readerships. To
insist on postmodernism as a particular kind of sensibility or language
rather than a play of styles, while not acknowledging this in the plainest
kind of political language that communicates one's commitments,
values, and interests, borders on the odious "political correctness" of
recent infamy.

Finally, it might be noted that perhaps the most intense polemics
about reflexivity nowadays can be heard in academic departments
among the dissertation committees that oversee graduate student projects. Is reflexivity a license or a method? Graduate students most want
to know pragmatically how to deal with reflexivity in the writing that
will credential them in a disciplinary tradition. How much reflexivity?
Where in a text, and in what form(s)? Finally, why?

Styles of Reflexivity

Reflexivity is an immense area of comment and interest. The following
discussions therefore need a controlling frame, the most appropriate
of which is structured by the fields for which ethnography has had a
special value, has been a regenerative practice, over the past decade of

revitalization in the humanities and related fields in the United States, often powered by a fascination with defining postmodern(ism/ity), but also institutionalized in the interdisciplinary centers (usually known as humanities or "cultural studies" centers) that have sprung up across academic America. These fields include:

—sociology of the sort theorized by Pierre Bourdieu and Anthony Giddens (but also the sociology practiced in British cultural studies and now in American cultural studies, for which ethnography has had a special appeal);
—anthropology, for which ethnography has been a signature practice;
—feminism, for which ethnography has been one among several related genres through which theory and research have been produced.

Before examining the reflexivity stakes in each of these fields, I want to outline a basic or null form of reflexivity with which the term is usually associated. The null form of reflexivity is the self-critique, the personal quest, playing on the subjective, the experiential, and the idea of empathy. It is this sort of reflexivity that most often evokes nervous responses or dismissals of reflexivity as dead-end self-indulgence, narcissism, and so on (as in Sahlins's joke, above). But we must be prepared to take this kind of reflexivity more seriously.

In anthropology, elaborate subjectivist accounts of fieldwork experience became the primary means of destabilizing the notion that fieldwork could be a method on a par with, say, surveys. Such reflexivity, previously limited to confessional framings of functionalist ethnography, exposed the epistemological and ethical grounds of anthropological knowledge to full critical discussion and opened the way for hermeneutics to become a major influence on anthropological theory and research practice. But here is where the main contribution of this kind of reflexivity has remained, and once its critical function became well absorbed, it lost its power and fell prey to those who would nervously dismiss reflexivity altogether. At most, such reflexivity opens up the possibility for the so-called polyphonic text or the completely collaborative project, but more often than not, it merely reinforces the perspective and voice of the lone, introspective fieldworker without challenging the paradigm of ethnographic research at all—to the contrary.

In feminism, the subjectivist kind of reflexivity has had much more weight. It is indeed the signature of a distinctively feminist cognitive mode that runs through many genres of feminist writing. As such, reflexivity is a performed politics and the means of overcoming the gendered character of supposedly value-free objectivist discourse. In feminism, this kind of reflexivity was pioneered in autobiography, and its appearance as a style of ethnography is simply a carryover. As such, ethnography has been fully integrated with a discourse in which subjectivist reflexivity is not only already legitimate, but where it has a special power and function.

The situation in anthropology is, of course, quite different: subjectivist reflexivity challenged the sacred boundaries of identity that differentiate scientific ethnography from travel accounts, memoirs, missionary reports, and the like. It had nothing like the preexisting legitimacy or purpose in anthropology that it had in feminism. Whereas subjectivist reflexivity dead-ends in anthropological ethnography, as I suggested, in feminist writing, including ethnography, it leads to the practice of positioning which manifests itself either as a doctrinal kind of identity politics or as an ambitious and comprehensive means of reenvisioning the frameworks and practice of ethnographic research and writing (and, practically speaking, as the interesting experiments marked as messy texts).

Sociological Reflexivity

The position on reflexivity in Pierre Bourdieu's sociology, which can also stand here in general for the kind of reflexivity in ethnography that has had appeal for British (and, by derivation, American) cultural studies (e.g., the use of reflexivity in Paul Willis's *Learning to Labour* [1981 (1977)]), is tied to the commitment to sustain objectivity, the distance and abstraction of theoretical discourse, and empiricism as distinct historical contributions of sociology (and a related social theory) as a discipline. With such a commitment, ethnography retains its identity as a method and reflexivity becomes valuable only in methodological terms as a research tool. As we have seen, Bourdieu is hostile to reflexivity as touching on the subjective. The following quotations from the preface to *The Logic of Practice* (Bourdieu 1990a) are revealing:

> In opposition to intuitionism, which fictitiously denies the distance between the observer and the observed, I kept on the side of the objectivism that is concerned to understand the logic of practices, at the cost of a methodical break with primary experience; but I never ceased to think that it was also necessary to understand the specific logic of that form of "understanding" without experience that comes from mastery of the principles of experience—that what had to be done was not to sweep away the distance magically through spurious primitivist participation, but *to objectify the objectifying distance and the social conditions that make it possible, such as the externality of the observer, the objectifying techniques that he uses, etc.* Perhaps because I had a less abstract idea than some people of what it is to be a mountain peasant, I was also, and precisely to that extent, more aware that the distance is insur-

mountable, irremovable, except through self-deception. Because theory—the word itself says so—is a spectacle, which can only be understood from a viewpoint away from the stage on which the action is played out, the distance lies perhaps not so much where it is usually looked for, in the gap between cultural traditions, as in the gulf between two relations to the world, one theoretical, the other practical. (Ibid.: 14 [emphases mine])

Distance is not abolished by bringing the outsider fictitiously closer to an imaginary native, as is generally attempted; it is by distancing, through objectification, the native who is in every outside observer that the native is brought closer to the outsider. . . . In contrast to the personalist denial which refuses scientific objectification and can only construct a fantasized person, sociological analysis, particularly when it places itself in the anthropological tradition of exploration of forms of classification, makes a self-reappropriation possible, by objectifying the objectivity that runs through the supposed site of subjectivity, such as the social categories of thought, perception, and appreciation which are the unthought principle of all representation of the "objective" world. By forcing one to discover externality at the heart of internality, banality in the illusion of rarity, the common in the pursuit of the unique, sociology does more than denounce all the impostures of egoistic narcissism; it offers perhaps the only means of contributing, if only through awareness of determinations, to the construction, otherwise abandoned to the forces of the world, of something like a subject. (Ibid.: 20–21)

In absolutely opposing any sort of identity between the worlds of the observer (the academic social scientist) and the observed (the peasant, for instance), while at the same time privileging, perhaps as the manifestation of reason, the domain of distanced "theory," Bourdieu positions himself outside postmodern sensibilities which find value in various strategies (e.g., dialogism) for collapsing high and low culture, the theoretical and the practical, the identities of narrator and narrated, and so on. As such, reflexivity, which Bourdieu *does* valorize, has a very restricted function. Self-critical reflexivity is for Bourdieu a renewed and more powerful form of the old project of the sociology of knowledge, but this time fully integrated as a dimension of sociological method.

In his fervent desire to assert (against the looming narcissists) the absolute priority of objectivity/objectivizing in the sociologist's work, even in being reflexive, Bourdieu's account is tone-deaf to the inevitable moments of *subjective* self-criticism that have always occurred in even the most scientific ethnography. By denying or ignoring this integral dimension of the most objectifying methods, Bourdieu misses the sorts of tensions that propel the ethnographer toward reflexivity in the first place, whatever ideological form it may eventually take in writing (e.g., subjective, methodological, etc.). Personal reflexivity is present in several of his own works (he even appeals to it ironically in the passages quoted above), but in the conventional way, that is, pushed to the margins.

Indeed, the great virtue of Bourdieu's cultural critique lies in the personal motivations that led him away from ethnography, which he eventually came to see in the politicized context of decolonizing Algeria, and back to the major educational and class institutions of France that shape "the scholastic point of view" (Bourdieu 1990b). This move from apolitical structural anthropology in Algeria, during the revolution, to the critical sociology of his home institutions, especially those that engendered him intellectually as an ethnologist/sociologist, reflects the process of producing an objectified form of reflexivity, making an object of that which shapes one's own knowledge, never giving into a romantic subjectivist fantasy. The objective, critical treatment of the contexts which produce objectifying modes of thought (reason) is indeed a valuable form of reflexivity with many possibilities for expanding/reconstructing the ethnographic research project. But more's the pity, then, to severely constrain such possibilities by assimilating this kind of critique as a method that does not seriously alter the forms taken by past sociological (and ethnographic) practice.

Anthropological Reflexivity

The most interesting form of self-critical reflexivity in anthropology (beyond its null form, discussed above) is one that emphasizes the intertextual or diverse fields of representation that any contemporary project of ethnography enters and crosses in order to establish its own subject and to define its own voice. This is reflexivity as a politics of location, as Fred Myers (1988) has termed it.

Such a revision of ethnography changes the understanding of what ethnography is generally about. In the past, ethnography has been associated with discovery, that is, with describing specific groups of people who have not been treated before. Restudying such groups has not been the norm in anthropology, and the full matrix of existing representations (by missionaries, travelers, journalists, the people themselves, etc.) within which an ethnographer produces his own text has always been downplayed. "One tribe, one ethnographer" has persisted as the romantic ethic of the way research is organized long after the European age of exploration and discovery. And a clear, sensitive etiquette about not working on another anthropologist's people, or at least another's group, has been the rule. Against this, modernist (or postmodernist) ethnography is supremely aware that it operates in a complex matrix of already existing alternative representations; indeed, it derives its critical power and insight from this awareness (or form of reflexivity). Of a deconstructive bent, modernist ethnography depends on not being the first account, on not discovering. It remakes, re-presents, other representations. Experimental ethnography thus depends on preexisting, more conventional narrative treatments and is parasitic on them. Such ethnography is a comment on, a remaking of, a more standard, realist account. Therefore, the best subjects for modernist ethnography are those which have been heavily represented, narrated, and made mythic by the conventions of previous discourse. Part of the experimentation is in revealing the intertextual nature of any contemporary ethnography; it works through already constituted representations by both the observed and previous observers. Modernist ethnography does not enact discovery, in the classic sense. It forgoes the nostalgic idea that there are literally unknown worlds to be discovered. Rather, in full, reflexive awareness of the historical connections that already link it to its subject matter, modernist ethnography makes historically sensitive revisions of the ethnographic archive while remaining conscious of the complex ways that diverse representations have constituted its subject matter. Such representations indeed become an integral part of modernist fieldwork.

The field of representations is by no means merely supplemental to fieldwork; representations are social facts and define not only the discourse of the ethnographer, but his or her literal position in relation to subjects. Fred Myers (1988) shows this well in his paper "Locating Ethnographic Practice: Romance, Reality, and Politics in the Outback." Called to mediate the appearance of a "lost tribe" of Aborigines (from a group with whom Myers had worked for years), who had made contact with white Australian society, Myers found himself involved in a complex set of interests and characterizations of the event (the government's, the media's, the people's own) for which existing anthropological modes of representing Aborigines had not prepared him. He had to think his way through various interests and associated representations in order to locate himself and his discipline's discourse in relation to them. As Myers observes:

> For many practicing anthropologists, the literariness of rhetorical self-awareness gives it a rather self-absorbed, intellectualist, elitist, or apolitical quality removed from the nitty-gritty of social life. It can be, on the contrary, quite sensitive to relations of power, conflict, and implicit judgments. The question raised may be appropriate to an anthropology that is less centralized, that has many masters—or many different sorts of audience. . . . So-called post-

modern anthropology is . . . asking questions similar to those generated increasingly by work under local auspices, that is, of a decentered and less Eurocentric anthropology. (Ibid.: 611)

The value of rhetorical self-awareness is in drawing our attention to the constructions through which, as professionals, we have learned partly to read but which still mask many difficult and misleading assumptions about the purpose and politics of our work. (Ibid.: 622)

In this episode of advocacy fieldwork, Myers literally had to renegotiate the meaning of "Aborigines" in Australian anthropological discourse through critical self-awareness of the overlapping alternative representations, with their different valences of social power and influence. The primary focus of his work is the group of Aborigines, and, as an actor, his primary commitment is to them as well. While his concern was not to further anthropology through experimental ethnography (which might have led to a "messy text"), at least he draws attention to the key importance of a kind of reflexivity which locates the ethnographer through a keen sensitivity to the complex overlay of related, but different accounts of almost any object of ethnographic interest.

Feminist Reflexivity

The feminist version of the highly valued and powerfully evoked null form of subjectivist, experiential reflexivity has more recently been discussed and theorized as the practice of *positioning*, which is not that different from the politics of location that have shaped reflexivity in critical ethnography within anthropology, as described above. Positioning as a feminist practice is most committed to the situatedness and partiality of all claims to knowledge and hence contests the sort of essentialist rhetoric and rigid binarism as a cognitive mode (male/female, culture/nature) that has so biased questions of gender or "otherness" in language use. The *ethic* and practice of positioning defeats these rigidities of language and makes it possible for different sorts of identities and concepts of race, culture, and gender to emerge.

On the one hand, the practice of positioning envisions a satisfying ethics of research (one that is a major motivation for the production of messy texts): any positioned or situated argument constitutes an invitation to critically respond to its partiality. Positioning assumes that all work is incomplete and requires response (and thus engagement) from those in other positions. This ethical concern of positioning carries with it the anti-essentialism so central to feminist thought.

On the other hand, the limitation of positioning is its focus as a deeply reflexive meditation upon a relationship which produces ethnography (see, e.g., Judy Stacey's [1988] article "Can There Be a Feminist Ethnography?"). As such, it yields the map, the totality, the social whole in which it is embedded, or it uses a "canned," monolithic construction to stand for this whole beyond the intimacy of ethnography, such as patriarchal, corporate, and/or late consumer capitalism. To yield the larger landscape in which it operates so as to avoid "totalizing" only leaves this landscape to be constructed in reception—by readers who will endow the ethnography with a larger context and not necessarily, of course, one that the feminist ethnographer might want. As noted, one goal of "messy" texts is to reclaim this larger, framing "whole" of ethnography without being totalizing.

As we will see in a moment, it is Donna Haraway's specific formulation of the positioning practice from within feminism that pushes it most strongly in the direction of ambitious, messy experimentation. Yet the practice of positioning can easily get stuck in a sterile form of identity politics, reducing it to a formulaic incantation at the beginning of ethnographic papers in which one boldly "comes clean" and confesses one's positioned identity (e.g., "I am a white, Jewish, middle-class, heterosexual female"). This kind of reflexive "act of location," while potentially a practice of key importance, all too often becomes a gesture that is enforced by politically correct convention. (Locating one's position by parsing it as the components of identity works most powerfully, in my readings, when it is done as a critique of monologic authority, such as in the brilliant conclusion of Aijaz Ahmad's [1987] critique of Frederic Jameson's "Third-World Literature in the Era of Multinational Capital," in which Ahmad deconstructs Jameson's identity into its unacknowledged gendered, racial, and cultural components.)

In "Situated Knowledges: The Science Question in Feminism and the Privilege of Partial Perspective," Donna Haraway (1988) extends the feminist version of reflexivity-as-positioning into a reimagining of the dimensions of fine-grained, interpretive research (in her case, the feminist study of science, but also fully congenial to anthropology's ethnographic study of ways of life as cultures). The following manifesto-like passages give a sense of her scheme:

Feminists have stakes in a successor science project that offers a more adequate, richer, better account of the world, in order to live in it well and in critical, reflexive relation to our own as well as others' practices of domination and the unequal parts of privilege and oppression that make up all positions. In traditional philosophical categories, the issue is ethics and politics perhaps more than epistemology.

So, I think my problem, and "our" problem, is how to have *simultaneously* an account of radical historical contingency for all knowledge claims and knowing subjects, a critical practice for which recognizing our own "semiotic technologies" for making meanings, *and* a no-nonsense commitment to faithful accounts of a "real" world, one that can be partially shared and that is friendly to earthwide projects of finite freedom, adequate material abundance, modest meaning in suffering, and limited happiness. (Ibid.: 579 [emphases in original])

Not so perversely, objectivity turns out to be about particular and specific embodiment and definitely not about the false vision promising transcendence of all limits and responsibility. The moral is simple: only partial perspective promises objective vision. All Western cultural narratives about objectivity are allegories of the ideologies governing the relations of what we call mind and body, distance and responsibility. Feminist objectivity is about limited location and situated knowledge, not about transcendence and splitting of subject and object. It allows us to become answerable for what we learn how to see. (Ibid.: 582–83)

A commitment to mobile positioning and to passionate detachment is dependent on the impossibility of entertaining innocent "identity" politics and epistemologies as strategies for seeing from the standpoints of the subjugated in order to see well. One cannot "be" either a cell or molecule—or a woman, colonized person, laborer, and so on—if one intends to see and see from these positions critically. "Being" is much more problematic and contingent. Also one cannot relocate in any possible vantage point without being accountable for that movement. (Ibid.: 585)

A splitting of senses, a confusion of voice and sight, rather than clear and distinct ideas, becomes the metaphor for the ground of the rational. We seek not the knowledges ruled by phallogocentrism (nostalgia for the presence of the one true Word) and disembodied vision. We seek those ruled by partial sight and limited voice—not partiality for its own sake but, rather, for the sake of the connections and unexpected openings situated knowledges make possible. Situated knowledges are about communities, not about isolated individuals. The only way to kind a larger vision is to be somewhere in particular. The science question in feminism is about objectivity as positioned rationality. Its images are not the products of escape and transcendence of limits (the view from above) but the joining of partial views and halting voices into a collective subject position that promises a vision of the means of ongoing finite embodiment, of living within limits and contradictions—of views from somewhere. (Ibid.: 590)

As with Bourdieu, in Haraway we have a committed return to objective knowledge, but what a difference in how Haraway's notion of objectivity is constituted, and what a difference in how the practice of reflexivity is defined in order to constitute it! Haraway's visionary program defines a space of juxtapositions and unexpected associations formed by a nomadic yet embedded analytic vision that constantly monitors its location and the partiality of its perspective in relation to others. Whether or not one fully appreciates Haraway's idiom and rhetoric, she has taken the locational and positioning conception of reflexivity (shared by both feminism and anthropology) and expanded it into a field of experimentation entailing both an openness to possibility and an open-ended ethics. With Haraway's experimental field, we have come full circle and back to my identification of "messy" texts as the most interesting current form that postmodernism specifically takes in ethnographic writing and as the way that certain strategies for practicing reflexivity might lead to such experimentation. In this, Haraway's program, within the frame of feminism, parallels and expresses more completely the implication of the sort of study encouraged by the locational politics of reflexivity in anthropology.

References

Ahmad, Aijaz
    1987 "Jameson's Rhetoric of Otherness and the 'National Allegory,'" *Social Text* 6(2): 3–25.
Bourdieu, Pierre
    1990a *The Logic of Practice,* translated by Richard Nice (Stanford: Stanford University Press).
    1990b "The Scholastic Point of View," translated by Loïc Wequant, *Cultural Anthropology* 5(4): 380–91.
Clifford, James
    1988 *The Predicament of Culture* (Cambridge, MA: Harvard University Press).
Clifford, James, and George E. Marcus, eds.
    1986 *Writing Culture: The Poetics and Politics of Ethnography* (Berkeley: University of California Press).
Coombe, Rosemary J.
    1991 "Objects of Property and Subjects of Politics: Intellectual Property Laws and Democratic Dialogue," *Texas Law Review* 69(7): 1853–80.
Fischer, Michael M. J., and Mehdi Abedi
    1990 *Debating Muslims: Cultural Dialogues in Postmodernity and Tradition* (Madison: University of Wisconsin Press).
Haraway, Donna
    1988 "Situated Knowledges: The Science Question in Feminism and the Privilege of Partial Perspective," *Feminist Studies* 14(3): 575–99.

1989 *Primate Visions: Gender, Race, and Nature in the World of Modern Science* (New York: Routledge).

Harvey, David
1989 *The Condition of Postmodernity: An Enquiry into the Origins of Cultural Change* (Oxford: Basil Blackwell).

Marcus, George E., and Michael M. J. Fischer
1986 *Anthropology as Cultural Critique: An Experimental Moment in the Human Sciences* (Chicago: University of Chicago Press).

Marcus, George E., with Peter Dobkin Hall
1992 *Lives in Trust: The Fortunes of Dynastic Families in Late Twentieth-Century America* (Boulder: Westview Press).

Myers, Fred
1988 "Locating Ethnographic Practice: Romance, Reality, and Politics in the Outback," *American Ethnologist* 15(4): 609–24.

Rajchman, John
1987 "Postmodernism in a Nominalist Frame: The Emergence and Diffusion of a Cultural Category," *Flash Art* 137(1): 49–51.

Sahlins, Marshall
1991 "The Return of the Event, Again: With Reflections on the Beginnings of the Great Fijian War of 1843 to 1855 between the Kingdoms of Bau and Rewa," in *Clio in Oceania*, edited by Aletta Biersack, 37–100 (Washington, DC: Smithsonian Institution Press).

Stacey, Judith
1988 "Can There Be a Feminist Ethnography?" *Women's Studies International Forum* 11(1): 21–27.
1990 *Brave New Families: Stories of Domestic Upheaval in Late Twentieth-Century America* (New York: Basic Books).

Taussig, Michael
1987 *Shamanism, Colonialism, and the Wild Man: A Study in Terror and Healing* (Chicago: University of Chicago Press).

Tyler, Stephen A.
1987 *The Unspeakable: Discourse, Dialogue, and Rhetoric in the Postmodern World* (Madison: University of Wisconsin Press).

Watson, Graham
1987 "Make Me Reflexive—But Not Yet: Strategies for Managing Essential Reflexivity in Ethnographic Discourse," *Journal of Anthropological Research* 43(1): 29–41.

Williams, Sarah
1991 "Suspending Anthropology's Inscription: Observing Trinh Minh-ha Observed," *Visual Anthropology Review* 7(1): 7–14.

Willis, Paul
1981 [1977] *Learning to Labour: How Working-Class Kids Get Working-Class Jobs* (New York: Columbia University Press).

Nine _____

Critical Cultural Studies as One
Power/Knowledge Like, Among, and
in Engagement with Others (1997)

IN OCTOBER 1994 I convened a seminar at the School of American Research in Santa Fe, ten years after the seminar that led to the well-known collection, *Writing Culture: The Poetics and Politics of Ethnography* (Clifford and Marcus, 1986). Including some of the same participants in that earlier seminar, this one was intended to consider broadly the current prospects of an anthropology that had become deeply embedded in the intellectual movements of which the *Writing Culture* seminar was both a reflection and a shaper. During the intervening decade there have been deep challenges to the founding assumptions of most of the disciplines that constitute the human sciences in the USA. Under the label first of "postmodernism" and then "cultural studies," many scholars in the social sciences and humanities subjected themselves to a bracing critical self-examination of their habits of thought and work. This involved reconsiderations of the nature of representation, description, subjectivity, objectivity, even of the notions of "society" and "culture" themselves, as well as of how scholars materialized objects of study and data about them to constitute the "real" to which their work has been addressed. Personally transformative for some, excessively skeptical for others, this trend was conducted in the name of "theory" and "critique," and in the U.S. was largely diffused through literary studies, which was trying to remake itself into a more inter-disciplinary cultural studies.

We are now at a critical moment of intense interest in how to deploy this intellectual capital in projects of long-term research, as well as in interventions in contemporary debates about politics, policies, and national problems—how to communicate and use in inquiry what was essentially a reformation of thought among scholars. Especially in disciplines that consider themselves empiricist, such as anthropology, there is interest in how the ideas and concepts of the past decade can be used to reformulate traditional protocols of research.

At the same time, I have noted a pervasive nervousness about the legacy of past self-critical ferment, a lack of confidence about the relevance of all the theory, a sense that maybe the so-called crisis of representation has only been an intellectual crisis, offering very little possibility of effective theoretical or analytic engagement with those outside academia. This sort of pessimism is easy to spot in conferences, publications, and corridor talk at present.

It is undoubtedly the case that the discussions that developed the intellectual capital of the past decade ideologically and theoretically for academics were hermetic, but the precise legacy of this capital is now being determined in the kinds of research projects that it has inspired. The 1994 Santa Fe seminar consequently took up two urgent tasks, mainly with the effects of the 1980s crisis of representation on anthropology in mind. One was to address the changing research process itself in anthropology. We wanted to demonstrate that the fate of the so-called postmodernist critiques of anthropology lay not in further discussions of postmodernism, but in the enactments of new kinds of research projects in anthropology, differently problematized and conducted (for a personal assessment of these changes in method, see Marcus, 1995).

The other task, and the one I want to elaborate upon in this essay, was to address squarely, by a kind of experiment in the ethnography of knowledge, the creeping lack of confidence regarding the integrity, worth, and relevance of the stock of critical ideas that had been introduced to American academics over the past decade and more. Indeed, we thought that this was the more urgent task of the seminar. We wanted to test (and, frankly, undermine if warranted) the sense that critical reflexivity has been an insular activity simply involuting upon abstractions and self-importance. Our idea was to affirm that social scientists, such as anthropologists, participate in a regime of power/knowledge (a term, derived from Michel Foucault, to designate formal institutions of modernity that exercise power through the creation and management of knowledge) such that self-critical trends in academia would be similar to trends in other power/knowledges, particularly those more directly concerned with the performance of instrumental functions in society: the professions, corporations, publishing, the military, finance, politics, public policy, science and technology. Because any self-critical trend is unlikely to take the same form of discourse, consciousness, practices, or contexts of activity across such disparate sites of power/knowledge, this task is eminently suitable for ethnographic research, deeply familiar as it is with subjects' views in the contexts within which it situates itself, and oriented to translating across them in a comparative way.

By recruiting a combination of practitioners within a range of institutions, and scholars who had conducted ethnographies within them, we hoped to provide a discussion about how widespread and relevant the crisis of representation had been. At the same time, we wished to assert an affinity between bureaucrats, officials, professionals, and left-liberal scholars, perhaps disturbing to the latter, but one that they would have to take self-consciously into account in pursuing future projects. Our experiment was thus to have been an exploration in ethnographic terms of Bourdieu's provocative designation of academics and intellectuals as the "dominated fraction of the dominant."

The relativization of academics along such a dimension of overlapping power/knowledges, often ignored or only superficially acknowledged by them in their own self-identifications, would be an important by-product of addressing the fear among scholars that they are only projecting their own problems or habits of thought upon the world. It would be very interesting to know whether similar crises of representation have appeared in domains of power/knowledge far from the self-identifications or sympathies of left-liberal scholars.

In the realm of social theory, the task that I have in mind has been discussed in terms of "reflexive modernization" (see Bauman, 1991; Lash, 1993; Beck, Giddens, and Lash, 1994). The construct of reflexive modernization specifies and gives a theoretical context for the task of cultural critique that I want to pursue here. It is indisputable that reflexivity as self-monitoring is pervasive in modern rationalist organizations and institutions. Rather, as Beck, Giddens, and Lash's (1994) critique of reflexive modernization suggests, the question worth addressing, both for the continued relevance of critical intellectual movements that have arisen in the academy over the past two decades and for the possibility of a future conversation of critical substance between the human sciences and the policy sciences, is the following. How postmodern (how critically reflexive, how hermeneutically open in rationalist cognition) are the conditions of reflexivity within the operations of various institutions and formal organizations of American life?

I argue that this is an urgent and eminently empirical question, requiring the sensibility of ethnographers, since the reflexivity of the sort I am interested in assaying is not likely to announce itself doctrinally, or say, in the planning departments and functions of organizations. Rather, it must be read as cracks, fissures, and shifts in cases and processes of dealing with phenomena, clients, and situations that don't fit operative traditional categories and resist easy fixes. In other words, the indications of reflexive modernization of the critical hermeneutic sort are likely to be registered not seismically, but in terms of tremors and cracks. At least this is my orienting supposition.

Clearly, I am not interested in the cultural studies cliché of "resistance" by often sentimentalized "Others," but in critiques relying upon affinities between critical academics and either "Other" academics or "Others" powerful in their institutional governing functions. Indeed, the future of critical ethnography itself depends on an understanding of its relationships and affinities to critical sensibilities within other power/knowledges. Far from taking the traditionally distanced perspective on the "Other," ethnographers involved in such new locations are altogether differently positioned. The fact of affinity with these powerful "Others" becomes "useful" knowledge for exploring this new terrain and modifying standard field-work assumptions and settings.

As a contribution to this task, I want to devote the remainder of this essay to the presentation of two occasional exercises of my own that probe techniques and possibilities for bringing critical cultural studies into a perhaps uneasy relationship of both identification and engagement with arenas of knowledge that it has had great distance from, or even actively opposed. The first brief exercise deals with the possibility of success or efficacy of different strategies of critical engagement. It confronts the daunting task of actually pursuing such dialogues. On the occasion of commenting on the inaugural issues of a new journal of *Feminist Economics*, I survey the various senses in which an engagement with mainstream economics by (mainly feminist) economists, deeply affected by the intellectual capital of diverse critical theories over the past decade, might be possible. In this case, the sense of developing engagements across power/knowledges happens to remain within the academy, though it does move beyond it to assess the vulnerabilities of the prestige of economics in its diffuse and derived practices in society, when the prospects of an engaged or dialogic critique of the discipline's academic mainstream appear bleak.

The second exercise deals with technique. It suggests how converging or intersecting genealogies of shared concepts and concerns might be established through a sort of ethnographically sensitive translation between "worlds apart" power/knowledge arenas, such that mutually relevant discussions might occur between scholars and experts who might never have thought they had much in common. Once convincing linking genealogies are established, then the agenda of critical anthropology is defined for the present in trying to exploit or explore them in further dialogues across very strange, and estranged, boundaries of academic/expert discourse. What is at stake is the movement of critical anthropology into conversation with policy studies and operations. Here the task of translation consists in making visible and conscious across domains the intertwined histories of conceptual frameworks that powerfully orient cognitions, practices, and senses of problems. The case developed in the second exercise, concerning cold war nuclear diplomacy, moves this project of critique outside a strictly academic frame, and in so doing also demonstrates how implicated the academy has been in forms of power/knowledge relating to high-level politics within and between states.

Exercise 1: The Case of the Journal of *Feminist Economics*: Strategies of Critical Work and Their Potential Efficacy

The recent founding of the journal of *Feminist Economics* presents an interesting opportunity to assess the prospects for the effective internal critique of a discipline, which in its methods and ethos seems to be the very antithesis of styles of analysis and discourse in critical cultural and/or feminist studies. The opening editorial of the journal gives a flavor of its intent (Strassman, 1995: 2–3):

> At issue is not merely the merits of one theory over another, but the relative merits of entire research agendas and disciplinary identities. Economists have rarely acknowledged the multifaceted character of research priorities or the consequences of socially constructed preferences in diminishing women's voices in economic conversations . . . feminists have begun to shed light on policy concerns integral to women's lives and conceptual flaws in the mechanisms by which economists have claimed the superiority of some ideas over others . . . feminists are exploring the historical construction of disciplinary categories in relation to the composition and other features of communities of economic practice.

Correspondingly, the articles in the first issues of this new journal exhibit work that ranges from the use of standard economic tools to address gender issues, to theoretical and methodological critiques of economics, empirical studies using nonstandard methods or theories, and contributions by non-economists.

For example, in the first issue of the journal, Sandra Harding, a prominent feminist critic of discourse and practice in science, addresses parallel issues in the critique of economics (Harding, 1995). In reading the responses to Sandra Harding's article, a line in the piece by Don McCloskey, who earlier pioneered the critique of economics based on its rhetoric, especially caught my eye (McCloskey, 1995): "My question is, is this or that argument by Harding going to persuade the kind of person I once was [presumably, a mainstream economist]? What *would* convince such a person?" It keys the question of what sorts of efficacy and transformative potential the authors of the various recent projects of cultural critique might desire. I especially have in mind those projects that seek to alter mainstream habits of thought and practices of work in paradigms of knowledge production, such as science, diplomacy, law, and for *Feminist Economics*, economics, all of which have great prestige as the intellectual engines of modern rationality with embedded institutional functions related to governance and social order.

So, is there any hope of "convincing" practitioners and scholars working within the mainstreams of such culturally prestigious formations of knowledge production? If so, then by what strategies of critique? Further, if there is not much hope, then what alternative, or rather supplementary, strategies of critique are available?

Of course, one could claim a much more limited purpose for feminist economics: merely to secure a domain for alternative work on its own merits. Engaged dialogue with the mainstream would not be sought as much as, at most, a legitimate, if marginal, space to operate alternatively within the discipline.[1] The real constituency for such a vibrant alternative economics is located within the contemporary interdisciplinary realm of critical literary/cultural studies, broadly conceived, from which it has importantly derived its intellectual capital. The work of an alternative feminist economics (among other critical social sciences) is the kind of complementary social science that cultural studies scholars, who are its inspiration, need in order to ground empirically their own more broadly based interdisciplinary endeavor. Satisfying by its own standards and supported by interdisciplinary alliances, a feminist economics can thus thrive in structural opposition to mainstream economics without any effort to engage with it on its own terms, or to transform it. It would then become, with viable institutional support, another "tribe" within economics.

Yet, to me, having worked with the signature ethnographic method of cultural anthropology and having attempted to practice cultural critique derived from it, this limited purpose is insufficient. However difficult, to find an engaged constituency within the disciplinary mainstream that might even be "convinced" (in McCloskey's terms) is irresistible for me. It also figures for me as the most important index of the power of a particular project of critique.[2]

The strategy of engagement with the disciplinary mainstream that I have in mind rests on finding and intellectually probing effective oppositional space within mainstream discourses. This means finding where the "fissures" are—that is, finding those concepts, methods, ideas, practices, and life experiences within the culture of the mainstream, about which there is self-doubt and uncertainty among mainstream economists themselves. This in turn means understanding these potentially self-critical cultural formations within mainstream economics, *ethnographically*, in their own terms and expressions.

To proceed ethnographically, one would address such questions as: What are the anxiety and rationalization structures supporting the maintenance of conservative modes of thought in economics? How are such anxieties and rationalizations expressed, in what cultural idioms, and to whom? (Perhaps, for example, they are not directed to the overt critics of mainstream economics, but rather to those who expect most from it in government and business.) What arguments could be developed to establish a sustained connection with embedded self-critical tendencies in mainstream economics? What are the perhaps buried intellectual affinities between these discovered and elicited self-critical tendencies within the mainstream and the manifest forms of critique which oppose it?

According to this strategy, the measure of the power of critique is involved response from within that mainstream. But this strategy does not argue against the mainstream with a counterdiscourse more powerful than its own, because it does not have one that is more powerful. Rather, this strategy depends on mapping the cracks, inconsistencies, and hesitations of mainstream discourse, such that if the critic pointed these out, the mainstream would become upset and moved to respond because it would recognize the critique *in its own internal idiom.* The test of such critique is that the mainstream would neither be indifferent to nor dismissive of what the critic says, but would at least partially recognize itself in such critique.

Now, what I am proposing may seem like "psyching out" mainstream economics in order to convert (or convince) it, but as I indicated, I prefer to understand this strategy in terms analogous to the practice of cross-cultural ethnographic research in anthropology. Based on recent critical discussions of this enterprise (Clifford and Marcus, 1986, and the decade-long stream of discussion that it has initiated), the creation of ethnographic knowledge is inseparable from its contexts of collaborative productions with specific others as informants (in the older terminology), consultants, associates, or simply interlocutors in the field. Indeed, its very form, substance, and purposes are entwined within the self-other negotiations so central to the formulation of translations and interpretations in anthropology.

I am suggesting analogously that any critique of mainstream economics seeking engaged response would proceed approximately like ethnographic practice. This requires working dialogically within the mainstream. In other words, this means being oppositional, without a clear "outside" bounded space of opposition. Certainly, the open-ended possibilities of the pursuit of ethnographic knowledge through dialogically working on the "inside" of another culture makes the idea of "converting" or "convincing" the other side far too simple and inappropriate a metaphor to describe this sort of critique. To be effective, one must put one's own position at risk in opposing and critiquing an "other's." There is no other way to be effectively oppositional from within.

The ideal measure of the success of such a strategy of critique—that those critiqued be motivated to respond and engage with the critique—derives from a parallel "ethos" of success or achievement in ethnographic practice, relating to central issues of cultural translation. Even though anthropologists have always produced interpretations and descriptions primarily for their own academic, largely Western community, they have always had a deep sense that the knowledge that they produce should be accountable to the "natives." In fact, anthropological knowledge has been rarely tested in this way, away from sites of fieldwork, but it is increasingly the case that as objects of study and world conditions change, the nature of the realms of reception of anthropological scholarship are both broadening and diversifying.

The simplest and ethically least implicated form of this concern is often expressed as a wondering whether the discourse that the anthropologist has produced would be meaningful at all to natives, and whether the latter would even be able to comment at all on what the anthropologist says (writes?) about them. The worry of the anthropologist is less that the native would be dismissive than that she would be indifferent to what the former produces as "knowledge." "Getting it right," about which ethnographers argue endlessly, is more about being meaningful to an "other" than being accurate about a particular detail.

The imaginary of such successful ethnographic engagement has been a very strong guide and self-critical measure in anthropological work, and would operate analogously in the strategy of engaged critique "from within" mainstream economics that I am proposing. At the level even of an imaginary, the requirement of accountable engagement serves to keep ethnography, and presumably would keep the critique of economics, honest, by not hardening the lines of its own inevitable self-promotions and morale-building endeavors.

However, practical as well as imaginary success is also at stake in most projects of critique. And there may be some mainstreams or dominant discourses for which the strategy of engaged critique will just not succeed in any way that satisfies the critic. Even if such connection is made, exchange might be endlessly frustrating or contentious. Or pure acts of institutional power, prerogative, and arrogance might summarily end overtures to engaged critique, even when such critique skillfully strikes the right nerve. Indeed, there may be some discourse domains in which, however good the strategy of engaged critique may sound, there is simply no "talking to it." Mainstream defenses (as well as those on the side of critique) may be too great: sufficient, minimal good faith may not exist. Such, for example, may be true for mainstream economics.

So, let's suppose, then, that such a project of critique by transformative engagement with reasonable openness as to the results is finally insupportable—not because the idea is naive, but because it will prove to be just too wearing on the positive spirit which powers a project of critique. To persist, engaged critique needs interlocutors "on the other side," for whom there is some possibility for movement and development in debate. This leads me, then, to the final suggestion of a critical strategy inspired by the project of feminist economics.

I shall call this strategy "oblique critique." The strategy that I have just described for probing mainstream economics suggested by the experience of ethnographic research in anthropology—that of developing engaged critique through finding affinities with the "other" critiqued by dint of the equivalent of ethnographic knowledge, itself derived through dialogue—remains the same. What changes is the field in which it is exercised.

The use of the concepts and modes of economic thinking are widely diffused beyond the activities of academics who centrally define the discipline of economics itself. The economics of the Wall Street broker, the judge, or even the middle-class investor are of course not the same as those of the economics professor, but they are related in complex ways and patterns of influence that have not yet been studied. Like literature and history, most college undergraduates at least pass through economics. Because of the general cultural prestige of economics as a specific expression of reason and rationality, its ideas and models permeate many other specializations and technical spheres of knowledge production. For example, in Exercise 2, I study the interesting career of the "prisoner's dilemma" from game theory (which itself has complex associations to economics) as an artifact of the epitome of the application of rationality, complexly distributed over time and space in recent American cultural history. Indeed, it was my effort to see the "postmodern" in this seminal formalist puzzle of strict rationality and its particular ramifications in the formation of cold war nuclear weapons strategies that led me to both clarify what I mean by a strategy of engaged critique and to see its most potentially successful applications. Those applications confront the practices, not of the ur-disciplines of rationality, such as economics, but obliquely, of those fields into which the ideas of economics have migrated as dominant, prestigious models of operation.

Thus, in establishing such an oblique and extended field of critique of economics, the point is to conceive of this branch of technical knowledge on a broadly cultural map. The prestige of economics is certainly based on its complex spread and genealogies of influence in different locations of American life as well as internationally. And it is the prestige of economics as a discipline at the core of this broad cultural field that most protects its mainstream practitioners from more direct critiques. So, if the path of directly engaged critique of the disciplinary mainstream is necessary to try, but fraught with difficulty, then the critique of economics as a derived mode of thought in locations and spheres to which it has migrated is perhaps a more promising, if supplementary project of feminist economics. If done systematically, the project of oblique critique could have, over time, a profound effect on the configurations of prestige which give the mainstream in academic economics the power to ignore or downplay either the challenges of marginalized sectors within its own disciplinary boundaries (i.e., Marxists, feminists, postmodernists), or its own very masked tendencies toward self-critique.

Finally, would it in fact be easier to "translate" through engaged critique the economic models and practices at work in the broader cultural field of oblique critique than to connect with self-critical hesitations in the thought of mainstream economists? Of course, this is very much an empirical question, but merely the effort to do so would shift feminist economics from being the critique of a discipline to being a powerful and broad form of cultural critique in the name of economics (and, of course, feminism). From the domains of application of the prisoner's dilemma, to those of rational choice theory, to the way that the contemporary middle classes manage their finances and plan for the education of children, the oblique critique of economics by those trained within its sanctum is likely to produce an immense amount of intellectual capital through which the frameworks of mainstream economics might be eventually transfomed.

Exercise 2: The Affinity between Postmodernist Critique of the 1980s and Nuclear Diplomacy by Way of a Modernist Avant-Garde Link to the "Prisoner's Dilemma"

This exercise is one of critical translation in a world of family resemblances of overlapping power/knowledges—moving beyond the critical field of discourses that have emerged in the human sciences to the discovery of affinities, parallels, and differences within other power/knowledges for which these critical discourses have meant little or nothing. If, indeed, overt styles of critical postmodern thought have cogently gestured toward conditions "out there," then through a kind of ethnographic translation, a similar de facto postmodernism "in its own terms," however subtly marked and even resisted, should be found in other power/knowledges. Such an exercise would at least indicate with great specificity what are useful and less useful ideas in the central trends of academic postmodernism of the past decade. It would also map with equal specificity a much needed and perhaps provocative expansion in the range of discourses of scholarship, technical thought, and expertise with which critical postmodernism and cultural studies might engage, other than in their distancing and clichéd "oppositional" stance to all that is "dominant" and "hegemonic."

This form of critique looks for affinities between postmodern academic thought and other power/knowledges precisely where they are *not* obvious, where they emerge in the latter as unintended consequences of trying to deal instrumentally with the contemporary world. For example, at what points is a power/knowledge that has comfortably dealt with constructs of integral selves and individuals, faced suddenly with multiple subjectivities (a key artifact of postmodern/feminist/cultural studies thought) in the course of its problem-solving? It is precisely at such points that two-way translations and engagement might be strategized. The fact that these affinities are discovered/negotiated within the "enemy" territory of the dominant/hegemonic, rather than imposed by the power of postmodern thought in brilliant applications, marks the difference between the project suggested here and the existing domains (reservations?) of postmodern critique.

I want to work through an example of this critical project focused on the power/knowledge of high-level cold war diplomacy at its twilight. I have decided to give my example at least a short historic perspective. I have selected nuclear/arms control diplomacy of the 1980s as the target "other" power/knowledge to try to discover affinities with moves and constructs of so-called postmodern critique within the academy for two reasons. First, nuclear diplomacy is clearly distant from postmodern critiques of academic disciplines. Second, it was at the very vortex of the most dramatic structural and cognitive real-world changes of that decade, including the shift in leadership in the USSR and the latter's eventual dismantling. My question is whether there are any affinities between the radical shifts of framework and representation practices suggested by postmodern critiques in the academy of the 1980s and the discourse of diplomacy of the same period, which, albeit insular, was having to navigate radically changed conditions and new assumptions.

At the Institute for Advanced Study, 1982–83: Storylines

I was invited to be a visiting member at the Institute for Advanced Study in Princeton, N.J., during 1982–83, primarily because of Clifford Geertz's interest in the paper that I published (with Dick Cushman) in the 1982 *Annual Review of Anthropology*—"Ethnographies as Texts." It was also during my time at the Institute that I planned the Santa Fe SAR "Writing Culture" seminar with Jim Clifford, and drafted (in partnership with Mike Fischer) the arguments for *Anthropology as Cultural Critique*. Clifford visited me at the Institute during this year, and met Geertz for the first time. There was clear mutual respect between them as writers, although at the time Geertz was attracted to, but also wary of, the coming "literary" turn—even though before the days of "theory" he himself had been associated with a literary influence on anthropology. The concerns with textuality, disciplinary history, critical modes of reflexivity, and the critique of realist practices of representation that informed my (and to a far lesser extent, Geertz's) thinking was just a local case of what was then happening in many disciplines. This was one clear "storyline" in the atmosphere of the Institute during my year that was to become a major story of the decade and beyond.

Amid the diverse other projects that were in play at the Institute that year, there were three other salient storylines being pursued, two of which figure into the exercise that I have designed for this paper. One of the other storylines (not directly relevant here) was the focused attention given to cognitive science that year.

Another of the storylines derives from the work that Charles Sabel was doing as a visiting member of the Institute during 1982–83. He was working on the manuscript that was to become *The Second Industrial Divide* (Piore and Sabel, 1984). This was to be one of the first major statements about the changing conditions of capitalist political economy in the West. In addition, in 1982–83, the middle of Reagan's first term, analysts were noting adverse changes for the U.S. economy in a rapidly changing world of competitive capitalism. The rapid changes in markets, production processes, and consumer choices were very apparent to the "person on the street" in the early 1980s. These realities, I would argue, played a crucial off-stage role in giving postmodernist critiques a sense of their own possibility. Indeed, this new work on emerging political economy was frequently referenced in works of cultural critique.[3]

This brings me to the final storyline, which circumstantially happened to be quite salient at the Institute during the 1982–83 year, and which I found perhaps the most fascinating of all. It dealt with the seemingly Spenglerian moment that the Reagan administration had begun to create with its departure from detente and its more aggressive stance toward the Soviet Union. This was the moment of the invocation of the "evil empire" and of debates about the feasibility of direct military intervention in Central America. I recall public debates between Richard Ullman (professor at the Woodrow Wilson School and visitor at the Institute that year) and Bill Luers (former ambassador to Venezuela, then visitor at the Institute, nervously awaiting reassignment) about the dangers of Soviet footholds in Central America. Most memorably, I participated in a weekly series of informal lunches at the Institute dining hall, that brought together a diverse group of international relations scholars from the Woodrow Wilson School, some weapons scientists, occasional persons who had moved between academia and government or diplomatic service, and always George Kennan, who had for many years been a member of the School of Historical Studies at the Institute.

In terms of sharp, edgy discussion about something that clearly mattered, about "events of the day," these lunches were for me the most stimulating events at the Institute that year, and have stood out for me since then. The discussions were dominated by young, very bright scholars of international relations arguing point-counterpoint over U.S. strategy in competition with the Soviets, with a narrow focus on nuclear arms policy. I was captivated by the elegance and intricacy of this very reductionist game, while finding the game itself obtuse.

Others on the sidelines at the lunches made commentaries or more philosophical glosses on the tight tension of U.S.-Soviet competition at the time. The strategic threat of revolutions in Central America and the background to U.S. policy there often came up. For Charles Sabel, the interesting developments in IR at that time concerned the evolution of a new international regime which was reorganizing world economies, but the group's main focus was on the narrow game/discourse of U.S.-Soviet nuclear strategy totally insulated from immense changes in political economy, thereby maintaining a surreal, but also very locally real, centering to the cold war order.

The major counterweight at these lunches was the quiet, but large presence of George Kennan, whose comments persistently undermined the assumptions of the revitalized neorealist game being pursued by the younger men. I later learned that Kennan was well known for his distaff view about the Soviet threat that powered cold war competition, but he was very involved at the time in rearticulating this view as the Reagan administration was heating up the cold war. Not long after his crucial early cold war articulation of containment strategy, Kennan had begun to argue for a complex and nondemonized view of the Soviets as "others" in the great game that would have precluded, for example, Reagan's return to a nuclear brinksmanship strategy. Kennan was thus once again the colossal rallying point for left-liberal opinion against what looked like a return to the old cold war in the early 1980s.

As we know from the 1990s, this early 1980s cold war strategizing discourse was to go through dramatic changes after Gorbachev came to power in 1985, moving from the challenge of the Spenglerian specter of the "decline of the West" at the beginning of the decade to a jingoist, but still not fully confident, heralding of the "triumph of the West" at the end, as in Francis Fukuyama's *The End of History*. Now in the 1990s, I want to juxtapose and mutually engage this power/knowledge of high-level diplomacy during the 1980s to that of postmodernist critical thought of the same period that was related to it only distantly (if at all), but was certainly spurred on and stimulated (through the off-stage real effect mentioned above) by the spectacle of the dramatic changes in post–World War II order that were centered in the terms of "the great game" of Soviet-U.S. relations. Was there any parallel sense of postmodernist moods deep within the distant power/knowledge of nuclear diplomacy?

The Avant-Garde (Post)Modernist Fascination with Simultaneity and the Prisoner's Dilemma

Working into the 1980s power/knowledge discourse of nuclear diplomacy in practice, starting from within "postmodernist" critical thought of the same period, requires the construction of intersecting critical genealogies between two domains apparently "worlds apart." I can only offer a sketch here of such an analysis of an opening, posited affinity. The specific locations I would like to probe are the long-term fascination with simultaneity in the discourse of avant-garde modernisms and postmodernisms, and an identifiable similar fascination with simultaneity in the construction of the key problematic of game theory—the prisoner's dilemma. In turn, the development of game theory (the prisoner's dilemma in particular) in the U.S. is intimately related to the formulation of early cold war strategies of nuclear diplomacy. Nuclear diplomacy was not in the hands of game theoreticians, nor is it clear that game theory was prominent in the thinking of the main actors of Soviet-U.S. relations, but game theory was certainly a powerful intellectual expression on the inside of the actual "great game" (if "game" is the correct metaphor) of nuclear arms competition and control. Thus, I am wagering that making the connection between a problematic of simultaneity in postmodernism and game theory will create a vehicle to probe the power/knowledge of nuclear diplomacy in practice for its parallel to critical postmodernism's evoked projections of immense change upon the contemporaneous world.

The Fascination with Simultaneity among Avant-Gardes

Techniques of juxtaposition have been at the center of avant-garde practices throughout modernism and postmodernism. Montage, collage, assemblage—these have been avant-garde critique's forms of representation or anti-representation, with sharp, implied challenges to construction of discourses of the real in conventional genres.

One of the most important moves in the so-called postmodernist trend in the academy has been the adoption in both spirit and practice of these avant-garde techniques of (anti-?) representation in humanities/social science writing as a means of challenging the academy's mode of realism: analytic reason. The power of this form of reason for scholarly practices remains overwhelming. Even when writing against it, one is writing in its terms, or least in reference to it. Thus, "reality"-testing lurks as a criterion even for the most distanced, theoretical uses of strategies of critique by juxtaposition. The key empirical question embedded in the practice of juxtaposition concerns the state and experience—the phenomenology—of simultaneity. This is the condition that the discourse of analytic reason might acknowledge, but must evade, and which postmodernist critique wants to address squarely, but for which it might not have a substitute discourse that would by any means satisfy analytic reason.

Analytic discourse about the real employs linear representation, and sequence, making possible statements about causation, if not rigorously articulated, then implied. It allows for systematic theorization and description of social and cultural life. Its basic representational mode depends on the taken-for-granted capacity to articulate *relationships* (of people, parts, distinctions, things, etc.) as the most basic object of study. A relationship, however complex and multilevelled, entails linearity and sequenciality in conception. This is the basic "work horse" of analytic reason that postmodernist critique's concern with simultaneity wants to address.

Instead of actors who respond to what has been done to them by knowable others—the basis of a relationship—let us suppose that actors are acting (maybe even responding) to what is being done by unknowable others as they act (the play with synchronicity in experimental film and fiction—Joyce's *Ulysses* being a prime example—or the idea of "utterance" in Bakhtin are good examples from very well established modernisms). The imaginary/discourse of simultaneity is quite different to anything that has been explored in the dominant analytic realisms in play in most contemporary power/knowledges. It is precisely this alternative imaginary/discourse that postmodernist critique within the academy—and centrally in the realm of the analytic real as the common sense of most power/knowledges—wants to explore. Observations about defining aspects of contemporary societies as postmodern (for example, the centrality of time-space compression as reviewed by Harvey, or of speed as focused upon by Paul Virilio), enhance the fascination of current critical thought with simultaneity and its potential as a condition through which to evoke an alternative vision of contemporary life. Thus, the unrelenting concern with simultaneity is one of the most distinctive, and certainly one of the most subversive, provocative, and irritating characteristics of many forms of thought called postmodern. It is something that realist genres have not been able to abide, dependent as they are on linearity and the construct of transparent reciprocity which simultaneity undermines.[4]

A Case in Point: Game Theory and the Prisoner's Dilemma

Of all the varieties of contemporary discourses of analytic realism, game theory, and specifically, its most central and influential puzzle, the prisoner's dilemma (hereafter, PD), is the only one that foregrounds in its construction the problem of simultaneity, thus sharing an affinity with this key provocation of (post)modernist critique. The other main postwar paradigm of analytic realism was cybernetics and systems theory, but it was fully constructed on the imagery of linear relationships and continuous interconnection (see Heims, 1993). The PD was thus an attempt of rationality to find a perfect solution in the environment of a key problem of modernity—the condition of simultaneity—while avoiding the assumptions of systems/cybernetics theory, which posited linear relationships and direct connections. While by no means equally sharing the spirit or ethos of avant-garde critique—in fact the condition of simultaneity is constructed for rationalist manipulation by the metaphoric notion of game itself—PD does come a cropper as a puzzle for elegant solution for reasons that are not unrelated to the fascination that simultaneity has for postmodernist critical thought.

The history of game theory itself is intimately linked to cold war history and the policy management of nuclear weapons, especially in its early years (see Poundstone, 1992). Game theory begins with the 1944 publication of *Theory of Games and Economic Behavior* by John von Neumann and Oskar Morgenstern. It concerns conflict between thoughtful and potentially deceitful opponents in which players are assumed to be perfectly rational. Thus, it is a branch not of psychology but of mathematical logic that underlies real conflicts among not always rational humans. A "game" is a conflict situation where one must make a choice knowing that others are making choices too, and the outcome of the conflict will be determined in some prescribed way by all the choices made. This is the (post)modernist's problem of simultaneity under the logician's control.

Game theory found its most important application at the RAND Corporation, which was the prototypical think-tank founded at the behest of the Air Force shortly after World War II. RAND's original purpose was to perform strategic studies on intercontinental nuclear war. The need for RAND's "operations research" was indeed stimulated by a sort of "crisis of representation" in military matters brought on by the appearance of nuclear weapons: generals and scientists became wedded in new ways.

In 1950, two RAND scientists devised the most provocative version of game theory. Merrill Flood and Melvin Dresher devised a simple "game" that challenged part of the theoretical basis of game theory. RAND consultant Albert W. Tucker dubbed this game the prisoner's dilemma, so called because of a story Tucker told to illustrate it. Not published as such until years after its invention, the prisoner's dilemma—a story that is both a precise mathematical construct and also a real-life problem—spread through the scientific community of the 1950s by oral transmission. From the 1960s, this dilemma paradigm became part of a much broader intellectual culture and even a marker of "cultural literacy." It has come to stand for game theory, its ethical ambiguities, and the tensions of the early nuclear era.

Flood and Dresher, the inventors of PD, were trying to take account of the fact that people are irrational within the realm of game theory. They thus dispensed to some degree with the narrow "game" assumptions of the original theory to make it relevant to everyday life situations of dilemma, choice, and calculation. Albert Tucker, a Princeton mathematician, gave the tale its classic formulation, of which Poundstone (1992: 118–19) presents a typical contemporary version:

Two members of a criminal gang are arrested and imprisoned. Each prisoner is in solitary confinement with no means of speaking to or exchanging messages with the other. The police admit they don't have enough evidence to convict the pair on the principal charge. They plan to sentence both to a year in prison on a lesser charge. Simultaneously, the police offer each prisoner a Faustian bargain. If he testifies against his partner, he will go free while the partner will get three years in prison on the main charge. Oh, yes, there is a catch . . . if both prisoners testify against each other, both will be sentenced to two years in jail.

The prisoners are given a little time to think this over, but in no case may either learn what the other has decided until he has irrevocably made his decision. Each is informed that the other prisoner is being offered the very same deal. Each prisoner is concerned only with his own welfare—with minimizing his own prison sentence.

The prisoners can reason as follows. "Suppose I testify and the other prisoner doesn't. Then I get off scot-free (rather than spending a year in jail). Suppose I testify and the other prisoner does too. Then I get two years (rather than three). Either way I'm better off turning state's evidence. Testifying takes a year off my sentence, no matter what the other guy does."

The trouble is, the other prisoner can and will come to the very same conclusion. If both parties are rational, both will testify and both will get two years in jail. If only they had both refused to testify, they would have got just a year each!

This story was not intended to be a realistic picture of criminology, but to serve the logician's challenge to game theory, by posing a puzzle without a perfect solution. In fact, an expected solution never came to the PD, and it remains a limiting case for the ambition of a theory which would impose perfect rationality on the (post)modern condition of simultaneity—the nonlinear nature of relationship as a *usual* circumstance of social and cultural life, and not just of dilemma situations.

So much for the disappointments of theory. In practice, no example of a prisoner's dilemma has been more popular, both in technical articles and the popular press, than nuclear arms rivalry. The "prisoner's dilemma" is sometimes taken to be part of the jargon of nuclear strategy, along with "mutually assured destruction" and "MIRV." At the time the PD was invented, the U.S. and the Soviets had embarked on an expensive nuclear arms race. The situation could be seen as a PD (and was seen as such at RAND, whose "thinking about the unthinkable" was of maximum strategic influence at the time), in which building the bombs could be identified with defection, and holding off could be identified with cooperation. Each side would prefer that no one build the bomb (reward payoff for mutual cooperation), rather than both build it for no net gain of power (punishment payoff for mutual defection). But each side may well elect to build the bomb either out of hope of gaining the upper hand militarily (temptation payoff) or out of fear of being the one without it (sucker payoff).

As the cold war wore on and the U.S. and the Soviet Union became implacable foes, whose relations remained focused on the politics of

CRITICAL CULTURAL STUDIES

nuclear arms competition and then control, the relevance of exercises in perfect rationality as embedded in the project of game theory (and within it, its internal critique and limiting case in the form of the PD) clearly lessened. Yet the problematic around which the PD developed and which it shared with avant-garde modernisms—the fascination with relations of simultaneity—seems to be of crucial relevance in understanding the development of high-level nuclear diplomacy in terms of which cold war reality was articulated and managed. It is just that avant-garde modernisms have nothing as elegant as the PD to offer with which to understand the actual course of cold war nuclear diplomacy.

This is where the ethnographically sensitive translation between power/knowledges and the probing for the PD in action, so to speak, come in. The basic setup of the PD—the condition of nonlinear relations of simultaneity—is probably useful to retain and quite ironic as a perspective on the actual playing out of U.S.-Soviet relations at the end of the cold war. But a richer set of theories and concepts is needed to describe the human experience of operating in conditions of simultaneous processes, where one's relations are with unseen, or only partly perceived, others. Classic social theory and analytic realism, as noted, offer very few resources for this re-imagining of the PD in messy, human terms.[5]

Let's move to a set of exhibits/artifacts from the late cold war history of nuclear diplomacy that detect something of the dynamic in practice of the mixed PD/postmodernist problematic of simultaneity. When *do* we reach the point in "real" life when the utility of maintaining the fiction that what we are doing above is a game at all is exhausted, and we look for other terms and descriptive frames to deal with "provisionary strategies?" This would be, for nuclear diplomacy, a parallel to the crisis of representation that pervaded academic disciplines. No such dramatic breaking of frame in nuclear diplomacy at the end of the cold war is apparent, but certainly the game metaphor, implied or explicit, wavered at various points in the events of the 1980s.

Finally, it seems to me that revisions in systems theories to encompass discontinuity, contingency, nonlinearity, and apparent simultaneity—or to put it simply, complexity—have generated theoretical paradigms, such as chaos, that have thoroughly displaced game theory in terms of prestige and also popularity. The new systems theories retain the goal of establishing principles of embedded or underlying order in accounts of much more complex phenomena. This is a heady brew that both promises order and yet recognizes in phenomena the contradictions, paradoxes, and processes of disorder, so focused upon by (post)modernist critical thought. It is no wonder, then, that the long-standing

CHAPTER NINE

practice of the borrowing of theoretical metaphors and analogies from the natural sciences to enhance the rhetoric of new ideas in the human sciences continues, with frequent references to chaos, complexity theory, fractals, and the like in contemporary discussions of global cultures, new social formations, etc. Game theory, although at one time addressing within its dilemma stories (like the PD) key aspects of the problematics of avant-garde modernisms that systems theory ignored, now pales against the ability of revised systems theory (theories of chaos and complexity) to excite, contribute to, and legitimize developing imaginaries within the human sciences.

Nuclear Diplomacy

Game theory turns out to be a very formalized portrait or calculus of the way that social actors think about interests in its *own* interest of pure rationality. However, because of its very specific intellectual and cultural history just outlined, it has a very close relationship to the mode of thought with which the cold war was identified and, in fact, produced as a practice of power/knowledge—the discourse of nuclear arms production, competition, and control. The purveyors of this discourse were not scientists, but establishment, or establishment-style, lawyers like Paul Nitze and Paul Warnke, who were brought into various administrations through political influence and alliance. Such nuclear arms negotiators presented a strange combination of the cultivated generalist/amateur posture of the establishment elite, and intricate, technical expertise about the character of nuclear weapon systems.

As noted, it is doubtful that game theory (the PD) itself had much presence in the actual "great game" after the early years of the cold war as it was articulated within the complex arena of those concerned with nuclear diplomacy. In practice, the "great game" has had all the characteristics of (post)modernist simultaneity and not "game" theory. Still, the PD its part of the elite lore of those charged with nuclear arms control. It is, therefore, I would argue, one prospective "mole" for probing affinities with postmodernist critique within the terms of this power/knowledge at the vortex of global change during the same period the critique emerged in U.S. academia. As I argued, there are aspects of the way that the PD is constructed—having to do with relations defined by conditions of simultaneity—which are at the heart of a perception of a condition of (post)modernity in avant-garde thought. Could these aspects be reconfigured for probing within the characteristics of "nuclear diplomacy" discourse in which the "PD" has a chimeri-

cal, marginalized standing, as a once-important constituting paradigm
of nuclear diplomacy, but is now an artifact of elite folklore? It is precisely in this latter capacity that it might serve as the bridge for a project of ethnographic translation between power/knowledges.

The insularity of actual nuclear diplomacy discourse is striking. With
few exceptions (the Cuban missile crisis, Paul Nitze's "Walk in the
Woods"), actual contacts and exchanges with the Soviet "other" are
highly ritualized and technical. The dynamics are generated by politics
among those in an administration charged with nuclear diplomacy—
the president, the national security advisor, the secretary of state, those
positions within the state department charged with arms control negotiation, and the community of various expertises—journalistic, academic, scientific, intelligence—oriented toward these "agent" positions
in nuclear diplomacy. Only former cold warriors on the outside—epito-
mized by George Kennan—could articulate the contrary wisdom that
argued for the recognition of the substantive alterity of the Soviets
which would have expanded or transcended the discourse of nuclear
diplomacy and conventionalized the relationship between the two
powers at the highest levels.

The stylized manner of U.S.-Soviet relations that was constituted by
nuclear diplomacy was disrupted by two events in the 1980s—Reagan's
SDI initiative unveiled in a speech on March 23, 1983, and Gorbachev's
accession to power in 1985. As nuclear diplomats struggled to deal with
the momentous consequences of both, to what degree did they self-
consciously, or even ambivalently—in subtly marked ways—come to
terms with the (post)modernist conditions of their power/knowledge,
embedded within their own history and folklore in the PD story?

Reagan's SDI: A Rupture in the Discourse of Arms Control

Reagan's announcement of the Strategic Defense Initiative ("Star
Wars") in 1983 took the nuclear diplomatic community by total sur-
prise, and the rest of the decade was in part a struggle on the part of
various factions to reassert their versions of the verities of arms control
while seeming to pursue the president's unconventional initiative (Talbott, 1988). This idiosyncratic, radical, and highly futuristic move by
the president to make nuclear weapons outmoded through space defenses, totally undermined the arms control efforts which were the
form that nuclear diplomacy had taken through the period of detente.
While the idea was to make the whole basis of the U.S.-Soviet relationship irrelevant, the SDI was in fact a keenly aggressive move, since it
would match the economic power of the two states in a way that had

not been done since the arms buildups of the early cold war, and both sides knew that the Soviet Union was not up to this strain.

Reagan's attempt to dispense with the great game could not be attributed to such easy-to-perceive cunning in retrospect (i.e., the move was designed to break the Soviet economy). It had its roots in a kind of idealism, surrealism, and American exceptionalism (the latter treated as a major theme of U.S. foreign policy in Henry Kissinger's (1994) retrospective *Diplomacy*) characteristic of Reagan's style of thinking. The byzantine efforts of nuclear diplomats like Paul Nitze and Richard Perle to continue to pursue their agendas through the new challenges that SDI imposed was the true game of nuclear diplomacy during the 1980s, as the Soviet Union continued to fall apart. These agendas, of course, had to do with the assumption of the possibility of nuclear war on which the simultaneously real and imaginary relationship of the U.S. and the Soviet Union had been based.

Reagan's initiative, in its dreamy unreality, can be understood as an effort that would end the prisoner's dilemma of U.S.-Soviet relations, in its (post)modernist inflection/affinity given here. The contemporary masters of the PD-in-practice embodied in nuclear diplomacy succeeded in sustaining this imaginary on which the focal cold war relationship of simultaneity was constructed (with all its psychological possibilities of paranoia and indulgent self-construction in the absence of any rich and broadly monitored contact with an "other").

What was not registered sufficiently in this insular, baroque game that guaranteed order in the world of the cold war was the appearance of real alterity for the first time in the person of Gorbachev. This event proved to be far more endangering to the assumptions of nuclear diplomacy than SDI.

George Schultz Lectures Gorbachev on the Information Revolution, 1987

In his memoirs, George Schultz records a meeting in the Kremlin with Gorbachev in April 1987. The text is remarkable. Schultz takes advantage of a short break in the discussion about nuclear weapons control for a long lecture (complete with "brightly colored pie charts") about changes in the contemporary world that reads much like the kind of understanding of political economy that inspired thinking in academia about conditions of postmodernity. For example, compare Schultz (1993: 891–92) with David Harvey (1989). In this interlude, Schultz was trying to break the frame of faceless "rational" nuclear contestation in the spirit of the prisoner's dilemma. The lecture apparently engaged Gorbachev's whole attention, and only came to a close when, "after about twenty-five minutes, Marshal Akhromeyev walked in with a jaunty step and upbeat, confident manner. We turned to START and SDI. Gorbachev said that the idea of a 50 percent cut in strategic forces, first agreed on at the Geneva summit, could now be described in numerical terms: 1,600 launchers and 6,000 warheads" (Schultz, 1993: 892).

Schultz, the Stanford economics professor, was trying to give Gorbachev the bigger picture—the sense of the dramatically changing "real" on which the cogency of developing postmodernist cultural critique of the 1980s was most directly based—the changed conditions of capitalist political economy. But this was a mere interruption in the insular narrow frame to which Schultz's face-to-face meetings with Gorbachev and other high-level Soviets was restricted. The relationship of the U.S. and the Soviets in simultaneity had been sustained in practice by the discipline of the discourse of arms control negotiation. Gorbachev was the first Soviet leader with the hint of a "face" that might be recognized in a normal face-to-face relationship. Schultz was trying to break through the rigid frame of the old world of U.S.-Soviet relations to an account of a new world in which, apparently through the information revolution, simultaneity would continue to be the medium of relationship, but through speed and time-space compression in the global economy, rather than through the mannered relations in the blind of the cold war leviathans, who were, true to the PD, prisoners rather than gamesters of the nuclear world that they had created.

After 1988, the unravelling of the Soviet Union had unexpectedly displaced the centrality of the (post)modernist, PD basis of Soviet-U.S. relations in high-level U.S. diplomacy. Definitely for Reagan and even more so for Bush, the arrival of Gorbachev meant for the first time a complex, actual interlocutor "other" to be imagined as counterpart by the U.S. president. This gave a literalness, an intersubjectivity, a linearity of back-and-forth interaction—in essence, an illusion of presence—to U.S.-Soviet relations that belied the conduct of their relationship in simultaneity, along with whatever insight into the nature of sociality in the (post)modern world that this previous condition offered.

The illusion of a relationship in the most conventional terms—an "affair," or partnership, as it were—impeded management at the highest levels of the speed of change in the late 1980s for which Schultz's lecture on the (post)modernist political economy was apposite and the conduct of U.S.-Soviet relations in the simultaneity of nuclear diplomacy was perhaps more relevant (see Beschloss and Talbott, 1993, for the most detailed account of the end of the cold war). The Bush-Gorbachev affair was the ultimate limiting case (and failure) of the conventional idea of a relationship in the (post)modernist world in which

Soviet-U.S. relations, centered on nuclear diplomacy, had been conducted through much of the cold war, and with special intensity during the 1980s.

Yet, within a U.S. context, the 1980s were a remarkable decade of new unconventional thinking (the exotic foray of avant-garde idioms into the human sciences with mixed results, thus far) and the struggle of old forms of unconventional thinking (nuclear diplomacy at the end of the cold war) with affinities and contradictory parallels between them (the [post]modernist fascination with simultaneity through the PD, for example). Critical work in the fin-de-siècle 1990s, I would argue, depends more upon the speculations of translating across the power/knowledges of this period, than on any self-conscious return to the eternal verities of existing metahistories (see Kissinger, 1994, for example), whose frames are likely to miss what is acknowledged by them as unprecedented, really different, and distinctively definitive about *these* times as they unfold.

Envoi

With a strong sense that the 1980s' intellectual ferment at the level of metatheoretical discussion is over and an equally strong sense of unrealized potential and irresolution of many of these "high" theoretical ideas in enactments of very specific genres of research and scholarship, what remains for critical cultural studies and its derivations is to seek not always comfortable engagements in arenas that it has been hesitant to enter, or frankly, has defined itself in opposition to. This would address unfinished aspects of the practice of reflexivity that has been such a major emblem and strategy of critical research in recent years. Critical cultural studies has produced impressive work on popular culture and the contemporary predicaments of those social actors conceived in subaltern positionings. Reflexivity in such work has aided the construction of these valuable research genres. What has not been done within the framework of these very same critical cultural studies is to incorporate the reflexive dimension that makes visible the established and *potential* relationships of critical cultural studies to forms of institutional power. This essay, with some tentative exercises in this direction, has sought to argue strongly for not only making these connections, but also for *developing* them.

The point is not merely to suggest this kind of provocative reflexivity (as others, like Bourdieu, have done) for theoretical purpose and advantage. It is to consider the radical implications of performing it in all aspects of the research process, for the standard ways that critical cultural studies scholars position themselves in relation to subjects of study and presumed audiences, how they materialize objects of study, and how they create rhetorics of political purpose, affiliation, and virtue for their projects. For example, from the standpoint of critical ethnographic work in cultural studies, the most radical move required of scholars who have repositioned themselves by establishing affinities between themselves and those operating in other power/knowledges is overcoming typical distinctions between elites (and institutional orders) as "others" that anthropologists largely do not study, subalterns as "others" who anthropologists do study, and anthropologists themselves in the position of ethnographers as "other" to either of these. The self-perception of the practice of ethnography as a power/knowledge like, among, and with specific kinds of connections to others, based on certain ethical commitments and identifications, forces the refiguration of the terrain of research—unfixes standard positionings—in which the concepts of elites, anthropologists, and subalterns get rearranged. Leaving aside power structures and conspiratorial groups as the defining features of elites, what we have attributed to elites is not "other" to us as scholars at all, but rather the play of institutional orders, which incorporates "us" as merely a different institutional interest.

Operating within reconfigured spaces of research has implications for the traditional sympathetic involvements of researchers with their subjects. Now these involvements are multiple, conflicting, and much more ambiguous. The nature and quality of field work in one site can be very different from others. This requires a different kind of resolution of a research persona than that which had normally constituted the anthropologist in field work, and which was a major component of the much-critiqued traditional conventions of authority in ethnographic writing (I know because "I was there"—I saw, I sympathized, etc.—see Clifford and Marcus, 1986). The construction of new personae and identities, both in field work and in writing, creates what I have called elsewhere a kind of circumstantial activism (Marcus, 1995) in these reconfigured projects, stimulated by a style of reflexivity that places critical cultural studies much more complicitly in the fields of power that it might have preferred to just as well leave as elite hegemonic "other."

But, finally, the stakes for critical cultural studies of cultivating a serious, performed view of itself as one power/knowledge among others are greater than just a revision of the research process and its habitual modes of preferred representation. It seems to me that to prevent cultural studies scholars from speaking only to themselves, and sometimes to those they presume to speak for as well—in other words, from occupying a place of "reservation" filled with both complacency and anxiety about "relevance"—the possibilities of relationship and discussion across the frontiers of standard positioning moves must be attempted. The process of trying to do so may not be any more satisfying. In fact, the risks for ethics, integrity, and confusion are much greater. But at the current juncture, there is little other choice. At least it gives a radically reflexive cultural studies the kind of activist engagement that it has in fact imagined for itself, but through stratagems that it might never have thought it would undertake.

Notes

1. Indeed, there has always been a legitimate "reservation" or "ghetto" for work critical of mainstream neoclassical economics, and such spaces have even found important patrons among revered figures of the discipline who in their seniority have had the license to cultivate a certain maverick position against the very mainstream that reveres them. In the past, such marginal domains have operated under the labels Marxist or institutional economics; at present, the designation "feminist" or "postmodern" more prominently labels this "reserved" space.

2. Engaged debate (dialogue? confrontation?) with the mainstream could, and often is, discussed in terms of metaphors of missionizing, warfare, or political struggle. And, indeed, a certain will to power always figures in projects of critique, such that images of wanting to overcome and replace dominant forms with something better are irresistible in characterizing the confrontational setting of critique. Critique is often powered by either the desire to convert (or merely convince), or the desire to subvert (calling up images of revolutionary action). Still, in trying to suggest here a somewhat hopeful strategy for a practice of critique that seeks engaged response from a glacial mainstream, at worst unlikely to listen to it, or at best, likely to marginalize it, I prefer to give it an anthropological expression, even though I am keenly aware of how anthropology itself has historically wrestled with missionizing and subverting, both as metaphorical and literal aspects of its own endeavors (Clifford and Marcus, 1986; and especially Clifford's [1988] essay on Marcel Griaule). But at least anthropology has squarely confronted, and in a reflexively active way, now deals with this past will to power, however ethically sensitive, in its new projects of critique (Marcus and Fischer, 1986).

3. The main channel of reference was through geographers who, among the theorists of changes in political economy, were most deeply and explicitly engaged with postmodernist critical thought, the must important statement being that of David Harvey (1989). See also the work of Scott Lash, James Urry, and the interesting "Theory, Culture, and Society" group for whom Zygmunt Bauman eventually became a key figure.

4. For example, it is a nub of the complaint of Habermas, who builds his system on conventional notions of intersubjectivity, against most of the post-structuralists, who in their concern with self, being, and presence, tie into the

modernist avant-garde legacy of posing issues of simultaneity against realist visions of society and culture.

5. Some of the recent forays into culture theory within the (post)modernist trend of critique might be promising. For example, it would be an interesting exercise to rethink the PD paradigm in terms of Mick Taussig's mimesis/alterity perspective derived from Walter Benjamin; alterity/otherness is a vital concept missing from the PD paradigm, necessary if one wants to follow it into the real life of nuclear diplomacy; and Taussig's/Benjamin's notion of the mimetic is suggestive of how involvements and relationships with others through conditions of simultaneity might be materialized for study.

References

Bauman, Zygmunt 1991: *Modernity, and Ambivalence*. Cambridge: Polity Press.

Beck, Ulrich 1992: *The Risk Society: Towards Another Modernity*. London: Sage.

Beck, Ulrich, Giddens, Anthony, and Lash, Scott 1994: *Reflexive Modernization: Politics, Tradition and Aesthetics in the Modern Social Order*. Stanford: Stanford University Press.

Beschloss, Michael R. and Talbott, Strobe 1993: *At the Highest Levels: The Inside Story of the End of the Cold War*. Boston: Little Brown.

Bourdieu, Pierre 1984: *Distinction*. Cambridge, MA: Harvard University Press.

―――― 1990: The Scholastic Point of View. *Cultural Anthropology*, 5 (4), 380–91.

de Certeau, Michel 1984: *The Practice of Everyday Life*. Berkeley: University of California Press.

Clifford, James 1988: Power and Dialogue in Ethnography: Marcel Griaule's Initiation. In *The Predicament of Culture*, Cambridge, MA: Harvard University Press.

Clifford, James and Marcus, George E. (eds.) 1986: *Writing Culture: The Poetics and Politics of Ethnography*. Berkeley: University of California Press.

Fukuyama, Frances 1991: *The End of History and the Last Man*. New York: Vintage Books.

Geertz, Clifford 1988: *Works and Lives: The Anthropologist as Author*. Stanford: Stanford University Press.

Halberstam, David 1994: The Decline and Fall of the Eastern Empire. *Vanity Fair*, October, 246–64.

Harding, Sandra 1995: Can Feminist Thought Make Economics More Objective? *Feminist Economics* 1 (1), 7–32.

Harvey, David 1989: *The Condition of Postmodernity*. Oxford: Basil Blackwell.

Heims, Steve Joshua 1993: *Constructing a Social Science for Postwar America: The Cybernetics Group, 1946–1953*. Cambridge, MA: MIT Press.

Kissinger, Henry 1994: *Diplomacy*. New York: Simon and Schuster.

Lash, Scott 1993: Reflexive Modernization: The Aesthetic Dimension. *Theory, Culture & Society*, 10, 1–23.

McCloskey, Donald 1995: Comment. *Feminist Economics*, 1 (2).

Marcus, George E. 1992: Review of Writing Worlds: Discourse, Text and Metaphor in the Representation of Landscape, edited by T. J. Barnes and J. S. Duncan. *Society & Space*, 10 (3), 361–63.

——— 1995: Ethnography in/of the World System: The Emergence of Multisited Ethnography. *Annual Review of Anthropology*, 24, 95–117.

——— (ed.) n.d.: *Critical Anthropology in Fin-de-Siècle America: New Locations, Nonstandard Fieldwork*. Santa Fe: School of American Research Press.

Marcus, George E. and Cushman, Dick 1982: Ethnographies as Texts. *Annual Review of Anthropology*, 11, 25–69. Stanford: Annual Review Press.

Marcus, George E. and Fischer, Michael M. J. 1986: *Anthropology as Cultural Critique: An Experimental Moment in the Human Sciences*. Chicago: University of Chicago Press.

Piore, Michael and Sabel, Charles 1984: *The Second Industrial Divide*. New York: Basic Books.

Poundstone, William 1992: *Prisoner's Dilemma: John von Neumann, Game Theory, and the Puzzle of the Bomb*. New York: Doubleday.

Schultz, George P. 1993: *Turmoil and Triumph: My Years as Secretary of State*. New York: Scribners.

Strassman, Diana 1995: Editorial: Creating a Form for Feminist Economic Inquiry. *Feminist Economics*, 1 (1), 1–6.

Talbott, Strobe 1988: *The Master of the Game: Paul Nitze and the Nuclear Peace*. New York: Knopf.

Taussig, Michael 1992: *Mimesis and Alterity*. New York: Routledge.

Von Neumann, John and Morgenstern, Oscar 1944: *The Theory of Games and Economic Behavior*. Princeton: Princeton University Press.

Ten

Sticking with Ethnography through Thick and Thin (1997)[1]

THERE CAN BE little doubt that cultural anthropology in this country has been in a state of transition of major proportions. The most senior generation of anthropologists are clearly most pessimistic or worried about this, even with statements in sotto voce that anthropology is dying just as they produce their own last works.[2] I of course will want to offer a different, more nuanced view of the current situation. Belonging to the "coming-into-senior" cohort—those in their late forties and fifties—I want to express here a sense of this transition from a perspective of those who are identified as both having brought about the transition and are most directly experiencing it in their scholarly careers. We are scholars who began in one paradigm or research program and are now most definitely operating in another, of as yet undetermined contours.

In expressing this view, I want to assiduously avoid a prophetic or visionary rhetoric, or even a mode of overview and sober forecasting. Although visionary discourse is perhaps natural in truly transitional periods, I have often been engaged in this kind of discussion over the past decade, and am personally exhausted with it. And further, given the evoked stereotypic moods of fin-de-siècles—let alone a fin-de-millenium as well—full of ambivalent hope and pessimism, I am especially wary of "taking stock" discussions since the appetite for them is so hyperdeveloped at the moment.[3]

Instead, as in the title to this essay, I want to stick with ethnography in at least two senses. After all, it was the focus of the critique of more than ten years ago (see Clifford and Marcus 1986) that was in part thought out at the Institute for Advanced Study, and that articulated and brought into discussion this watershed transition of the discipline. Ethnography is still worth focusing on to understand more recent developments. Nothing has as yet displaced ethnography, the tradition encompassing both fieldwork and the writing that it engenders, as the key research practice and emblem of cultural anthropology as a distinctive form of knowledge production. A continuing reflection upon ethnography is no longer simply about the critique of anthropological authority in its traditional forms and rhetorical expressions, as it was in the 1980s. Rather, ethnography remains the ground for a continuing debate about form that is in the present really about the research practices themselves of anthropology, which are in transformation. There is just a lot more variety now in the nature of research projects that begin as ethnography, and in the textual forms that these are taking.

I want to give some systematic sense of these changes which represent the profound critique of anthropology of the 1980s working itself out in projects conducted under interdisciplinary ethos, or at least on the borders between anthropology and fields such as feminist studies, science studies, media studies, and cultural studies, rather than in the name of some debate or trend of theory that is by and for anthropologists as shaped by their previous century of controversies. In my view, this latter kind of centering of the discipline where it defines itself and its interests in continually renewing its tradition as such is gone forever. That tradition while still immensely valuable is reinvented in the diffusion and centrifugality of anthropologists' research interests, pulled by interdisciplinary movements external to its own historic definition. And this process can only now be glimpsed by attention to how ethnographic research is being reshaped in the playing out of careers.

In a second sense, then, I want to stick with ethnography to provide a micro view, a participant observer's sense, of these changes rather than a macro, prophetic one. Characteristic of ethnography, I want to understand the changes as a structure of professional experience, as practices, rather than as a major trend. We are at present rather "stuck" in transition, which would not be a good thing if we were perpetually "stuck," but being stuck is best understood by a kind of ethnographic perception where a trend is not foreseen beyond a close attention to change in disciplinary practices. I present the following commentary, then, as a set of related observations generated systematically from a key one that has struck me as the most important ethnographic "fact," so to speak, about the present transition. These all derive from what I have learned as an ethnographer from my routine professional activities—in particular, reviewing manuscripts for publishers, recruiting and training graduate students in my own doctoral program, reviewing cases for promotion—and engaging in the sort of corridor chat and gossip that gives me some continuing sense of the typicality or exceptionality of my perceptions.

If my own position in this exercise is distinctive in any way it is because I have been personally identified, among others, over the past decade with the 1980s critique of ethnography, and thus I have had a special interest and stake in gauging responses to the critique and assessing its legacies. I want to begin with an observation about a distinctive pattern in the development of research careers among my own cohort, and that is also characteristic of younger scholars coming into their own. It is both illustrative and symptomatic of the transition, and has, I believe, considerable ramifications, which I want to trace.

First Projects, Second Projects among the Coming-into-Senior Cohort and After

From the 1980s onward, I have become aware of an interesting career pattern among a striking number of the most noted anthropologists within my own and adjacent cohorts. There is a distinct break between first and second projects of research that surely has something to do with broadly changing trends, that in turn reflect the new intellectual capital that swept the human sciences from the late 1970s through the 1980s, but this characteristic of careers also has deep implications for anthropology's changing sense of its own identity. First projects of such anthropologists can be fully understood within the frame of stable disciplinary practices in place for the past fifty years and still define at least formally the categories by which choices of dissertation projects are channeled, jobs are defined, and curricula—especially undergraduate curricula—are shaped. Fieldwork with the aim of making a contribution to the world ethnographic archive divided into distinct culture areas (e.g., South Asia, Southeast Asia, Latin America, Oceania, Middle East), each with a distinctive history of anthropological discourse and trajectory of inquiry still orients graduate training, and certainly did so in the coming-to-senior cohort of which I am part. The initial training project of ethnographic research—two or more years of fieldwork in another language, dissertation write-up, followed by the publication of a monograph—constitutes the capital on which academic appointments are attained and then secured through tenure. As I will argue, these first career-making projects for current and younger scholars have changed dramatically even in conformity with the traditional mise-en-scène of anthropological research oriented to the cumulative archive. But for most of my own cohort—who are in their forties and fifties—at least these first projects were consistent with the variety of genres defined by the established discourses of the different culture areas before the distinctive break through 1980s critique of anthropological representation.

Since that period of critique, which spoke of the emergence of a trend of experimentation with the ethnographic genre, those who have looked for marked changes, worthy of the name "experiment," in first projects might have been disappointed. Maybe they have looked in the wrong place, since for my own cohort and the ones following, the most interesting source of experimentation in the conduct of research has occurred very commonly at the break point with the initial career-making and conservative-tending research project when the scholar attempts to do something very different than he or she was trained to do. Since the initial project, often lasting more than a decade, by no means achieves deep ethnographic mastery of another form of life even of research situated in a very focused space such as a village, town, or urban neighborhood, as most conventional fieldwork is, there has always been virtue attached to returning again and again to the original site of work and moving both geographically and conceptually beyond it in a painstaking manner. In contrast and more commonly these days, I find breaks with first projects to be real departures and de facto experiments both in the conception of research and in its production. Yet, since careers do not depend on such projects, they tend to be more quietly developed, more intensely personal, and more ambitious, and pursued less confidently. It is in the relatively silent production of second projects that the experimental trend, posited by the 1980s critique, exists on a broad scale in contemporary anthropology.

The basic problem of these projects is precisely that of redesigning the conventions of ethnography for unconventional purposes, sites, and subjects—particularly moving beyond the settled community as site of fieldwork toward dispersed phenomena that defy the way that classic ethnography has been framed and persuades. For example, moving from a study of Italian villagers to the multinational European Parliament, from the Amazon jungles to pain treatment centers in Boston, from a study of a Japanese factory to the international fashion industry, from the study of ancestor worship in village Taiwan to medical and popular understandings of bodies and the immune system, from Transylvanian villagers to Romanian intellectuals, from the study of Sherpas in Nepal to one's own high school class, from the study of an Australian aboriginal people to the circulation of aspects of their material culture as collectibles in Euro-American art worlds, and many more shifts of careers like these each involves testing the limits of the ethnographic paradigm, and especially altering the form of the ethnography and the conditions of fieldwork on which it is generated. While there has been much explicit debate about the critique and transformation of anthropology's central practice of ethnography, this transformation is actually occurring broadly in the quiet career predicament of evolving second projects, which is very much the predicament of how to work and conceptually write one's way out of a tradition that one both wants to preserve and change.

Most importantly, this transformation is occurring not so much within the space of disciplinary debates and discussions, but rather in that of various interdisciplinary arenas. Indeed, this most diverse and innovative work in anthropology is only barely or indirectly registered in self-identified disciplinary discussions. What was at one time the most marginal work in the field has become its most vital space of innovation, while the center, represented by first projects and the historic ethnographic archive of diverse peoples, has become increasingly fragmented and decoupled from historic questions about the nature of traditional societies in relation to modern ones. These questions have become specialized pursuits, among others, rather than continuing as the general orientation of anthropology's research program.

In cohorts younger than my own—among the thirtysomethings— who have managed to secure academic careers, the pattern that I have just described is even more prominent and compressed. Even as their first books are in press, many of these scholars are already engaged in second projects that differ markedly in style, orientation, and commitment from the first, and are shaped by interdisciplinary discussions of various sorts rather than by a sense of identification with a developing intellectual agenda strictly within disciplinary terms.[4] I am not suggesting that first projects of younger scholars are pro forma, or done under the duress of discipline. Rather, they are innovative contributions to a core disciplinary tradition, and indeed, this tradition is kept alive and sustained by these career-making first projects. But I would say that they are also both an homage and a parting tribute to that older tradition, and in many of the first books the transition to second projects of different sorts is legible. It is perhaps unique to anthropology that its core traditional context of work continues ironically to be produced through this powerful break or transition in the careers of its best scholars.[5]

This increasingly distinctive break in the patterning of research careers should also be seen for its implication in contemporary graduate training. Often, it is the second projects of senior and established scholars that are "a lure to the talents," so to speak, in combination with the stimulation of interdisciplinary trends. But training modes and curricula in anthropology are still defined and shaped by its core tradition. This defines an obvious dissonance and tension for both teachers and students in most departments. The overwhelming tendency is to reproduce students and projects according to the central tendency of the discipline, with shadings of difference and innovation negotiated into the construction of the dissertation project. In any case, this tension is being negotiated, sometimes productively, sometimes not, in every major graduate program in cultural anthropology. If there is a central debate that animates departments these days it concerns mediating the two kinds of research endeavors that shape the careers of professors, and increasingly of graduate students in every major department—determining its identity and at the same time the discipline's. This debate is about both the limits and resilience of ethnography and anthropology's traditional research process rooted in fieldwork. It is reflected in the flux of graduate teaching—what to teach, what to have students read, to what degree the teaching involves sustaining the first-second project distinction that I have described, or bridging it.

The First Books of Younger Scholars

As noted, first books of younger scholars are by no means passive contributions to the tradition of the ethnographic archive. Indeed, for many culture areas, they represent the efflorescence of long-standing traditions of writing, bringing new ideas and concepts to provide magisterial discussions of very old tropes and discourses in these culture area domains (note, for example, the concern with gender replacing kinship studies, studies of the person and emotions opening up areas of experience never probed as deeply in earlier ethnography, and the focus on popular culture and media displacing previous tropes that dominated the ethnography of particular regions, such as hierarchy for India, or honor and shame for the Mediterranean). But this is efflorescence perhaps at the end of a tradition about writing about peoples largely outside of history. The line of current innovation in the traditional arena of the ethnographic archive is the massive historicization of the previous subjects of study of ethnography under the influence of recent movements of cultural critique, especially colonial/postcolonial discourse studies. This represents an alliance with history, and critiques of representation to preserve the subject, rationale, and methods of cultural anthropology. These are progressive projects within the traditional domain and show the influence of new intellectual capital coming from outside anthropology on its central tendencies.

These progressive works within the traditional mise-en-scène of ethnography nonetheless begin to evidence interesting shifts signaling the more radical departures from the ethnographic paradigm in second and later projects. I have registered this especially in my reading of manuscripts as first books for either press reviews prior to acceptance for publication or promotion cases. I want to mention here two tendencies in the form of first books that signal the deeper transition that I have alluded to beyond merely the progressive remaking of the tradition.

First, there is the work, rich in ethnography and theory, that is over-
burdened by theory. That is, I often read manuscripts in which there is
a problem of "fit" between the ethnography presented, and the aspiration of the theory-framed argument. Often, the fieldwork was done
under the more traditional regime, and the material collected and
available does not directly address a theoretical interest that was either
acquired later or for which anthropological training provides no guide
as to conducting the fieldwork that would be cogent in relation to it.
Regardless of theoretical interest, most fieldwork is oriented toward the
long history of functionalist concerns in anthropology so that little
fieldwork in the traditional program is conceived to answer or work
through questions that would require a different kind of research design and agenda. This problem of adapting ethnography becomes explicit, and less resolved in second projects by the awkward conjoining
of a framing argument under one inspiration and a research process
undertaken with different and contradictory deep assumptions.

For instance, as an example of this symptomatic lack of fit, I read an
excellent manuscript on agricultural reform and policy at the grass-
roots in India, that was informed by postcolonial theories of the state in
India. Yet, the fieldwork, largely oriented to understanding changes at
the local level, and not where issues of the state were of primary concern, could not fully support the quite stimulating theoretical reflections that framed the ethnography. So here is a first book legitimated
within a traditional domain of anthropology, yet out of line with the
theory that most motivates it.

Another work, worth noting in this regard, is Anna Tsing's much
discussed *In the Realm of the Diamond Queen* (1993) since it is explicitly
conceived as an effort to bring the ethnography of an out-of-the-way
place (but in a much written about and well-troped part of the traditional ethnographic archive) to bear on the concerns of "theory" of
interdisciplinary realms affecting contemporary anthropology. It thoroughly examines in the anthropologist-subject relation within the traditional mise-en-scène of fieldwork the idea of marginality—its prag-
matics and imaginaries—as a contribution both to theory and the
ethnographic archive. It is self-consciously and experimentally in this
regard a transitional work produced as a first book.

The other kind of first work that signals the second project is the
text of connected chapters, rooted in a focused fieldwork experience,
but ranging widely beyond it and diverse in its concerns. It is as if
ethnography is the legitimating anchor of the work, demonstrating a
traditional kind of "I was there" authority but then its concerns migrate
beyond the locus of a village or community where most of the fieldwork period was spent. For example, I read recently a manuscript on

contemporary China which covers various interesting topics, a chapter on debates about population policy, a chapter on a case of an impostor that was made known in newspapers and caused quite a stir, among others. There was one solid traditional ethnographic chapter from village fieldwork on exchange and gender relations—topics which have been important in defining the tradition of ethnographic work on village China. There were a number of themes that skillfully held the studies of this volume together, but the form itself of a fragmented and multi-sited set of "studies" in which the traditional ethnography is only one mode of analysis among others is what is diagnostic of transition in this work. It is as if the author chose to write about many things tangential to the focused ethnography of her original research plan. Texts of "related studies" like this one that discover a new space of investigation from a beginning as a traditional fieldwork research design are increasingly common as first works, and again, signal the less certain, more venturesome conditions fully explored in second projects.

Before passing onto these conditions, I should say that first books while they look progressively backward do not mark an end to area specialization. Anthropologists who later shift radically to studies in their own society, or elsewhere as second projects, tend to maintain a continuing interest in area studies—investments in an area scholar identity continue to be worth a lot professionally—but this becomes a secondary interest, a lost first love to be met again at various times. Or they sustain work in the same area, but it is not done in a traditional area studies frame. Rather, it is developed in a far more interdisciplinary and transcultural comparative cultural context instead of in terms of the aims of the ethnographic archive available for the topics that have defined a science of "Man." So while second projects sometimes take place in the same area—Japan, China, the Middle East, South Asia, etc.—of the first, they are informed by issues that are distinctly outside the tradition of area studies. In any case, the impetus giving rise to second projects where they occur in the same area or repatriate themselves is radically different from the older idea of developing second projects continuously out of the base of first, career-defining projects.

The Uncertain Conditions of Second Projects

The key genre of the second project among my coming-into-senior cohort is the essay collection. While these second projects may eventually generate recognizably professional monographs, as just one kind of output, they tend to be reflected more commonly and much earlier by collected essays. And these essays, far from indicating a resoluton of these second projects in writing, suggest instead a hesitation, even reluctance, about how to write-up such research in encompassing forms that evoke the traditional ethnography. Such collections may be seen as "on the way to" or just "in the meantime" in relation to such projects.

In the past, essay collections were the prerogative of the most senior scholars nearing the end of their careers and summing up certain themes tangential or in the interstices of the production of major monographs—they were definitely supplementary. Now such collections are published routinely by younger scholars. Early on, in the midst of second projects, they collect "reports" on a project hard to grasp otherwise, and are written for occasions—invited seminars, invited lectures, etc.—rather than independently stimulated by a personal writing regime.[6] If there were not such occasions, one might ask whether the work would be written at all in any conventional way for academic disciplinary communities. Such essay collections thus reflect the uncertainty of conditions that produce second projects. They are "reports to the academy" about evolving projects of uncertain relation to the traditional frame of anthropological research. The form of the fieldwork and the book are both in productive question.

Second projects arise partly out of the intellectual capital that has powerfully critiqued human science disciplines over the past decade, mostly through calling into question past means of representation and taken for granted conceptual apparatuses. The result has been analysis more comfortable with multiplicity and difference within past senses of unity and coherence of concepts. This concern with the discovery of ramifying difference of course has an appeal for anthropology's long-term ethnographic project. Yet, the shape of second projects would merely be the result of the influence of an intellectual trend, or even fashion, if it weren't for the fact that the traditional subjects and objects of anthropological study were literally changing and that these subjects themselves were becoming more reflexive, even more self-consciously deconstructive, about their own forms of life. It thus certainly makes sense for anthropology in this era to be involved in these transformations by means of intellectual capital that parallels in its deconstructive tendencies the changes in the subjects, peoples, and cultural processes in which anthropology has always been interested. These second projects then represent most clearly as much an empirical imperative for the discipline as an intellectual transformation alone.

There are at least two features that are distinctive of second projects. First, they are generated out of undisguised passion, identification, or some clear personal connection, more than through given repertoires of study in disciplinary research programs. Method in these projects is a matter of shaping the personal into the objective and shared discourses of scholarly communities.[7] Second, these projects, while familiarly beginning with ethnographic foci conceived within the site-specific mise-en-scène of traditional anthropological research, demand elaboration and expansion by ethnographic means into other realms and literal places, challenging the coherence of the specified ethnographic object. This leads to a multi-sited work which deserves some discussion since it most challenges the limits and sense of what anthropology can do within its traditional frame of fieldwork and ethnography. Second projects literally move over discontinuous realms of social space in order to describe and interpret cultural formations that can only be understood in this way. Now they must understand the operations of institutions (e.g., information systems, corporate cultures, media technologies) as much as the modalities of everyday life lived in communities and domestic spaces, which have been the most usual sites of anthropological study. Single projects must traverse and work through systems and lifeworlds in the very same frame, needing to keep eyes on both institutions and everyday worlds in transcultural space. And this greater ambition evident in second projects adds immense scope and complexity to traditional research processes.

The fieldwork case was made explicitly or implicitly for the old ethnographic archive and the largely nineteenth-century questions about "Man" that it informed. Historicizing ethnographic traditions in their colonial and postcolonial contexts have updated this pursuit of the anthropology of peoples. But outside the old ethnographic archive, it is uncertain what the mere ethnographic case informs. Often the ethnographic case is a supplement to someone else's framework, be it the public or other fields in the ecology of disciplines. In second projects, the nature of the ethnography as a mere case or instance is dissolved in the ambition to understand and map an object of study in all of its disseminations and traces—recognizing cultural formations that are both local and in circulation. A full study of the modalities of such formations requires that the ethnography, or the evolved research project from the ethnographic base, conceive different forms of research relations and expectations.

I want to give some sense of the changing practices of research required to map multi-sited objects of study and what this means for the bulwark of fieldwork-ethnographic process which is important ideologically and pragmatically in sustaining the self-identity of anthropology in this transitional moment. The possibilities signaled by second projects, their uncertain conditions and forms, around multi-sited objects, establish a center of discussion in anthropology that generates both excitement and anxiety (with worries about the limits and definition of the field) to which we will return later.

Second projects involve anthropologists in domains of study where they are not the only ones producing representations. This is a key fact and recognition that can no longer be evaded by the assertion of a disciplinary authority and privilege (the weakening of anthropology's capacity to bound and justify its own representations was one of the major effects, for better or worse, depending on your interests, of the 1980s critiques). Often their specific subjects are producing representations that have a resemblance to the anthropologists' own. In fact many of the spaces in which anthropologists work call into question the use and value of anthropological representation. The active constituencies for anthropological study also overlap with its subjects. This requires a different definition of relationship with subjects and the media in which they are involved. I have discussed this elsewhere as ethnographers being involved with and submerged in other writing machines than their own. Anthropologists compete in the same space with other scholars, journalists, pervasive visual and print media, and the representations of the subjects themselves. As Sherry Ortner remarked to me, the others that we choose now tend to be more in the same business that we're in: one form or another of cultural production. Both they and we tend to be engaged in some variant or other of the business of trying to talk about the hard-to-grasp world.

Anthropological authority is no longer a purely academic or disciplinary matter, since the representations that anthropologists produce overlap and are shared with those they study. Anthropologists find themselves in collaborations rather than create them out of their defined and controlled field projects in their traditional mise-en-scène.[8] And the de facto collaborations of second projects involve a different sense of ethics and politics of research than those discussed for traditional projects of ethnography. As anthropologists move in and out of different sites, as identities shift, among, say, elites and others of lesser standing who are in complex relation to them, the coherence of the anthropological project is in constant question and only is rescued in disciplinary terms by the forging of second projects as a part of a revised practice of research and sense of problem in anthropology.[9]

The issues developed in second projects are built from the inherent advantage of special personal interest and connection, objectified for academic communities into ethnographic projects of undefined parameters. This is where the new research modalities are being formed in anthropology's participation in science studies, media studies, policy studies, and cultural studies.

The professional anthropological constituency for these second projects is only one, among others, but a key one, since it legitimates the work being done, gives it purpose as knowledge, and connects it to a tradition of scholarship. The mainstream response in anthropology to second projects is one of openness, excitement, and anxiety—a tendency to see them as marginal. But understanding this work in the frame of its multiple constituencies might perhaps relieve the sense of anxiety and malaise and perhaps allow it to be normalized.

For anthropologists who view the arena of second projects as personal and relatively undisciplined, as not quite anthropology, what does seem to be lost at present for them is a certain accountability that did exist in the past among anthropologists themselves. Missing is a community of sustained discussion among anthropologists which provides a scrutiny of the integrity of ethnographic facts, constructed in the work of individual scholars. The community of discourse has been interrupted such that the close assessment of arguments and ethnographic claims has been curtailed. There are no debates that depend on sustained empirical testing—nothing like a center of argument such that any claims get considered for very long. For example, there is nothing like the old debates of kinship, for which the British were known. Perhaps we do not want the return of such debates in the same manner and on the same topics, but we probably do want something to fill that space, if only because we want to share each other's current work in a more substantial way.

I think that the loss of this style or mechanism for discussion has been perceived as a loss of science, objectivity, rigor, etc., and the influence of the humanities (the dreaded postmodernism, the literary turn, followed by cultural studies) is held responsible. For myself, I am not sure that this is the loss of science in any general sense, but it is certainly the loss of intellectual weight in the old center of the discipline. And perhaps in a very specific sense this is indeed a loss of science in the practice of anthropology in the only way that science ever had meaning in anthropology anyhow. Beautiful theories have given rise to beautiful monographs in which the aesthetics of argument, their moral power, and their manner of achieving these—their exemplariness—are judged more closely than their content. Each work's value is judged by what it comes to stand for, or symbolize. Thus, a certain art world–like practice of critique and assessment of individual works has substituted for an older style of sustained assessment of shared objects of study which overwhelm the capacity of individual works to define their own unique objects of study in their own way. It is this attenuated condition of the discursive community in anthropology that is more precisely at stake in any feelings within the anthropological mainstream that the discipline is in decline.

But this account is only of the old center of the field and has little capacity to tell us much about how the most innovative and adaptive projects of research are evolving among anthropologists—that is, in the arena of second projects. In 1994, I participated in a School of American Research advanced seminar (the same venue that in 1984 produced *Writing Culture*) which turned out to be about the evolution of contemporary research topics in anthropology in unexpected contexts, among shifting constituencies, and according to new agendas. The participants all had worked in U.S. society on the study of complex cultural and social formations that spanned institutional orders as well as everyday life situations of subjects located outside such orders. Subjects of study ranged from the Waco/Branch Davidian affair, to the emergence of PCR technology, to the issue of intellectual property and the NET, to the origins of the "Generation X" category, to the situation in Union Carbide after Bhopal, to family values politics, to the massive expansion of the non-profit sector in the U.S. In each case, the collapse of "system" and "lifeworld" dimensions within the same frame of research required the modification of standard ways of situating ethnography. While most of the participants had been influenced by recent critiques of representation and objectivity in anthropology, all had originally planned their work in conventional ways that have consistently defined the data, descriptions, and arguments of any past anthropology that its practitioners had deemed "scientific." But, the traditional distance of the ethnographer became impossible to sustain in locations which had already been thoroughly treated by the representations and writings of others, some of whom came close to the role and function of ethnographers themselves. Mainly, media representations and legal discourse had been there first, so to speak. And in each case, the anthropologists had to pass through and negotiate a discursive space with these other representations in order to form his or her own by writing that derives from the distinctive process of classic participant observation. But this passing through and negotiation of other representations of a defined subject of study turned out to be thoroughly transformative.

Participants in the seminar found circumstantially they could no longer constitute themselves as "anthropologist" in relation to "subject." Instead, they became activists in spite of themselves as a function of operating across a number of sites of fieldwork, in each of which they tried to act as ethnographers, with often mixed success. The profound politics of knowledge involved in weaving together the unanticipated fragments and pieces defined by the trajectory of such projects has led in each case to a highly activist practice of anthropology, defined not by commitment to some external social movement or by the self-image of the committed intellectual in some imagined vanguard role, but purely by the involvements and uneven interventions internal to research that becomes multi-sited in the ethnographic pursuit of discontinuous social and cultural processes amid dense and diverse genres of already existing descriptions and analyses. Figuring out and representing the relationships that compose the resulting assemblage out of disjointed fieldwork have unavoidable political implications internal and external to the conditions of research.

I think that in the future such projects of research that very much have the present quality of muddling through, having started off with very different assumptions and expectations, will be very much a matter of design and innovation as anthropology revises its emblematic methods. Is this anthropology any less scientific than it has ever been? I think not. In any case, it need not be. What remains to be seen is whether anthropologists can reestablish any centers of substantial discussion among themselves that will create the rich and dense internal assessment of their own work, comparable to the past. Will anthropologists have the capacity to fascinate themselves once again with their new locations, methods, and objects of study as much as they have been able to fascinate other constituencies involved in the complex terrains in which anthropological work now haphazardly intervenes and will soon be more systematically conceived?

Thus, it is not that anthropology is vacant of focusing and self-identifying debates, but that these occur on its borders with other constituencies. Anthropology participates strongly in these spaces, and there is no way that it could if its contributions were not distinctive and valuable for these constituencies. The problem is to register and legitimate this development of anthropology on its borders within the heart of the discipline itself.

As noted, there remains a sector of work in anthropology that is defined by the discipline's historic questions in which the ethnographic archive still has uses as cases for others and for the general questions about humankind that anthropology itself has always asked. But this sector can no longer focus and centralize the discipline, however much it should remain a vital part of the field. Outside the effective contextualization of this historic center of the discipline, the meaning and use of ethnographies are left to others. The great advantage of second projects is that they build their own contexts of significance— they don't factor in political economy or history, but construct these contexts as part of the scholarship of the case. They resist the idea of the ethnography as *merely* a case. As a result, anthropologists find themselves in much more interesting domains of discussion—ethnography becomes not just the data, case, or support for someone's argument, but it becomes the engine of major argument itself, pushing itself into new contexts of interpretation and levels of debate. As its relation to other "writing machines" changes so does the identity of anthropological knowledge itself—not as the marginal, the exotic, the extreme case, but as cultural accounts of spaces that have not had them. This is the promise of second projects once they are recognized by the discipline as more than addenda to the regime of first projects in which anthropology's traditions of work have been reproduced up to now.

Anxieties and Adaptations

Finally, I want to discuss the sense of anxiety to which developments that I have described have given rise among many anthropologists. Second projects, and changes in first ones as well, under new intellectual influences and widespread recognition of the transformed ways that the empirical objects of anthropological research in the world are being constituted have generated considerable fear about the loss of integrity and effectiveness of the ethnographic form and process, governed by their traditional rhetorics and regulative ideals. I want to address here the state of this mood by focusing on the issue of the seeming loss of "depth" or substance in fieldwork-based ethnography as the conditions of multi-sited research in second projects emerge more prominently. To do so, I want to report on a conversation I had with James Clifford about this prior to the 1996 American Anthropological Association meetings.

Clifford said that the practical problem of sustaining fieldwork in multi-sites is the loss of depth of interaction, on which the entire ideology and ethos of fieldwork has depended in anthropology. His point is that the criterion of "depth" has been at the heart of anthropology's sense of itself as a profession. On its evaluation has rested anthropology's sense of standards—how well do you know the language? How long did you live among the X?

This set off the following ruminations on my part. The first question I had was: depth for what kind of knowledge and in relation to what kind of self-identified community of anthropologists? Both of these factors have changed dramatically in the practice of anthropology over the past decade, and therefore the issue of depth has to be thought about in different terms.

If it is the traditional Malinowski model concerning the virtues of depth in fieldwork, the specific terms in which this is defined is to attain a functionalist knowledge of another way of life by a complete outsider who goes through the process of "passing," of becoming a fictive native through achieving "rapport" with those among whom he lives in order to eventually convert information from the native's point of view into a form of professional knowledge. However, after the critique of the 1980s, depth is no longer the modality for getting at certain agreed upon functionalist topics such as kinship, ritual, religion, etc. Rather, depth is understood as interpretations of cultural experience—ideas about subjectivity, personhood, the emotions. This is a much more demanding sort of depth required of ethnography—one that goes beyond the ability to respond in detail to the "Notes and Queries" inventory that defined classic ethnography. It is a kind of depth that challenges sensibility; knowledge and the understanding of experience in a particular way of life become much more intimately entwined. And this leads to much greater pressure on what methodologically and personally was required in the past of mostly Euro-American anthropologists working among mostly non-Euro-american peoples.

As such, the standard of depth in ethnography must be understood with reference to a differently identified community of scholars in relation to subjects. This is a result of the emphasis on reflexivity—of the personal—in the construction and design of ethnographic projects. Identity questions (and politics) have thus entered, for better or worse, into the way that ethnography is shaped (cf. Lila Abu-Lughod's well-known paper, 1991, on "halfies"). The old question of *depth* in the creation of functionalist ethnographies by complete outsiders is now mediated by questions of *identity*—the anthropologist's preexisting extent of relationship and connection—to the object of study. Indeed, in very pragmatic terms, it is very much the case as I can attest from tendencies in my own graduate program that ethnic affiliations and identities give students an immense advantage in shaping research within traditional area studies. There is control of language and a well of life experience that are great assets for achieving the sort of depth that anthropologists have always hoped for from one- to two-year fieldwork projects, especially when the analytic categories of cultural analysis are much more now about the nature of experience across cultures than about the functioning of institutions.

Indeed, very few people are recruited now from Kansas, for example, to work in the Middle East or South Asia. Such students, unless extraordinarily gifted, are at a comparative disadvantage in relation, say, to diasporic South Asians from Canada who wish to develop fieldwork in India. It is not so much that the former "natives" are now becoming anthropologists, but rather that the demography of anthropologists themselves is far more cosmopolitan than ever before. And this fact is combined with the trend in which objects of study are becoming more transcultural such that the demands on the fieldworker for depth and breadth are much greater than ever before. In some ways, only cosmopolitan fieldworkers with fluency in more than one language and who are at home, or at least familiar, with several culturally distinct places through their autobiographies can meet the challenge of developing a satisfying sense of depth of ethnography in the trend of second projects. Indeed, perhaps this is the reason why so many ambitious second projects by U.S. anthropologists are "repatriated."[10]

Envoi

The challenge of this essay has been not less than that of classic ethnographic puzzles of traditional social organization that anthropologists used to face in figuring out, for example, double descent, kula rings, acephalous segmentary lineage systems, or matrilineal kinship. The transitional predicament in anthropology is as complex and unfamiliar. For the present, and for the foreseeable future, from the way that prominent research careers, patterns of publication, and relations in graduate training are unfolding, we can posit two creative engines of production institutionally shaping cultural anthropology. What makes these modes complex is that they overlap in careers rather than run parallel in their own spaces. While they thus may institutionally be in awkward association, causing some sense of displacement and anxiety for individuals, defining of particular generations, situation, and commitments as to what the limits or boundaries of anthropology are, they are both fully in line with cultural anthropology's historic evolution as a field. The dual identity of cultural anthropology is by no means schizophrenic, but fulfills a promise that it has long had within it. Its present condition is not a perfect, internally coherent knowledge machine—far from it—but it is a vibrant sustainable one.

What is reconfiguring are the traditional valences in the discipline of center/periphery and the hierarchy of priority between these two projects within anthropology. I personally find the developments in one more interesting than in the other—the one that defines itself in more experimental terms and has more explicit tolerance for the uncertain conditions of its production, that is, the anthropology now most strongly being developed as second career projects in the interdisciplinary arenas of science studies, media studies, and cultural studies, broadly conceived.

As I have attempted to outline, the one project marks the efflorescence at dusk of the traditional ethnographic project in anthropology
but ironically freed of its moorings in a century of historic controversy
and debate. This has made for the uneasy contemporary atmosphere
of continuing to build the historic ethnographic archive but without a
firm sense of what that archive is for. This is by no means a static engine of production in contemporary anthropology—it is infused with
new ideas but worked out within a traditional sense of the field. Its
ecology, at least formally, is still that of its association with the other
major subfields of anthropology—archaeology and biological anthropology—and it is paced by slowly changing categories and a sense of
continuity with the past. Within this regime of production, students are
led to specialization by existing problematics within the discipline,
however restated under the influence of external trends, rather than
being pushed by a spirit to bring the discipline to problematics the
formulation with which it is relatively unfamiliar. But as I have tried to
indicate, even in this self-consciously traditional domain of production,
there are distinctly new configurations, for example, the alliances with
history and critiques of representation in the arena of postcolonial
studies, and the importance of identity and reflexivity as new modalities for assuring the depth and substance of ethnography.

These changes are centrifugal in direction, so that one of the characteristics of the period is the relative absence of focusing debates among
anthropologists, and the eerie silence of its own professional public
sphere. This is perhaps the most unnerving of anthropology's contemporary conditions. For example, whereas fifteen years ago, the recent
lively debate between Gananath Obeyesekere (1992) and Marshall
Sahlins (1995), two of the most distinguished anthropologists of the
present senior generation, over their Captain Cook/Hawaii researches
would not only have been noted by virtually all cultural anthropologists, but it would have been the subject of intense interest and elaboration as well. Today, however, while the controversy has been a matter of widespread note among anthropologists, it has hardly been a
touchstone of ramifying debate and intense intellectual interest across
the discipline. It is a classic controversy conducted with great brilliance,
but in the absence of classic response. Indeed, this controversy is a
surrogate for a debate of much more intense interest having to do with
the confrontation between anthropology's traditional modes of cultural analysis and that of cultural studies, but it only registers it lightly.
So what at one time would have advanced the solidarity of the field in
dialogue, no longer works effectively to do so. And nothing else does.
There are many specialized discussions and debates within the disci-

pline arising from the multiplicity of subfields and specialities, but no longer any discourse at the center that self-consciously engages the identity of the discipline as such.

Of course, such debates and discussions are not absent altogether. They are only absent within the traditional sense of a strictly disciplinary identity in terms of its own history, of and for itself (and here, as noted, they are registered indirectly by surrogates as in the recent case of Obeyesekere and Sahlins). Rather, the core debates that now define anthropology are on its boundaries and peripheries as it diversely revises and re-creates its modes of research, writing, and regulative ideals and as it establishes effective forms of authority in its participation in various interdisciplinary spheres such as science and media studies. This is what the conditions of production of second projects—the other creative engine to which I referred and in which many anthropologists are sooner or later involved in their career paths—develop.[11]

Expanding on my opening observation of the unusual pattern of contemporary careers, we can see that anthropology is developing from two structures of authority, but in which its achievements and innovations on its borders are the more powerful source of its authority as a field of knowledge than the thoroughly fragmented situation of its tradition. Anthropology, then, is perhaps unique in drawing on interdisciplinary participations to continue to define a distinctly disciplinary authority for itself.

Does this condition of cultural anthropology foretell its death as a discipline or its dissolution into postmodern surfaces? Hardly, on either account. Rather, anthropology is becoming perhaps the first human science of this era that lives with its own tradition and builds new forms of authority as well, based on interdisciplinary participations of various sorts. Of course, a strong internal politics of anxiety accompanies this transition, but that has always existed to some degree in anthropology, in less millenial moments, and in every generational transition which reflects unfulfilled personal longings and power shifts played out as familial drama. Indeed, anthropology may be less easily positioned or identifiable to its publics and constituencies, which increasingly overlap with the subjects and found collaborations that define its new research programs. But what matters is that anthropology's peculiar dual relation of a fragmented core tradition and experiment on its borders—manifested in the break between first and second projects in contemporary individual career paths—be sustained with vitality, open-mindedness, curiosity, and above all, tolerance for complex organization in the production of knowledge.

Notes

1. This is a slightly revised version of a paper I presented at the 25th Anniversary Conference of the School of Social Science at the Institute for Advanced Study, Princeton, N.J., in May 1997. Each discipline had its speaker, invited from among past visiting members at the Institute.

2. I do not believe anthropology as it has been known is dying, but there are displacements—such classic issues as cannibalism arising from the study of tribal societies continue to be worked on, but do not remain a center of gravity for the discipline. At their most vocal, a number of senior anthropologists feel that anthropology has been lost to the anti-science, so-called postmodern crowd. Here, I hope to demonstrate that the perceived loss of science in cultural anthropology is more precisely a complaint about the loss of a community of sustained discussion among anthropologists focused on a common object of study in which ethnographies focus issues, and get sustained scrutiny and discussion. The community of discourse has indeed been interrupted such that the close assessment of arguments and ethnographic claims has been curtailed, but this is not strictly the loss of science. I find the intention and design of most current anthropological projects to be as objective, empirical, and scientific as they were in the past—in the only way that science was ever practiced in anthropology.

3. Since 1992, I have originated and been involved in editing the *Late Editions* series of annuals published by the University of Chicago Press, with the final volume to appear in the year 2000 (see the first volume, Marcus, 1993, for the series' rationale; there are currently five volumes published and three more in various stages of preparation). These volumes do evoke the fin-de-siècle, but they also avoid prophetic, forecasting discourses that savor the moment of transformation either in terms of marveling or of fear and loathing. Rather, we opt in the series for in-depth ethnographic interviews, for expressions and exposures in diverse contexts of the great changes in process. I develop my remarks here in the same spirit about perceiving a major transition in anthropology through ethnographic-style close observation of disciplinary practices.

4. I do not want to give the impression that the distinction here is simply: first project means work in a traditional culture area abroad; second project means work back home in one's own society, that is, the U.S. For my own cohort, this distinction seems to hold more regularly. But what is really being reflected in second projects is (1) the adaptation of the core disciplinary tradition to the new theoretical capital developed largely in the West in interdisciplinary arenas such as feminist studies, science studies, media studies, and cultural studies, and (2) the generation of projects out of personal agendas and knowledge of cultural contexts (this involves generating ethnographic projects from biography and autobiography, but it does not imply literally writing autobiography which many anthropologists have come to see as self-indulgent when it is not uniquely powerful). This of course has meant involvement with one's own society and its issues in second projects, but the composition of anthropology is more diverse and self-consciously diverse under the influence

of identity discourses and those of postcolonial theory. Therefore, second projects are often conceived in terms of transcultural or transnational spaces, rather than simply in terms of the distinction between work back home and work over there. This mode of thinking about research raises much more difficult methodological questions for anthropology than merely "repatriation," from say, first projects in New Guinea, to say, second projects in the U.S.

5. As the differences marked by second projects become more institutionally developed and as more careers are "made" on these sorts of projects, they will become characteristic of first projects. But this is not the present situation of protracted transition or of the foreseeable future. What generates second projects is not institutionalized in how department cultures are currently constituted. With some exceptions, work in the U.S. or in interdisciplinary arenas such as science studies, or with forms of ethnography that do not arise out of long-term situated fieldwork is still marginalized, however much the prestige of and curiosity about such projects are increasing. My own department is an exception in that we normalize in graduate training a much wider range of dissertation projects—projects defined more by an interdisciplinary rather than disciplinary influence—and our challenge is to adapt the disciplinary tradition to them, rather than to continue to test these projects against some central tendency of the discipline. We do, however, always counsel students about the career risk of doing this, while at the same time suggesting that for intellectual reasons the risk is perhaps worth taking.

6. Of course one could say that the essay genre is an artifact of the whole hyped-up celebrity system that cultural studies has brought about, where scholars are increasingly kept busy on speaking/conference circuits. Maybe so. But this does not preclude the "writing" or "genre" problem as an intellectual predicament of the second project. Indeed, it is unclear how much writing at all would get done, if the celebrity circuit did not create opportunities for essays.

7. The debates or controversies over second projects are often about their form and style, the level of tolerance for incomplete remakings of the personal into a variety of genres—personal narratives, stories, and the like, that are unfamiliar to mainstream objectifying discourses of social science writing.

8. In the 1980s critique, showing the de facto collaborative basis of ethnography was an attempt to give informants voice and a partnership in the explicit creation of knowledge which had elided or marginalized such participation. The current situation is quite different in that collaboration is neither a choice nor a prerogative of the anthropologist to give in a definition of the relationships which he controls; rather, it is a question of giving, taking, and sharing representations in collaborations that evolve in different ways and not strictly in the frame of the controlled definition of fieldwork. (See Marcus 1997.)

9. There are today interesting discussions of the different sorts of methods needed to work in institutions rather than in villages and neighborhoods, among elites and notables rather than among those who take you in. For example, I attended a seminar recently on "shadowing," the "fly on the wall technique" of following for extensive periods of time officials and other notables without really being in interaction with them. There is quite a different pres-

ence and ethics to this than living with subjects, yet current projects combine both with different sets of subjects in different settings.

10. Of course, there is a very sensitive matter about exclusion, and a certain kind of ethnicism or racialism in this development—crudely that "it takes one to know one." The practical point is that there is an immense *potential* advantage to studying places and peoples with which you are already familiar, even though you are methodologically required to make this familiarity strange or distant. The less innocent side of this trend is something that anthropologists have only been indirectly willing to discuss thus far, and it is what fuels the growing dissatisfaction with identity politics, at least in the U.S. context of cultural studies. Only a rigorous openness to the talents, regardless of connection, can keep the ethnicist implication of this tendency controlled.

It is clear in my own graduate program that a person follows a personal line to a research project, but we insist on distance or a complex engagement with that connection rather than arguing indulgently in terms of it. But there is no question that depth of the traditional, impersonal, and professional sort (*any* person learning *any* language, crossing *any* cultural boundary) cannot equal the depth created by the reflexive production of research through a given identity or personal connection in the control of cultural detail and nuance.

In some sense, by crafting research out of personal history, the "ante" on depth has been raised which could never be matched by anthropologists of the West studying the non-West. The community of anthropologists is far more diverse now in composition and self-identifications, and ideologically so as well. Old standards still reign, but the projects with the complexity of second projects require a level of commitment and language knowledge that can only be developed through the turning of the reflexive mode, explicitly realized, but not dwelt upon as such, into a theater of inquiry.

11. Of all of anthropology's established subfields, medical anthropology is perhaps the most prosperous, and not only because it ties itself to the prestige of medicine as a science and institution. Rather, it bridges effectively both engines of production. It is a major context in which the traditional ethnographic archive continues to be developed, in its newer progressive forms, and it also has been the main channel for anthropology to participate in the interdisciplinary domain of science studies, for example, through the research on reproductive technologies, in turn strongly mediated by work in feminist and gender studies. Medical anthropology develops its own subfield debates, but it also creates new generalized authority for anthropology through its interdisciplinary participations.

References

Abu-Lughod, Lila. 1991. "Writing Against Culture," in *Recapturing Anthropology*. Ed. by Richard Fox. Santa Fe: School of American Research Press.
Clifford, James and George E. Marcus, eds. 1986. *Writing Culture: The Poetics and Politics of Ethnography*. Berkeley: University of California Press.

Marcus, George E. 1993. "Introduction." *Late Editions 1 Perilous States: Conversations on Culture, Politics, and Nation.* Chicago: University of Chicago Press.

Marcus, George E. 1997. "The Uses of Complicity in the Changing Mise-en-Scène of Anthropological Fieldwork." *Representations*, no. 59, pp. 85–108.

Obeyesekere, Gananath. 1992. *The Apotheosis of Captain Cook: European Mythmaking in the Pacific.* Princeton: Princeton University Press.

Sahlins, Marshall. 1995. *How "Natives" Think: About Captain Cook, For Example.* Chicago: University of Chicago Press.

Tsing, Anna. 1993. *In the Realm of the Diamond Queen.* Princeton: Princeton University Press.

Index

postmodernism (*cont.*)
  as everyday life, 49, 53
  and modernism, 58, 76nn.2, 4
  in 1970s and 1980s, 88, 203
  and nuclear diplomats, 9, 92, 206–7,
    211, 212–26
  as object of study, 82, 86–89, 186–87
  as other, 181–82
  as Toyota of thought, 191
"Postmodernism in a Nominalist Frame:
    The Emergence and Diffusion of a
    Cultural Category," 184, 191
poststructuralists, 19, 36, 181, 182, 228n.4
Poundstone, William, 219
power, 42, 65, 79, 135–50. *See also* com-
    plicity; rapport
  of ancestral leader, 162, 171
  and cultural studies research, 8–9,
    27n.5
  of elites, 27n.9, 166–67
  as object of study, 19–20, 59, 197
  relations in the field, 120–21, 173
  trope of, in modernist ethnography,
    74–75
"Power and Dialogue in Ethnography:
    Marcel Griaule's Initiation,"
    128n.11
power/knowledge, 27n.5, 61, 86, 203–29
  defined, 204
predicament
  in anthropological writing, 182–87
  common, of ethnographer and sub-
    jects, 119
  of declining elites, 165
  of ethnographic subjects, 34, 79
  generational, of anthropology, 9, 25n.1,
    234, 247, 251n.6
  identity, 68–69
  local historical, 41–42
  of loss of systemic grasp of political
    economy, 81
  moral, as object of study, 19
  shared, of ethnographer and subject,
    58, 62, 118, 119
  of subalterns, 226
  of students, 4–5, 11
  transitional, in anthropology, 247
Predicament of Culture, 128n.6, 182
presence, 50, 128n.10, 228n.4, 252n.9
  of ethnographer in the field, 90, 99,
    119–20

of ethnographer in text, 62
metaphysics of, 36, 153, 154, 156, 157–
    58, 160n.3, 225
*Primate Visions: Gender, Race, and Nature in
    the World of Modern Science*, 188
primitives, 12, 153, 154, 159n.2, 168, 174.
    See also other; peoples
Princeton, New Jersey, 214, 219, 250n.1
prisoner's dilemma, 211, 212, 216, 218–
    26
processes, cultural. *See* cultural processes
production, cultural. *See* cultural produc-
    tion
production, knowledge. *See* knowledge,
    production of
professions, the, 50, 158, 162, 204
Public Culture (journal), 88, 129n.19
public, 15, 167–68
  and private, 64, 97
  spheres, 95
publishing, 192, 204, 232, 236–38

Rabinow, Paul, 41, 42, 43, 51, 72, 75n.1,
    88, 190
race, 59, 76n.2
RAND Corporation, 219–20
Rajchman, John, 184, 191
rapport, 6, 190, 246. *See also* complicity
  defined, 6, 105–6
  fiction of sustaining, 109–12
rationality, 154, 159n.2, 211, 218, 222. *See
    also* reason
Rationality and Relativism
readers, 12, 36, 72, 75, 130n.34, 189
  natives as, 210
  subjects as, 68
  Western, 155
reading, metaphor of, 186
Reagan, Ronald, 92, 214–15, 223–24,
    225
real, 62, 203, 217, 225
  changing, 225
  discourse of the, 217
  modernist sense of the, 68, 70, 184
realism, 217, 221, 228n.4
  ethnographic, 41, 59, 75, 159n.1, 214
  modernism as, 58
  new old, 40–42
  social, 39–40, 57–58
reason, 195–96, 211, 217
reception, 58, 68

George E. Marcus is professor and chair of the department of anthropology at Rice University where he directs a graduate program that is attempting to develop new modalities and uses of ethnographic research. This effort is reflected currently in his editing since 1992 of the fin-de-siècle series of annuals, *Late Editions*, published by the University of Chicago Press.